LANDMARK COLLECTOR'S LIBRARY

# The History of the
# Cheadle Coalfield
## Staffordshire

Herbert A Chester

LANDMARK COLLECTOR'S LIBRARY

# THE HISTORY OF THE
# CHEADLE COALFIELD
## · STAFFORDSHIRE ·

Herbert A Chester

Landmark Publishing

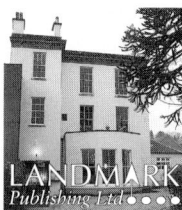

Published by

LANDMARK
Publishing Ltd ● ● ● ●

Ashbourne Hall, Cokayne Ave
Ashbourne, Derbyshire DE6 1EJ England
Tel: (01335) 347349 Fax: (01335) 347303
e-mail: landmark@clara.net
web site: www.landmarkpublishing.co.uk

2nd edition
1st edition: Privately published in 1981 as "Cheadle Coal Town"

ISBN 1 84306 013 2

Printed by Bookcraft, Bath

Design & reproduction by James Allsopp / Mick Usher

Editing by Trevor D Ford & John Shouksmith

Production by Lindsey Porter

**Cover captions**:

**Front cover**: Cheadle Park Colliery
**Back cover & page 3**: New Haden Colliery, 1903

# CONTENTS

## MAPS

## ACKNOWLEDGEMENTS TO THE FIRST EDITION

The author wishes to thank the very many who have helped with the production of this book, especially my friends, George Chandler, George Rushton and Harry Scragg, who have worked all or most of their lives in coal and later in life turned their work into their hobby. Also thanks to George W. Short, President of Cheadle Historical Society, for all his willing assistance in research and loan of material and Mr. J. S. Plant for his untiring attention to the photography.

Mr. F. Stitt and his Staff at Stafford Record Office.
Mr Henstock and his staff at Nottingham Record Office.
Mr H. B. Cart :for use of his work on the Bank's papers.
Mr. Lloyd and his Staff at Lincoln Record Office.
Dr. J. A. Edwards, Archivist, The Library, University of Reading.
The Director, Ian Chisholm, Paul Strange, for information from
   unpublished material now at British Geological Survey, Keyworth,
   Notts.
Peter Lead for documents and map making.
Lindsay Porter and John Robey for documentary information.
Clifford Barnes and J. Gilman for photographs.
Dennis Tweedy for script reading.
Ann Brown for the typescript.
Valerie Aspey for the pen and ink line drawings.
The National Coal Board, Messrs. Stanway, Wheelhouse,
Wheatcroft and John Eyre.
Mr. John Wood for documentuy information.
Messrs J. Slack and W. Harris for map information.
Mr. R. Gamble for open cast information.
Mr. A. W. Jeffery for Brindley documents.
Mr. Campbell, Editor of the Cheadle and Tean Times for permit
   ting a search through old numbers of the paper.
Mr. F. Whitehurst and Mrs. Heaton for documentary information.

## Publishers Note

Landmark Publishing wish to thank George Short and the author's daughter, Mrs Ann Brown; John & Jodi Peck and Gordon Johnson for assistance with photographs for this book. The OS maps used are from the 1879 survey, produced to 25 inches to 1 mile scale. The accounts on pages 51/52 are reproduced by permission of the Duke of Devonshire and the Chatsworth Settlement Trustees, from the Devonshire Collection, Chatsworth. Dr T D Ford offered editorial and geological advice on the text and further assistance was produced by Wes Taylor; thanks to both of them. This is a historical account of the industry. For recent thinking on the geology, readers are directed to the Bristish Geological Survey Memoir for Ashbourne & Cheadle, 1988.

*Left: Map from Barrow's Geology of Cheadle Coalfield, 1903*

# INTRODUCTION

This book was first published in 1981 and is a detailed history of the working of the Cheadle Coalfield. The Cheadle Coalfield lies to the east of Stoke on Trent and the North Staffordshire Coalfield. It covers an area of about 20 sq ml (53 sq km) and the area is bounded by Cheadle Park – Woodhead – Lockwood – Foxt – Ipstones – Belmont – Consall – Dilhorne. Within this area there is a region of about 5 sq ml (13 sq km) which is rich in ironstone (hematite) and this mineral was mined as a raw material for the iron industry of the area; the ironstone area lies between Far Kingsley Banks and Frogall.

The coal and ironstone has been worked for a number of centuries and there is documentary evidence of working the coal from before the 17th Century. The 1880 approx edition of the Ordnance Survey 25 in to 1 mile plan of the area shows 66 coal mines, 15 coal/ironstone and 28 ironstone mines. At this date many of the mines shown had already ceased to operate. The OS map does not show the many mines which had been worked other than by vertical shafts i.e. adits, levels or footrells.

Nowadays there is very little evidence of the former industrial activity of the coalfield. Most of the evidence of mining activity has been destroyed or it has become overgrown. Tramways have been converted to metalled roads and it is only with an experienced eye that evidence of the past industrial activity can be identified. These include the coppiced woodland in which charcoal was produced and samples of iron ore, shale and ash on public footpaths. The names of some of the villages and other areas in the district give an indication of the industrial activities that took place in the vicinity.

The Cheadle Coalfield was at one time an extremely prosperous mining area but the last deep coal mine in the area, Foxfield Colliery, closed in 1965. Opencast coal mining continued in the area after this date but all coal production ended in 1994.

The last ironstone mine was the Cherry Eye Mine in the Churnet Valley which closed in 1923. At the time of closure this mine was producing iron ore for colouring purposes rather than the production of iron.

The Cheadle Coalfield is detached from the North Staffordshire Coalfield but geological analysis of marine bands in the mid 20th Century correlated the seams in the two coalfields. The coal measures are covered with alluvium and marl which is of varying thickness across the coalfield. The coal was at a relatively shallow depth that simplified the access to the coal via the shafts.

A section of the coal measures was prepared Barrows in 1903 and the workable coal seams were identified. The coal seams, in descending order, and the thickness of each seam, as shown on Barrows section is shown below:

| Coal seam name | Approx thickness | | Depth to next productive seam |
|---|---|---|---|
| | Feet | Metre | Feet |
| Delphouse | 2.5 | 0.77 | 50 |
| Two Yard | 5.0 | 1.54 | 65 |
| Getley | 2.0 | 0.62 | 30 |
| Half Yard | 2.75 | 0.85 | 55 |
| Yard | 3.25 | 1.03 | 35 |
| Upper Litley | 2.5 | 0.77 | 65 |
| Four Feet | 4.0 | 1.23 | 35 |
| Little Dilhorne | 2.75 | 0.85 | 150 |
| Dilhorne | 5.0 | 1.54 | 65 |
| Alecs A | 4.0 | 1.23 | 195 |
| Woodhead | 3.0 | 0.92 | |

Unfortunately, no location was given by Barrows for this section

# FOREWORD

My earliest recollection of Cheadle was of loads, large and small, of coal from carts hauled by small ponies or horses tipped onto the High Street and overflowing on to the pavement.

There was little other traffic to worry parents in 1911, so I could cross the street to explore Alcock's furniture shop and more exciting builder's yard, now the Post Office sorting office yard; stare in the window of Mr. Cope's butcher's shop, now belonging to Jack Heath, and savour the smells of Johnson's bakery and shop, now belonging to Hammersley's. I could call to see if Jacob Lowndes was taking photographs in what is now Grace Eyre's handbag shop. That was the end of my route for I was too young to call on Jabez Noden at the Unicorn, though it was part of his practice to serve hot coffee to miners going to work at six a.m. A tot of rum improved it; two tots gave a roseate hue to the sight of the pithead gear. It must be admitted that three tots often had the opposite effect!

The following year, my parents moved, with their employer, Felix Wedgwood, to the South Durham coast where my father could fish on Tees Bay, but was at a loss to explain why most of the sands we should have played on in the morning were covered with a layer of tiny grains of coal, left by the receding tide.

The gathering of this black coating or seacole, as they called it, was the privilege of a certain group who scraped it into heaps with their wide scraping boards fixed to a broom handle, filled it into sacks and loaded it onto pony carts to hawk around the district. This fine wet slack served to back up the fire at night and, having dried out into a lump, it could be broken in the morning to provide the instant fire.

We returned to Kingsley Holt in 1915 where the garden had a grey band of shale, which daily annoyed the gardener in my father, but come 1926 and the miners' strike, he began to change his mind. The colliers came out of the Potteries in sixes and sevens looking for opportunities for 'outcropping' and found them just two hundred yards behind the house. It was hard, dry work sinking those half dozen shallow pits. Mother felt they would be pleased with a large can of tea. The fact that the level of coal in our coalhouse was getting lower, we were informed, played no part in making her decision, but having delivered the refreshment, I usually returned with a small bag over my shoulders to keep the home fires burning! On one such occasion I was met by the senior among them, 'Owd Jack', and, having passed the can, he turned and said "Com thee dine 'ere". We walked some eighty yards further down the field, he with his large shovel over his shoulder, until he stopped and carefully examined the turf. Down swung the shovel to lift a square foot of it and reveal a black layer below. "Dust say thet'n?" I gave a surprised "Yes" "Dust noa wo tis? Tak owd er ondful." I picked out a handful of the damp, soft, perished coal. "Nar that'ns Wudyed". I did not understand this but was convinced that Jack was an expert in these matters and often wondered why I could not be as clever.

Some twenty years later I met George Chandler at a class with the W.E.A. at Cheadle Senior School. He had spent a lifetime in Cheadle coal mines with the exception of his years in the Army during the first World War when he ranked as Company Sergeant Major. He continues my education in coal and mining to this day at a sprightly ninety-two years young.

For a recent account of the geology of the area, readers are referred to the British Geological Survey Memoir, *Ashbourne and Cheadle*, 1988. It was the first to be published since George Barrow, the geologist, completed his survey at the turn of the century and had it printed for 1903. Some twenty years before, the local coal master, Robert Plant wrote his *History of Cheadle and Neighbouring Places* but introduced another, geologist, William Molyneux, to give his account of the coalfield. Between them there was little history of the subject, mainly because, though they were able to give excellent accounts of the geology of the place, later twentieth century facilities such as Record Offices and libraries were not then available to the local historian. Whilst this account does not, in any way, claim to be the complete story, it is hoped that, despite the destruction of documents by many generations, it will prove to be as full and interesting a history as is possible at this time.

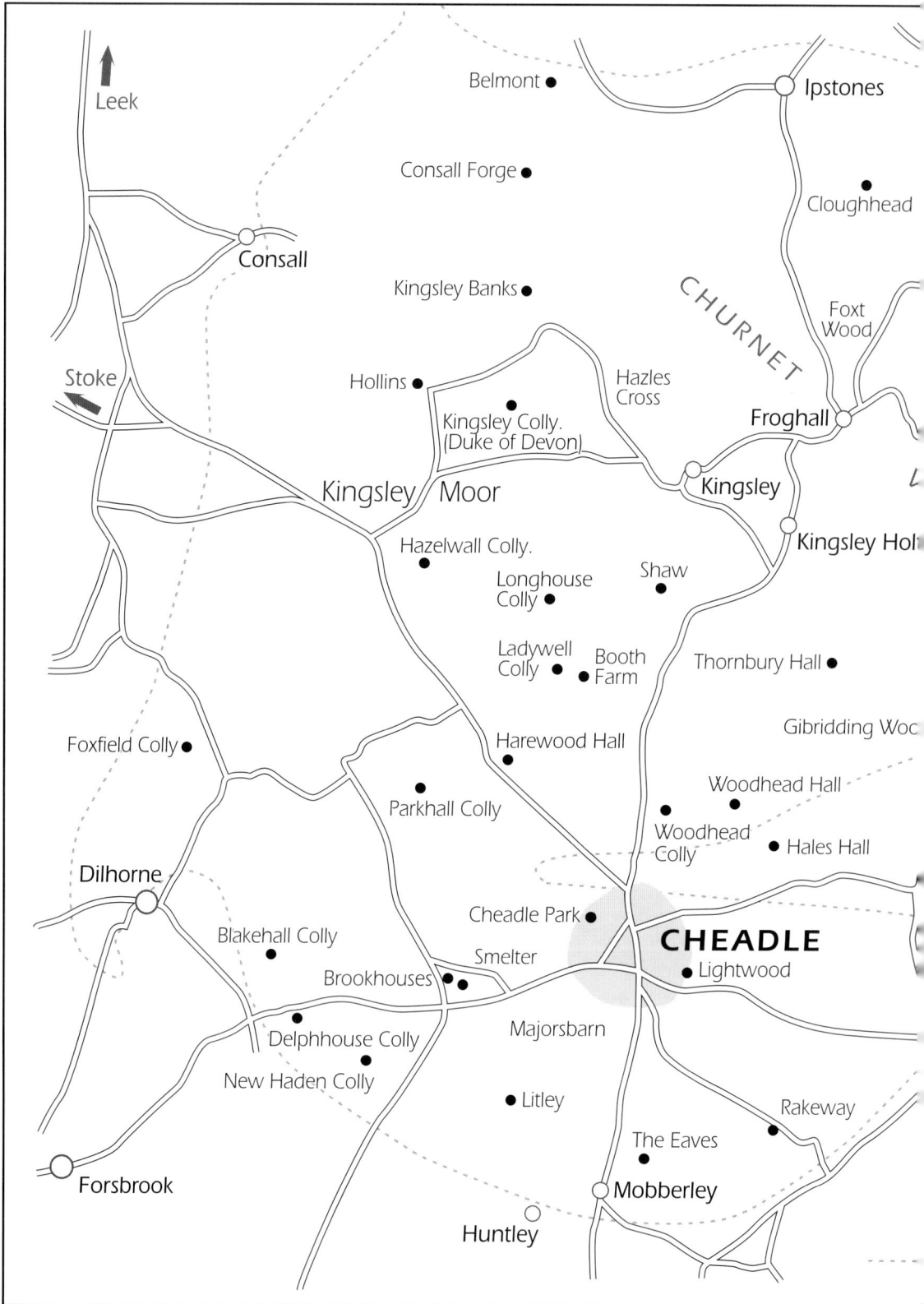

Leek

Belmont •

• Ipstones

Consall Forge •

• Cloughhead

○ Consall

Kingsley Banks •

CHURNET

Foxt Wood

Stoke

Hollins •

Hazles Cross

Froghall ○

Kingsley Colly.
(Duke of Devon) •

Kingsley Moor

○ Kingsley

○ Kingsley Hol

Hazelwall Colly. •

Shaw •

Longhouse
Colly •

Ladywell
Colly •

Booth
• Farm

Thornbury Hall •

Gibridding Woc

Foxfield Colly •

Harewood Hall •

Woodhead Hall •

Parkhall Colly •

Woodhead
Colly •

• Hales Hall

Dilhorne ○

Blakehall Colly •

Cheadle Park •

**CHEADLE**

Smelter

• Lightwood

Brookhouses •

Delphhouse Colly •

Majorsbarn

New Haden Colly

• Litley

Rakeway •

The Eaves •

Forsbrook ○

○ Mobberley

Huntley ○

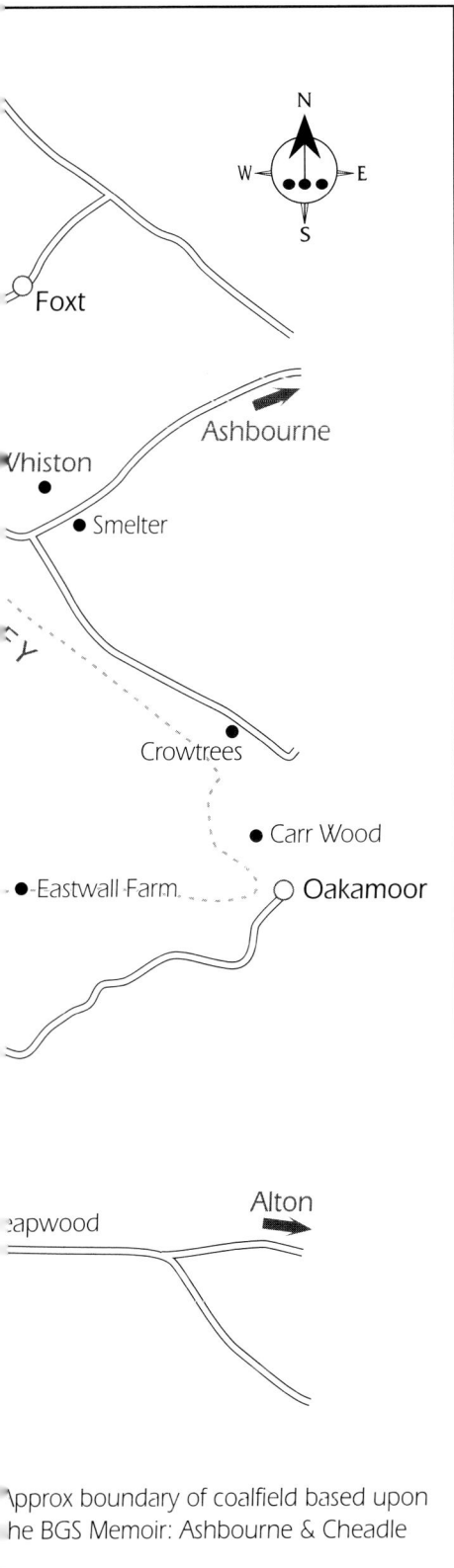

N
W E
S

Foxt

Ashbourne

Whiston

Smelter

Y

Crowtrees

Carr Wood

Eastwall Farm

Oakamoor

Alton

apwood

Approx boundary of coalfield based upon
the BGS Memoir: Ashbourne & Cheadle

# WHEN ADAM DELVED

Place names of an area have often given clues as to the shape of the countryside, its hills, dells, open spaces or rocky promontories. Other places were often named in later centuries from some activity or other taking place there. In this district we have our Skinners brook, Tanyard, Cattle Hill and Abbots Hay. But what of Dilhorne? Here is an example of a name, many times changed, for at Doomsday this was Delverne and along the Common another appeared later as Delphouse. These were digging places, not for the usual cultivation as we could have found in that larger community down the Tean Valley now known as Checkley. The folk at Delverne were digging for fuel, the coal they found under their feet, for the geologist tells us that five or six seams outcrop around the place which became Dulverne before today's Dilhorne. The coal became of major interest to the surrounding area for, as the population increased, this was a most important commodity in a district not blessed with ample windblown timber for burning. One geologist has suggested that this coal may have been used for lime burning, only since it was 'stinking' or sulphurous on burning, but most of this outcropping coal was good domestic fuel and would be so used at that period. Although the lime kiln was known in these early days it would not be a common feature on the Delverne scenery as it would be further east where, in the Dove country, heavy limestone took no carriage to the kilns though the lighter coal did!

## *The Broad Delph*

There was, however, one area of the Cheadle Coalfield where coal and limekilns could have some connection. The Manor of Hounds Chedle, or Dogge Chedle as it became nicknamed in the twelfth and thirteenth centuries, was registered in the Doomsday Book of 1086 as a 'Waste Manor'.

Our Norman French conquerors intended keeping we vulgar English slaves in our places and promptly conferred practically all land to the Norman soldiery who had helped in the conquest. That other half of Cheadle, the waste half, between the water of Bedbrook and Cecilly Brook over High Shutt to the Churnet, was granted to that worthy, John de Sacheveral. He usually resided further south at Radcliffe on Trent, (the family tombs can still be seen in the church) and decided with his son and grandson in around 1290 to give the manor to the Abbot and monks at Croxden in the Vale of St. Mary. There were, however, one or two reservations of value to the donors such as their *Capital Messuage, Le Parchuses* today's Parkfields, the old forges and mines of iron in addition to his *vetus minerium que vocatur anglice Le Brode Delph* (the old mine which the English call the Broad Delph) and the limekiln.

This information, with that on the early iron industry, came to light comparatively recently since the documents such as The Prima Carta de Chedle of around the late 12C and The Secunda Carta de Chedle of around 1290 (First and Second Charters of Cheadle) had been in the hands of the Abbot of Croxden until the Dissolution in 1538-40.

At this period there was, on the market a surfeit of land from the old monastic estates. Croxden was one of the poorer institutions of only some eight thousand acres, but there were also business men buyers, among them the brothers Leveson, wool merchants of the south of the County, who set about the climb to country-gentlemen status. Not only did they acquire the Cheadle Grange land of Croxden, but also those of Trentham Priory and Lilleshall Abbey in Shropshire. The Cheadle documents went to Trentham and, although the Cheadle land changed hands, (first to the Countess of Kent, daughter of Gilbert and seventh Earl of Shrewsbury, thence to her favourite and legal adviser, Seldon, and next to his four friends of whom Chief Justice Hales was one) the documents remained at Trentham. The partition of the estate into four quarters in 1694 allowed for the marriage of Hales' granddaughter to Archibald Grosvenor and the building of Hales Hall in 1712.

In 1634 the Countess had renewed the lease of a large part of the estate to Leveson's servant, Thomas Crompton, but both mines of coal and ironstone were reserved to the owner.

The Brode Delph, therefore, was the earliest coal working on the coalfield to be given a name which was recorded. Not only did this give a lead to work in the area, but also, within two or three centuries, to the naming of one of the most important seams. It was on the west side of the Churnet Valley, to the north of the present Gibridding Wood, near the top of the valley side and overlooking the land and water of the Hesteswelle on which East Wall farm has more recently been built. It was broad compared with the smaller delphs on the coalfield.

## *Early Coalworkings*

Of these early coalworkings only the names of the fields or areas were left for future use. Dud Dudley described them in a petition to the King, Charles I, in 1638 some twenty years after James I had frowned on coal burning in London:

> *"But where the coals are deep, and but little earth upon the measure of coals, there the colliers rid off the earth, and dig coals under their feet; these works are called footrids, but of these works there are now but few."*

References to this type of outcropping is made in the Kingsley lists of Terriers, i.e. the lists of Church properties and Glebe land the incumbent was expected to make every few years for submission to the Bishop.

After describing the Parsonage House, barns, crofts, etc, he proceeded to list the pieces of land retained specifically for his use. At Kingsley in 1681 he listed:

> *"Item. The Colepitts fields and two other fields.*
> *By 1693 this had become:*
> *It. 4 pieces of ground called ye nearer Cole pitts field adjoining to Pig Lane*
> > *7 acres*
> *2 other pieces of ground called ye Further Colepit Field*
> *5 acres $^{1}/_{2}$*
> *A later year it became:*
> *One Piece midnips with Cole Mine 20 acres."*

This first area from Kingsley Brook on the left of the main road to Kingsley Moor has a most uneven surface as have other pieces that were much later mined in the same way.

At around this period the village vestry meeting, the local government of the day, began to mention coal in its minutes:

> "1678 Spent on Coales and carriage to Church        10d.
> 1697 Given to Thos Clarke being hurt in the Colepitt        2-6d."

Since the village was responsible for the upkeep of the Church in addition to other village affairs these charges were met by the Overseers from the lunes or rates.

## Dr. Plot's Visit of 1680

When Dr. Robert Plot, the Oxford don, had completed his *Natural History of Oxfordshire* he was invited by Walter Chetwynd to write on Staffordshire. He was already surveying in the county in 1680 preparing for publication of his *Natural History of Staffordshire* in 1686. He spent a considerable time in the north east moorland quarter, i.e. that north of Uttoxeter, then commonly recognised as the Moorlands.

While visiting the iron working in the Churnet Valley he saw the coal mining around Cheadle and Kingsley and was able to describe some of the workings:

> "The coaliers can work a curriculus into the side of the Hill as they do at the Footerill at Apedale. He says that this is easier than the other more common hanging mines in which they are forced to follow the coal to a great depth. However these are as preferable to the other Hanging Mines as those are to the rearing ones which are the worst of all: the Colliers quickly reaching to their utmost workable depth every way: though it must not be denyed but that the coal of these and the common hanging Mines is most times more firm and better for burning, than that of the others."

## Barrow's description in 1903

Before Barrow goes into geological detail on the coalfield in his *Geology of the Cheadle Coalfield* he gives a survey of the sites, many around the perimeter of the field, where he found evidence of very early workings of the outcrop type, although this evidence was becoming more difficult, with the passing of time, to identify.

The district possesses a peculiar interest on account of the great antiquity of these workings they can be traced back as far at least as the reign of Richard III.

This is a surprising assertion since this monarch had but a short reign, 1483-5, and I have not found it possible to discover this reference from any other county sources. He does, however, find many interesting examples which are all but lost at this end of the century. He mentions:

> "probably 19th Century workings in Carr Wood through 90ft-100ft. of grit to reach coal. In a small valley one mile due N of Foxt coal is exposed and has been worked."

At Whiston Lees coal was again worked leaving a largish spoil bank and between Whiston and Oakamoor (probably the Ross Lane area).

Only a short distance to the east of the stream (between Froghall Wharf towards Foxt) a bore hole passed through a 2ft deep hollow where the coal had been mined.

Of the Eavesford and Whiston Eaves district he says:

> *"Over all this area the Crabtree coal has been worked some distance in from the outcrop. A shaft 500 yds S. of Eavesford passed through three seams of coal below the Crabtree."*

The Crabtree all over the area was extensively worked at times but was untouched in the Cheadle area but may some day be mined.

There are old outcrop workings some 500 yds north of the Kingsley Moor road junction and east of the stream flowing from Kingsley Moor to the Hollins Wood. Old workings are seen East of the steam as far as Hazles Cross.

Some of the oldest workings in the Woodhead coal are around the Woodhead Hall and the seam is named after it.

In other areas on the opposite side of the field Barrow mentions other old workings.

Above Park where workings in the Alecs Coal can still be traced. Below Hatchley numerous pits are seen round about sunk to the Alecs or stinking coal.

Further proof of these old workings were discovered when the striking miners of the 1920's accidentally came across them and had to move away before sinking more of their own shafts.

One such mining agreement was made in 1632 when Thomas Crompton and his sons of Cheadle Grange, yeomen tenants of considerable standing, (whose family were to be involved in the partition of the Manor of Hounds Chedle (sic) at the end of the century,) agreed with four other gentlemen including Mathew Cradock of Caverswall Castle, to exchange for 12 acres of land, lying in:

> *"the Comon Fields of Cheadull' for threescore years the right to have all those their Coles, Cole mynes, rowes Delphes and quarries of coles settlying or beinge in the Psh of Cheadull af'sd where in coles are now gotten or lately were gotten commonlie called or knowne by the name of Great Harwood als Coate Harwood being bound on the south west side by a lane called Harwood Lane and on the north west side with a lane wich goeth from Booth Hall and meeteth with the said lane called Harwood Lane at the corner of the said Close called Harwoods being now the land of Thomas Harrison of Hassele Waull."*

*The old mine which the English call The Broad Delph.*

They were to have the rights of:

> *"Ingresse, Egresse and Regresse, sinking, diginge, soughing, gusteringe, daminge'*
> *and to have 'Ingen or ingines or other wayes' for 41 years paying weekly and every*
> *week 'two compelent horse loads of coles."*

The agreement was signed by John Murhall, Thomas Mylles of Rakeway, Thomas Fyott [? Pyott] of 'Dillon' and Thomas Crompton both the latter made a mark, and the cobble coal was mined at less than thirty feet.

Nearly three centuries later, Mr. Sam Wheat was farming Little Harewood Farm near the large Harewood Hall. The 1926 coal strike brought the miners in the district looking for likely areas for outcrop or shallow mining. They approached Mr. Wheat for permission to try the area between Harewood Road and Clamgoose Lane and shortly started activities. Within an hour or so they reported that they had found considerable evidence of old men working within five or six feet and invited Mr. Wheat, a one time collier himself, to inspect their findings. He descended but for no longer than was necessary. This was one of the old workings that Barrow in 1900 had overlooked. The Booth Hall (see above) was the predecessor of that building standing today and would probably be a stone house of some character. The lane mentioned took a straight line from the Booth's corner and joined the Harwood Lane to make a simple cross road junction opposite the Perkins Lane to Dilhorne.

Some of the terms used in the document came down to the last century but such as soughing gusteringe daminge were new in the mining context and with the exception of gusteringe came into common use for the seventeenth and eighteenth centuries. The meaning of gusteringe has not been defined among the old coal men of today and indeed I only once found it in later documents when it was partially explained being written as gutterings.

# Blackdamp and Fire baskets

2

*"Thy getst a ruck er crocks, piled up rate thee nowst, grete lung mate dishes er borrem m goein litler dine to doll's ise sowsers a top. Thems thee coe saimes rind Chiedle. Bite er duzon em!!"*

This was *"one er thowd uns"* as he described the seams of the coalfield at the beginning of the century while we drank our pints in the quieter corner of the bar some fifty years ago.

He had read a little of George Barrow's geological account of the area published in 1903 and the diagram had provided him with a vision of the washing up on the kitchen table. He might have mentioned that the pile leaned dangerously to the west so that the smaller components rested under the Delphouse and Dilhorne district whilst the larger pieces could stretch the whole five and a half miles east to west and north to south. It was, however, arranged most conveniently around Cheadle and district so that all the town and villages within that area could draw some benefit from this distribution as the centuries went by.

## *Early Mining Activity*

From the Middle Ages by far the greater part of the coal dug from the out cropping seams went for domestic use as only one industry could make use of this coal as a secondary product. The old iron industry along the Churnet Valley could use nothing but charcoal made from timber for any of the early attempts to smelt and refine iron. With a charcoal made from this 'pyt cole' all attempts or experiments proved failures. It was not until early in the seventeenth century that attempts were made to ease the timber position. Legal restrictions on timber use were overcome by using coal to re-heat iron bars before bending or slitting into rods and even then with much suspicion. Many makers of iron bar and rod reckoned that their products would have to be sold at £2 per ton less than that heated solely by charcoal.

Despite this general adverse opinion the early Oakamoor furnace and forge supplied themselves with coal although little note of this is made in the accounts. just one note mentions this:

*"27 Oct 1593 Pd to Wm Thornbury for repair of the wheales for the collemyne."*

This seems to refer to a pit with a horse gin to raise coal – the mechanics preceding steam. Although the words pyt and myne had crept into the language at this period they usually referred to ironstone. Before mining the stone in the area around Lightwood and the east of Cheadle, however, miners would most likely contact the seam of coal, called the Woodhead, most respected by those concerned with either mineral. So little, however, was known about the winning of them that most was guesswork and good fortune.

Others have mentioned the mining of coal for the burning of limestone to produce lime for agricultural use or later building with stone. There is little evidence of such activity on the western side of the coalfield, the major part of construction at this early period being of the half timber, lath and plaster type until they could afford such fine stone buildings as the 1635 example of the Mylles House at Rakeway.

The result was a comparatively slow development of the field. The smaller populations, up to the beginning of the seventeenth century, being adequately supplied from the out-cropping seams already mentioned.

It should be remembered that the total population of the parish of Cheadle, including Huntley, Draycott Cross, Kingsley Holt, part of Oakamoor and Freehay only numbered one thousand in the religious census of 1676.

Towards the end of the early furnace period the operators were changing the terms delph for foot rids or footrills, thence to pyts or Pitts and on to mynes, or more popularly mines. A shallow form of mining with shafts follows naturally when the footrill has gone down as far as is safe. These came to be known as bell pits according to the shape of the pit. The shaft was sunk to twenty-five or thirty feet to reach the coal where the miners dug out spoil above the coal which could then be quickly removed, without danger, to a radius of twelve feet from the shaft bottom. Having succeeded in this, a bell-shaped hollow was left to subside whilst the miners proceeded to replace the spoil and repeat the exercise some thirty feet away.

## Seventeenth Century Mining

By the middle of the seventeenth century, however, it would appear that more experiments were being tried to win the coal where conditions of roof and floor were favourable. One such example occurred in 1655. The story really begins in 1585, according to the Cavendish documents at Nottingham, with the ownership of:

> *"certaine messuages cottages, lands and tenements within Cheadle and Huntley by Thomas Pyott who wills these to his sons on his death."*

Four years later in the thirty-first year of the reign of Elizabeth I the son, William Pyott, wills the lands to his six sons Thomas, Charles, Henry, Francis, John and Williarn and again eleven years later, just before Elizabeth's death the lands had been contracted to a Derby family for £50 or £60.

Disagreement about the full ownership continued through the early Cromwellian period when members of the illustrious Cavendish family had to seek refuge abroad after making what arrangements they could to keep down fines and sequestration of property by the various parliamentarian County Committees. By 1654-5 these troubles were concerning Viscount Mansfield the son of Elizabeth Basset, who had inherited her father's property in the Manor of Cheadle:

> *"Wm Basset Esq being seized in Fee of the Manor of Cheadle of w$^{ch}$ the lands in question were and are parcell about Decemb. Ao 44$^0$ Eliz: dyed thereof soe seized, leaving Elizabeth, his only daughter & heir to whorne after his death the same descended."*

Although there is another document of May 1655 which reads:

> *"I Charles Cavendish Lord Viscount Mansfield Have sold unto Thomas Pyot of Huntley.... for the sum of one hundred and Eighty pound etc. etc. followed by a second which reads "Upon ye Contract Between ye L$^d$ Mansfield & Thomas Pyott concerning ye purchase of certaine lands."*

The question of ownership came before two courts in 1660 and the following year. The last document is of greatest interest so far as coal and mining are concerned:

|  | £ | s | d |
|---|---|---|---|
| *"The Lord Mansfield was to have in money* | *180* | *0* | *0* |
| *The Ld Mansfield has ye dispossing of a colernyme which he* | | | |
| *leased to Mr. Coleclough at £10 a yewe for which he abated* | | | |
| *in ye Purchase* | *100* | *0* | *0* |
| *Spent by Thomas Pyott two journeys to London, Many* | | | |
| *journey to Welbecke Bloore and other places and one* | | | |
| *Journey to Mr. Huttons house in Yorkshire all upon yt Account* | *20* | *0* | *0* |
| *Cost Thomas Pyott and his Father in Building upon* | | | |
| *Ye misses Five Bays & a half built by him and a Bay* | | | |
| *& an half by his Father & bought all ye timber well worth* | *100* | *0* | *0* |
| | | | |
| *Which is in all* | *400* | *0* | *0* |

*Note yt although ye Colemyne was sett at £10 a yeare yet it was really worth £40 or £50 a year, for ye workmen have reported yt they have taken £80 a weeke & yt 40 or £50 a weeke was ordinay in ye Summer tyme. Ye, !essee having 4 pitts constantly going And which is reputed to be worth in ye whole at least £1,000."*

The Coalmine was reported:

*"to be sett soe cheape because ye Lord Mansfield had a particular kindness for Mr. Coleclough."*

We have no detailed accounts of these workings but I would imagine that Adam Colclough had introduced the use of timber for propping at this date.

This mining enterprise introduces us to the Colcloughs, who, within a short period, had become linked by marriage to the other three gentry families in the Dilhorne area, who eventually followed suit and became interested in coal mining.

Adam Colclough lived at Delphe House just west of the junction of the turnpike road and the pre-turnpike road, plainly marked by the two yew trees which are on the left, half-way up the Boundary Road. Colclough's father was Sir Caesar Colclough, so that two gentry families were well joined when Adam married Elizabeth Bamford from Cheadle Park or the Park Hall which stood in one of the sites enclosed by the moats behind the farm, the old manor house.

Adam's second wife had a daughter, Jane, who married William Adderley of Blake Hall, just three hundred yards across the road from Delphe House. The Adderley's had been leading gentry in the Dilhorne district for two hundred years.

A generation before this time, a Johannes Whitehurst from Whitehurst, Dilhorne had married an earlier Elizabeth Bamford from Park Hall. Had this quartet formed a partnership, it could have governed the coalfield much earlier than when Samual Bamford took control a century later.

According to the figures of £40-£80 weekly production, this colemine venture must have been the biggest enterprise around the coalfield through the rest of the century. The reported figures of the year averaged around £60 weekly. The price of coal at that period was 1d. per cwt or approximately that weight, or for larger sales for other than domestic use. There was a slight increase by the time the iron works were buying some thirty years later. In 1593:

> *"3 horse loads of Seecoles*                                         *21d*
> *By the time the Consall works were buying in 1695 they bought by the stack (more than a ton) we find:*
> *Pitcoles. OfDilhorne Coles 10 stacks@ 4/10*             *£2      8      4*
> *Of Kingsley Coles 1 ¹/₂ stacks at 7/-*                     *10     6"*

At these prices the amount of coal raised from the four pits, which were in the Huntley area, would represent a very large quantity for 1655. In 1900 there were traces of a group of four shafts, between Mobberley and the River Tean, which would work in the Dilhorne coal which stretched down to Huntley Hall. At an average £60 weekly, much less domestic use in summer than winter, this would mean an output of some thirty tons per day from each of the four pits and this must be taken to be a more advanced mining method than the bell pit method. At this early period this coal would be raised at about 1d. per cwt, although the terms tons and cwts were in more frequent use by the end of the century.

At one Quarter Sessions at Stafford in 1656 a Kingsley woman, Margaret Mosse, gave evidence that her husband, James Mosse, was a collier and worked at *"our coal mines in our Parish"*. She mentioned mines in the plural:

> *"In the 1680-90 period the bulk purchasers such as the iron works paid as follows:*
> *1688 33 doz pitt coles for ye clark and workmens fydring @ 7*
> *£11 16      3*
> *1693 50¹/₂ doz Pitt Coles for mill use 7d doz*
> *£17 13      6*
> *So spent to draw out 77 Ton 10 C of iron @ 3 doz per ton."*

By the early nineteenth century such unusual measures were still in use. Dr. Wilkes of Willenhall, in his *History of Staffordshire*, tables them as follows:

> *"A corf is almost the same as a skip; only there is no winding done about the edges of it to keep the coals upon it….This loaded, or a corful, as they call it has sometimes been sold for 3d. but is now worth no more than 2¹/₂d. They called twelve of these a ruck and double this number is called a dozen, so that every ruck is now valued at 2s-6d and every dozen at 5s. Of this sum the colliers have 1s 10d for getting the coal and finding all things necessary for the work as candles, ropes, corfs, mandrils etc."*

During the Interregnum the costs were much lower than in Wilkes' time but Colclough's pits were prosperous while they lasted and this Delphouse family knew what the Dilhorne coal was worth in those days. Before the end of last century the old miners related to their collier sons the finding of four shaft markings between Mobberley and the river Tean. There were a number of old shafts in the district though not of that antiquity.

## A New Partnership

In 1668 three well known townsmen formed a partnership intended to be a coalmining company. They were George Mylles of Rakeway, William Chaloner and Philip Hollings all paying rents to Thomas Banks of Revesby Abbey in Lincolnshire, landlord over considerable lands in both Cheadle and Kingsley.

The Mylles family were mining ironstone in the Lightwood district in the 1590s and lived in Rakeway House which stood on the site of the new Rakeway Grange. It faced the lane to Freehay and had a remarkable small rectangular staircase of oak in the Elizabethan style. Later other sections were built on back and front so that the new house faced Cheadle. By 1633 the Mylles were preparing to build a new larger house across the road as part of a marriage settlement and by 1635 was completed Cheadle's best example of this stone Jacobean dwelling. The Family became wealthy and were magistrates before the end of the century. Today the house is called Mill House Farm.

This partnership intended mining under the Town Field and others belonging to them but had also decided that it would be necessary to unwater the coal from this area which ran up towards the Lid Lane district. To do so, they found, it would be necessary to dig a sough to take the water into the river running towards Mobberley. It would, therefore, be necessary to tunnel under the close of Richard Fowell and his son, George, called Castle Croft.

The indenture reads:

> *"Agreed by Richard Fowell Huntley Yeoman and George Fowell his Sonne that 'Mylles and Co.' have free leave, liberty and licence for their workmen to digge gutter sough and drive a level through certayn lands of them the said Richard and George Fowell called the Castle Croft and also free entry, egresse etc for carrying all tymber and other materials necessary for the ymediate dreneinge or else for future cleansing repayring during the continuance of a certain Colemine intended to be sett on foot by the said partners through their severall and respective lands lying between Mobberley Brook and the Townfield of Cheadle af'sd rendering paying proportionally to Fowells every fortnight of the construction of the said mine three fourpenny horse loads or twelve pence of good money in lieu at the choice of the Fowells."*

The document laid down terms agreed for the payment of charges for this expensive venture which at this date had not been commonly practised, although Barrow claimed that some three hundred years before his survey, such an enterprise had been successful between Belmont and Ipstones to unwater a specially good coal presumably into a tributary of the Churnet.

> *"And when the level or sough shall have taken the foure foote coale each party shall measure his lands and account for the money layd forth or disbursed."*

Here again is something new for the period. One or other of the three prospectors knew what seam of coal they intended to find and then mine. For the first time we find them naming a particular seam, an indication that those interested in coal mining were acquiring a rough knowledge of the seams in the upper layers of the strata. Unfortunately, Mylles and company had not the benefit of the later geologists' research which would have told them that the Fourfoot outcropped just beyond the Tean brook at Brookhouses and that the larger stone bridge there, of the early nineteenth century, was actually built on a foundation of Fourfoot so that they were more likely to find the Dilhorne seam in the direction they were driving their sough. There is no record as to how much or what was mined. This partnership was not one to retreat empty handed, but we do have evidence that the sough was laid for, when about 1960 the whole of this area was opencast mined from Majors Bun to the brook by Litley, the men operating the huge machines struck the brickwork of the sough and George Chandler had to explain its function to them.

Further clauses were added to safeguard individual partner's rights once the mining had started:

> *"Item: each parties heirs shall haw entry to the lands of the others while partnership lasts for workmen agents etc, horses cuts all fetching carrying equally filling Pits, making ways etc. Hollings to pay to Mylles twenty shillings per year in March - Sept. after the mine set on foot. When partnership ends, if Hollins wished to continue he shall continue at thirty shillings per year.*
> *9tem: If Fowells get coals they shall pay an agreed portion.*
> *9tem: If the sough is stopped before it reaches Challoners Land it is repaired by Mylles and Hollins only."*

These upper layers comprising first, on top the babby's sowser covered only a comparatively small narrow area stretching from Delphouse east of Blake Hall and Madge Dale and the boundary turning to rejoin under the Bunter sandstone hill to the west of the New Haden site. This was the Two Yard named after its thickness of seam of good quality most of which was outcrop mined or with shallow pits or domestic use around Dilhorne and Cheadle.

Below the five feet six inches Two Yard seam by some seventy feet was the two feet six inches Half Yard seam followed lower down by some sixty feet by the three feet nine inch seam known as the Yard coal. These stretched over a much larger area under the same district but stretching from the Litley, Farm and over the Boundary round by New Close Fields and back to the Litley area.

These three seams supplied the demand for fuel into the first quarter of the eighteenth century although much of the deeper parts of the seams remained unmined until the later half of the nineteenth century when the early Delphouse Colliery re-opened.

Two other seams, one varying from two feet to two feet nine inches, more often called the Litley seam fifty feet below the Yard Coal, and the Fourfoot, of three feet nine inches before mentioned – another thirty feet deeper-covered a much wider district as far north as the Dilhorne Old Engine area and west approaching Callow Hill Farm to be mined near the Boundary at a colliery known as Commonside, above the Delphouse District.

The above seams came to be known as the Middle Coal Measures and were worked generally to the west of the coalfield, about a quarter of the total area.

## *Cheadle Grange*

By this time two important developments were happening in the east of the district where they had found the Brode Delph. Mining men know that the coal was beyond their reach by the end of the fifteenth century unless new methods were tried. These were started in and around the Gibridding Wood on the east of Woodhouse and in the fields crossing the track to Eastwall from the Lockwood Lane. One record of the changes in the district now known as Cheadle Grange concerns the passing of the manor from the Countess of Kent to her legal advisor, Seldon, and in 1653 he left it to his four friends of the Inner Temple.

Although the manor was left as a form of trust they soon began to use legal means to split or partition it into four quarters. By 1654 each of the recipients leased a quarter of the manor to his servant for three months at a fee of five shillings, at the end of which time they took back what were virtually separate quarters. It only remained to hold a lottery to determine which candidate should hold which quarter and none seemed concerned except the possible exception of Chief Justice Hales who, as stated earlier, had in mind a use for his quarter. The partition took place in 1694. The north east quarter, with its land running down to the Churnet, went to John Vaughan who promptly leased to Wrm Lee or Leigh as it became later, who had already occupied a part of this land, as did his father, Gervaise Leigh, in 1649.

A Thomas Crompton – I have already referred to this family in the 1632 Harwood Venture – leased the remainder including the old Grange buildings. Although the Cromptons do not appear to play a part in the area for much longer their neighbours, the Leighs, are to act a most important role here through the next century. Gervaise Leigh had been the second largest occupier of the Grange lands in 1649 and his family soon became gentry as is seen in the Kingsley Church registers:

> *"1708 Mr. Thomas Leigh departed this life Nov 7 buried Nov 11. (Note Mr.)*
> *Dec. 30 1719 Wm son of Mr Edward Leigh and Madame Ann Leigh. Bapt*
> *Jan. 2 1719 John Wardle Psh of Bosley and Judith Horden Nurse to Madame Leigh's Child*
> *Mar."*

It will be noticed that the old calendar was still in use and January belonged to the previous year.

The partition deed of 1693/4 mentions what is left of the old mill pool at the old Furnace and The Counting House and buildings lately erected at the "Woodhead". This collection of buildings was for the use of those mining the coal mentioned as crossing the Eastwall track. The lease of 1634 from the Countess of Kent to Thos. Crompton, mentioned in the last chapter, had reserved all Coles colemines etc. so that Crompton could do nothing about them, but once the manor had passed into other hands these coals were mined. One statement appears in notes on the documents *"The colemine opened 1690"*. A spur of the Woodhead coal stretches under three fields on the cast side of Lockwood Lane and the old workings show plainly the extent of the mining. Within a few years the Counting House became the Reckoning House and the three fields by the laneside became the Reckoning House Fields. The Barkers lived in the Reckoning House and accounted for all the coal sold from the mines. By 1700 William Leigh knew the value of this particular seam now named the Woodhead seam. Barrow, casting a geological eye over the district in 1900, says *"someof the oldest workings in the Woodhead coal occur in the neighbourhood of Woodhead Hall, and the seam has derived its name from this fact"*. Though less than three feet thick, more often only two feet nine inches, the coal is probably the best in this coalfield and, with a good roof and floor is much more economical to win. Barrow says *"the cost of timbering is unusually small."* He was reporting in 1900 when documentary evidence was difficult to find so he concludes:

> *"The workings near the outcrop in the northern and eastern area are of great*
> *antiquity and, as a rule, no details of them can now be obtained."*

Barrow did not realise that this Reckoning House enterprise had grown through two centuries into the Woodhead Colliery complex and would continue, with the Bowers, into the twentieth century

## The Cheadle Coal Seams

The Woodhead seam set a target for the many ambitious leaders in the industry but most had to be satisfied, owing to the ever increasing technical difficulties in the deeper digging, with exploring the seams above. This middle range of seams could be tackled over the rest of this field where that upper range we had found around Dilhorne did not reach. These were seven such layers, though many were quite thin and only economic to work where near to the surface or where the shaft passed through and this fuel would serve to work engines when steam power reached the coalfield.

Of the seven middle layers of coal the uppermost is known as the Dilhorne or Big Dilhorne since in the northern section it was often near six feet thick but towards the south it deteriorated to about three feet and was known as the Huntley seam. It was, like the upper seams, to the west of the town and outcropped in places down a boundary line from the Godley Brook and Birchenfields area by Majors Barn, down to Huntley where it turned under the sandstone hill. It was worked much later by both New Haden and the later Delphouse concerns, though its quality was suspect in places. It will probably be best remembered by those who worked it at Foxfield over its last twenty years. They found that, because it was near the surface, their boreholes indicated a great number of old workings with no records of when they were operating, or by whom.

Some sixty yards below the Dilhorne the next seam of note was the Stinking better known as the Alecs which gave about three feet of coal split by six inches of rubbish which the miners called pricking. It was found in an area from south of the Hazlewall colliery by Harewood Hall where some shafts had been sunk in the old racecourse fields. To the west the seam reaches under the boundary sandstone and was, during the last century, mined from a shaft on the Dilhorne Road side of Callow Hill farm, at a depth of fifty yards though little was taken from it.

Below the Alecs there followed four other thinner seams, all mined in various places and circumstances. They were the Foxfield, Mans, Cobble and Rider. The first is so named because the Dilhorne mining folk found it outcropping in the Foxfield, long before any major operations were contemplated, near the field looked upon as a game area. Its quality and thickness at about one foot six inches did not encourage much serious working in the later days of coal getting, though it was nicknamed Wallsend. It was mined at Park Hall Colliery in 1885. The Mans coal is so named in the Dilhorne Foxfield area because it was said to be worked from outcrops by the Manns brothers just before they touched the Woodhead near the brook just west of Dairy House farm. Of the Cobble and Rider coals only the former made any impact on the industry. It had been extensively worked by outcrop in an earlier period all around the inner coal field and during the later part of last century it was worked more seriously. In fact, one mining family headed by Mary Plant decided to change its name to Lucksall perhaps hoping in this way to influence the fickle fate governing coalmining. This seam, usually about one foot six inches of very good quality and one hundred and thirtyeight feet below the Foxfield, was good enough to be worked at the Cheadle Park colliery from 1904 until it had worked to its boundary in 1913.

The Rider coal also covers a wide area of the inner coalfield around the town itself, but since it could only offer a foot of coal and was a mere eighty feet above the Woodhead, which was the goal of all nineteenth century coalmasters, they tended to ignore it and dig away to the coal they fully expected would make their fortunes.

Below the Woodhead seam there remain but the two lower layers like the bottom two large dishes on which all the upper layers rest. These are the Crabtree coal at some four hundred and sixty feet below the Woodhead seam and a further varying great depth to the Third grit or Sweet coal. Although these are at great depth around most of the field, the great fault down the Churnet Valley reduced the depth to be dug at Ipstones, Foxt and Whiston and these seams, especially the Crabtree, sometimes again called Stinking, have been of the greatest importance there. When the Froghall ironstone was rediscovered in the 1850s between these coal seams the Crabtree was invariably included in the mining leases along with the red iron ore. The Sweet Coal was mined on the outer fringe of the field on the north and east beyond the villages named and many traces can be found of this working two miles beyond the valley.

The Cheadle coalfield, therefore, carried but some twenty feet of coal, a quantity which could easily be matched by one seam in the South Staffordshire coalfield or three seams worked by our neighbours in the Potteries district. That twenty feet, however, gave this comparatively small town and the villages around a certain independence and a most important aid to growth. This growth was of necessity slow since the dip of the seams, which Plot mentioned, kept the operators waiting for new developments in mining and changes not too expensive to be tried on these thin seams.

Although there were amateur geologists working in the pits at the end of the 19th century, we had to wait for the professionals to point out that despite the break of two or three miles between the Cheadle and the Potteries coalfields they were, in fact, one field. Prof. FW Wolverson Cope had made a study of what life there had been in each of the layers and matched up the seams conclusively by 1945. What we called the Woodhead, the Potteries called the King but unfortunately all our seams were some twenty-five per cent thinner. Some had also pointed out that the Cheadle seams were at a higher level than their neighbours accounting for the loss in thickness.

We have followed a few enterprises through the seventeenth century but must have missed some quite important operations through lack of documentary evidence. Dr. Plot found activities in the Cheadle area which might well have put our local workings in the forefront of the industry.

## *Dr Plot's Description of 1680*

During the 1680s he wrote of the dip of the Cheadle seams but later, having introduced the subject of gas and its dangers, he wrote about his experiences of the workings and damps found in them:

> *"Of Damps caused when they make great fires to soften the rocks to make them yield to the pick axe. Damps unfit for respiration. Such Mines as above are seldom or never free from damps. And of this sort, perhaps, are the damps of the coalworks about Chedle."*

He did, however, go on to explain:

> *"Unless the rocks above being hard have the fire put to it"* the miners *"would not work away so much in a day as will fill a hat   And yet these damps are neither visible nor noisome nor will they take fire but are so gross and moist that they extinquish it and are suddenly mortal."*

Having described the dangers he went on to show how we at Cheadle tackled the problem of clearing these damps from the workings:

> *"The second sort of damp occasion'd by srnoak they dispel either by water where they haw no Air pits and in winter time but chiefly by fire which they let down in an iron cradle they call their lamp into the shaft or bypit next to that they intend to work. The smoak damp must necessarily come away and fresh air come down the other pit which very way they use at Chedle and tis a secure one too but very chargeable."*

Plot described how coal workings in other parts of Staffordshire were troubled with fire damp and tells of some bad accidents but since he makes no mention of these around Cheadle he must have learned what later geologists and mining men have come to accept.

Apart from the fire basket, further precautions were taken against the dangers of smoak damp as time went on. Testing with naked candle flame was used around Cheadle as candles were to light dark passages and haulage roads.

In addition Plot used mining terms that had not been written previously in 1680 and many of them remained for the next three centuries. He spoke of the decision whether to boar or sink a pit", of the *"diping of the seams"*, of *"footrill and setings and pillar"s* and whether the mine would *"dip to the water"*, or *"crop to the grass"*. In the actual winning of coal he mentioned the wallings or stauls and ribbs left called thurlings. He then considered laying their coales dry with such variety of expensive Engines and use of Sough or by Gin. Of the latter he wrote of the use of the small gin called a jack which was either turned by men or the larger by horses. These could be either chains with leather suckers to bring up water or by *'barrells whereby one goes up as the other goes downe will also void great quantities of water provided they be constantly followed day and night, which Engines being so common'*.

Plot continued to describe how large amounts of limestone were quarried by hand and increasing quantities of coal were being used in lime burning in the moorlands:

> *"When they have gotten the Stone they burn it in oblong pits, made in the ground about seven yards long, 3 wide and but 6 or 7 foot deep at the but of the pit: wherein first they lay a little wood or gorse to keep the coal from the ground, which is laid under the Stone, the first stratum but thin, not above 3 inches thick; then a stratum of stone about 6 inches deep; the next floor of coal they make 10 inches thick, andthe layer of stone above that, 18 inches: the next coal above that is usually about a foot thick, and the floor of stone over it double the thickness; then the 4 layer of coal is but 10 inches and the 4 of stone but 18: then above all another stratum of coal about 2 or 3 inches, which they cover with parget or mortar, made with flak't lime and water to keep in the heat: the coal laid in this manner with the Stone S.S.S. burning it gradually into Lime in about a weeks time."*

The eighteenth century opened with more people thinking of coalgetting not necessarily for personal use but rather for profit making. Politics were not occupying the minds of our gentry about the turn of the century since it appeared, for a few years that William III had been accepted and the quiet accession of Queen Anne had banished, for a while, any Jacobite troubles.

One such example is found in the Alton Rolls headed:

> "Farley Coalmine
> 1702 Rec'd Rents from Coalmines    £3
> Poles sold to miners           £3     6     8.
> 1717 Arrears due for the Coale Mine   £24
> 1720 Sep 29 Farley The Coale
> Mine being at an end.
> 1729 Farley No 30 Heretofore
> Coale Works non Gott."

This would appear to be one of the less successful efforts to mine at the Cotton end of Farley. It is likely that some one had found an outlying area of the Sweet Coal which at that point could not have given the miners much satisfaction, though it would give Richard Bill, the Steward of the Shrewsbury estate, some experience.

Other mentions of coal are documented at this time though none of any consequence. The Povey Charity dated 1702 listed in Cheadle Parish Church porch includes coals under certain lands left to the charity but no subsequent mining operation has been found.

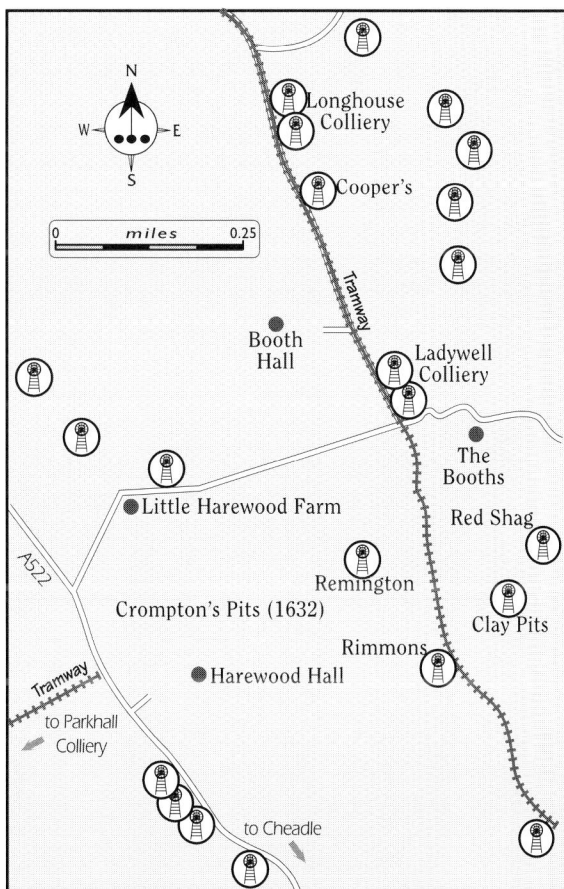

*Crompton's Pits, plus later shafts.*

# Mining in the 18<sup>th</sup> Century

In 1719 Mr. Joseph Banks of Revesby Abbey, Lincolnshire had become the Lord of the Manor of both Cheadle and Kingsley having held lands in both manors some sixty years previously. Within a short time he was approached with a view to mining on the west side of Kingsley. In September 1721 an agreement was made with a John Philips, Gent., Lord of the Manor of Checkley and Tean, father of John and Nathaniel both of whom developed, from 1744 the thriving textile industry of Tean:

*"to dig, delve sink and make Pitts drains in that part of ye wastes of ye said Manor called Churchs Gorse and from the Dumble or Valley at the North Side or bottom thereof to bring up a sough or gutter underground to drain all the coale that may be found in his" grounds comonly called the Oxleasers Colepitt Fields and Empty Shaws Lying near the said Church Gorse."*

This sough was also to drain any coal *"in a little farme of the said Joseph Banks in the possession of John Mosely."*

This farm would appear to be one called Hollows Greene in a later sale catalogue. Having gone to the expense of digging the sough, Philips was to pay a rent of Twenty shillings a year and was to:

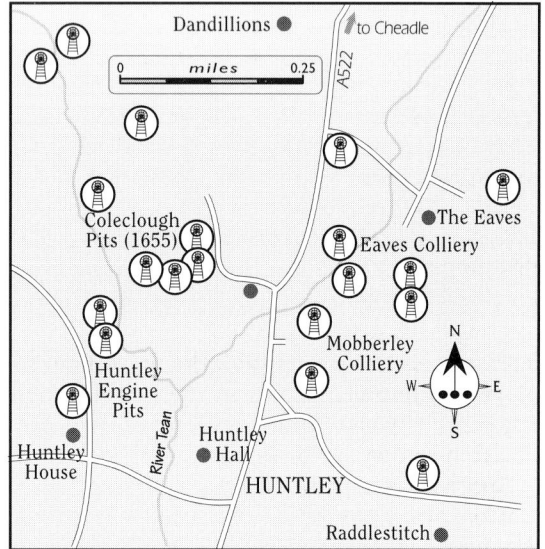

Colclough's Pits and later shafts.

*"allow the said Joseph Banks half the moneys for which such coals shall be sold free of all charges."*

This was a most important agreement for Kingsley people at this date mainly because of the extent of ground covered in one document and the length of time the lease was to run. In this district it would be possible to get down to the Woodhead coal at about forty yards and the sough probably cut as the document states. The Church Gorse land was the Glebe and stretched from the brook up to the Hollins and the remainder was on the left side of the road. In 1721 this was a vast area for mining. The important section had to do with the sough for at this period it was the only method by which an area of coal could be drained or unwatered. This agreement was witnessed by brothers George and Thos. Gilbert of Cotton, two gentlemen of a family destined to play a most important part in the district's history for a long period.

A further clause was added to the 1721 lease in 1730. This imposed certain further conditions on John Philips in that not only was he to get a minimum of coal:

*"as will at 8d per doz amount to Five pounds p. Ann."*, but also *"to commence the carrying up the said intended sough to the said Mr. Banks coals. Which sough at the*

*level it is now begun shall be carried on to lay Mr. Banks coales dry and not stick at Mr. Philips coal to hinder the same"*. The last three lines appear to have been included in Mr. Banks' own handwriting and witnessed by George Gilbert and Henry Browne.

By the end of the same year, Joseph Banks had completed a further lease to John Moss, William Carr and Edward Johnson, probably a Kingsley trio, *"to get coals in my works at Hassells Cross ....... at 20d p.Doz to allow me 12d a week for my burning – Coals 2 corfulls to John Mosley and 2 Corfulls to ye sough to allow 2 Corfulls to ye Banksman for every day he attends ye Bank. When they neglect to come to work and everyone neglecting a Day without being hindred by sickness to forfeit his days wage to the others coming to work"*. The Banksman was appointed to check on the amount of coal sold from the pit bank to satisfy both parties to the agreement that payments were correct. Other conditions of payment to miners varied locally but, in general, followed the formula for this early period. These leases served to turn Kingsley into a mining village as the Churnet Valley iron industry began to cut back in manpower. The Banks had held many properties in Cheadle and Kingsley through the seventeenth Century and lists of such holdings, including the old Cheadle Manor house, Park Hall, are recorded in 1679 and 1686 though most are but cottages.

Joseph Banks the second visited Cheadle in 1767. The account follows at the end of this chapter. This famous Botanist with the same name, who sailed with James Cook in his 1768 voyage round the world and had something to do with naming that part of Australia as Botany Bay. Cheadle's rose grower, Colin Thompson, informs me that many later species of flowers took the word Banks in their names and that he, later Sir Joseph, played an important part in the establishment of Kew Gardens. They do not, however, appear to have had time to attend to their properties in this area until there was a sudden decision to dispose of them in 1790.

Another enterprise of note ws also progressing during the 1730's. Thomas Gilbert of Cotton and Robert Bill of Farley were neighbours. The Bill family had come into the Alton district early in the seventeenth century and by the end, one had become the steward of the Shrewsbury properties in that area. He was living in the Lodge, near the Farley end of Alton Park, a building designed to accommodate the Earl and his retinue when he came on his hunting trips. At this date this premier Earl of England had taken a final step up in The Peerage and was titled the Duke of Shrewsbury, so that Robert Bill had an important post, obviously well paid and privileged since he now held the lease of the old water corn mill in the valley. Indeed, he had become something of an industrialist by subleasing the mill to the new Cheadle Brass and Copper Company of 1734 and bought a minor partnership in that enterprise. At the same time he had joined with Thomas Gilbert in a lead mining venture on Thorswood hill near Stanton three miles to the east and in a coal mining partnership on Gilbert's property at Clough Head, lpstones. Robert Bill also had an interest in the Ecton Copper Mine. See *The Copper and Lead Mines around the Manifold Valley*, pp 67, 204, 244. The Gilberts later built themselves a larger house, Cotton Hall, more a gentleman's residence than their previous home in the district at Licks Head.

## The Clough Head Colliery

We have a few pages of the coal accounts at Clough Head, Southeast of Ipstones, and these, though not inaccord with today's accounting standards, give some idea of the workmen, costs and problems of mining in this period. They would be mining the Crabtree Coal at approximately 40 yards deep.

An account of Clough Head Colliery from 24 Dec 1737 to 24 Dec 1738:

| | £ | s | d |
|---|---|---|---|
| *Elijah Hodgkinson & Brigs Cr Slack 9447 cwts @ 14d ton* | £33 | 0 | 8 3/4 |
| *Elijah Hodgkinson Sinking a pit @ £1 10, another @ 5/10* | £1 | 15 | 10 |
| *all Walter Snow banking 286 days @ 8d p.d.* | | | |
| *Coveling wood 3s all* | £9 | 13 | 8 |
| | £44 | 10 | 2 3/4 |
| *Mills & Moss Cr Slack 7791 @ 14d per score to ye 100* | | | |
| *all six scores* | £27 | 4 | 11 1/2 |
| *Mills 150 load of Slack got in bringing up ye Sough* | £1 | 5 | 8 |
| *at 14d price* | | | |
| *Pd Mills remaining part of Sough* | £1 | 5 | 0 |
| *Francis Ford Banking 220 days at 8d per d.* | | | |
| *A present to him 10s* | £7 | 17 | 0 |
| | £37 | 12 | 7 1/2 |
| *Totoll both* | £82 | 2 | 10 1/4 |

*26th Dec 1737*

| | £ | s | d |
|---|---|---|---|
| *Spent and gave the Colliers Ernest in Lowing and sinking Pits* | £1 | 2 | 5 |
| *Jos Allin 2 pare headstakes & a caurfe 2s 2d Boal dishes 2 @ 8d* | | 2 | 10 |
| *Faulkner filling Pitts @ 3s 6d and Banking* | | 14 | 6 |
| *22 days @ 6d Slack 300 load got last year went this year* | £1 | 1 | 0 |
| *@ 14 d p score getting* | | | |
| *Wid: Fearney slobs 1s Carridg 6d Packthread 3d Flower 2d* | | | |
| *Cars for A ring 8d* | | 2 | 5 |

*10th June*

| | £ | s | d |
|---|---|---|---|
| *Pd Richard Scarratt for caurfs reppairs 8s* | | | |
| *Jo Botham 21d @ 6d is 10s 6d* | | 18 | 6 |
| *Gave Walter to buy paper 2d Ditto to give* | | | |
| *Feleck to drink 6d I gave carriers to drink 2s* | | | |
| *Also Banksmen & lads 2s all* | | 4 | 8 |
| *Mr Beardmore 15 coards of Postwood @ 12s p coard laid down* | 9 | 0 | 0 |
| *Francis Snows team carring Pitt Lowes and Stone* | | | |
| *to the Causey 16 days @ 3s 6d per day comes to* | 2 | 16 | 0 |
| *Ditto himself 24 days labouring @ 10d per day* | 1 | 0 | 0 |
| *Jo Bradshaw 22 days at Causey @ 10d per day* | | 18 | 4 |
| *James, Berisford 10 days @ 10d Causey* | | 8 | 4 |
| *Thos Gidsall 25 day @ clearing Pitt Lowes @ 8d per day* | | 16 | 8 |
| *Matt Faulkner 7 days @ clearing Pitt Lowes @ 8d per day* | | 3 | 6 |
| *Miller 5 days @ clearing Pitt Lowes @ 8d per day* | | 3 | 4 |
| *Robert Eatons Team clearing Pitt and stone to Causey* | £1 | 5s | 5d |
| *John Eatons Bill Smiths work 9 days @ 3s 6d* | 1 | 11 | 6 |
| *my Troble* | £5 | 5 | 0 |
| *Mr James Hall a heape left out last year* | | 9 | 0 |
| *Left out clearing Pitt Lows Geo Salt 6 days* | | | |
| *Miller 2 @ 8d p day* | | 5 | 4 |
| *Mr Faulkner's Charges cordwood more* | | 4 | 0 |
| | 110 | 15 | 8 1/4 |

| | | | |
|---|---|---:|---:|---:|
| *Colliers Slack with our owne 17517 @ 2s 6d per score comes to* | 132 | 2 | 3 |
| *Coals 210 loads @ 3d per load haulso ours comes to* | 1 | 6 | 3 |
| *Slack and Coals Totoll* | 132 | 8 | 6 |
| *Charge Totol* | 110 | 15 | $8^1/_4$ |
| *Proffit* | 21 | 12 | $9^3/_4$ |
| *Mr Bills Moiety* | 10 | 16 | 5 |
| *Mr Bill made that Year* | | | |
| *Coal Mine* | 10 | 16 | 5 |
| *Lime Kilns (half Profit)* | 5 | 3 | 4 |
| *Thorswood Lead Ore* | | | |
| *One 24th Profit of £357 15 9/4* | 14 | 18 | $1^3/_4$ |
| *Totol* | 30 | 17 | $10^3/_4$ |

*Lime My Troble £10* (This was Gilbert's fee).
Later annual accounts show little detail.

| | | | |
|---|---|---:|---:|---:|
| *1738 Clough Head rent* | 7 | 10 | 0 |
| *1 739 Clough Head Profit* | 2 | 0 | $7^1/_2$ |
| *Coals to Alton Mill charged wrong in former acct.* | | 6 | 6 |
| *1740 Clough Head profit* | 9 | 15 | 0 |
| *1741 Clough Head Profit Mr. Bills Half* | 12 | 7 | $0^1/_4$ |
| *1742 Clough Head Colliery profit Mr. Bills Half* | 8 | 4 | 6 |
| *1743 Clough Head Coalmine Rent* | 7 | 10 | 0 |
| *1744 Due Lady Day Clough Head Coal Mine* | 7 | 10 | 0 |
| *1741 Slack from Starwood 289 loads @ 2/6 p score* | 2 | 1 | $1^1/_4$ |
| *1748 Acct by 7400 bricks from the Star @ 9/- per thousand* | 3 | 7 | 0" |

This mine, which had been working before 1737 appears to have produced mainly slack and served the furnaces in use at the Alton Mills brass wire works. The manufacture of brass wire entailed the preparation of the brass sheets, which had been transferred from the Cheadle works, by repeated heating in furnaces and rolling through cast iron rollers until they were reduced to the thickness easily cut by the slitting machine. This required a constant supply of fuel and Robert Bill was in a position to supply the demand.

The underground winning of slack was the work of the butties, Elijah Hodgkinson and Brigs as one team with Mills and Moss in charge of the other. The former worked in tons and cwts while the latter used the older measures.

Whilst most of the charges covered work normally undertaken in the mines of this period there are some items demanding further attention. The sough had been previously dug to the earlier pits and was now being extended to unwater the coal from the pits further north on the estate. In this case it would be cut to take water down into the Churnet. From all the documents of this period and over the whole of the field the successful mining of coal depended upon employing effective methods of dealing with water and the deeper the coal, the more necessary it became to invest money on the digging of the sough which has now become a common feature in the industry.

The filling of pits and levelling of pit lows so that the surface can return to its former use is also of great importance in any agreement for mining. One unusual item mentioned in these accounts is the causey. This was an abbreviation of the word Causeway, meaning in this case, much more than a path but more likely a horse or cart track.

Above the Clough Head estate running along the eastern boundary of lpstones, Foxt and Whiston the narrow road across the ridge is know today as the Casey. From the

Whiston end it runs easily onto what later became the turnpike road down into Oakamoor and both Casey and Oakamoor track would be of the utmost importance to Gilbert and Bill to get their slack to the Alton brass works or any other users around the district.

It will be noticed that the labouring wage gave the men four shillings per week of six full days whilst Faulkner managed only three shillings and the slack which cost the management fourteen pence per score was sold for two shillings and sixpence. The caurfs, later termed corves, were a strong form of wicker basket for dragging the corful along the pit bottom and required regular replacement.

Mrs. (Widow) Fearney's consignment I find some difficulty in explaining but the manager's £5 5s.0. fee, called *"My Troble"*, seems a reasonable salary to add to his *Proffitt*.

It may be appropriate in passing to point out that Thos. Bolton & Sons Ltd. were mining in the same seam but some quarter mile further south and some two centuries later!

## Hounds Cheadle

In 1733 the widow, Francis Grosvenor, had died without children. She had occupied Hales Hall and she and her husband, Archibald, had purchased three quarters of the old Manor of Hounds Cheadle. She willed it to Dr. Wilkes of Willenhall, the historian, and Caesar Colclough of Delphouse. This led to the break up of the estate and the possible last use of that title. Both Edward Leigh of Woodhead and Edward Mountfort of Wall were interested in its disposal.

### Mining at Kingsley

At about this period, the first half of the eighteenth century, a certain John Cliffe of Kingsley was setting his small piece of land to coal mining. His name appears in the vestry minutes book as being a supplier of coal to the parish church in 1738:

*"Mr Cliffe for 9 cartfuls of coal and carraige 3/-"*

He was a Church-warden in 1741 under Rector Wenman but by 1743 he became more of a small busi-nessman by leasing the coal below his two

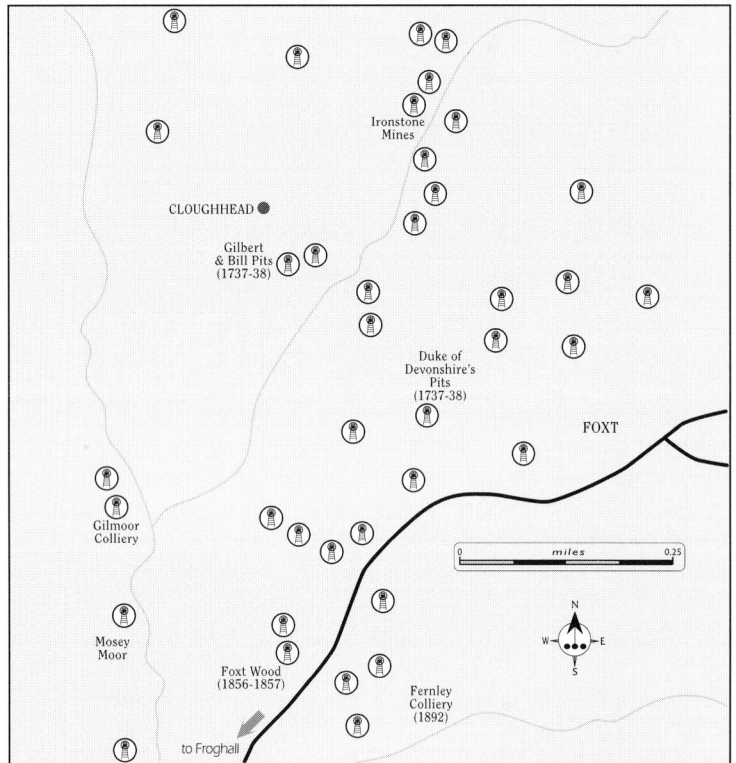

*The Gilbert and Bill Pits and the Duke of Devonshire's Foxt Wood Colliery.*

tenements to a certain "*Francis Smith of Penkrich (Penkridge) and to Thos Brian of Woodlain a collier, in the Psh Stoke on Trent*". The lease for 21 years is in an unconventional form in that Smith had financial responsibility for the whole concern and is repaid by taking the coal at 8 $\frac{1}{2}$d for every twenty-four skips of two hundred pounds of coal in each skip. From this John Cliffe was paid the rent for the mines. The name, Cliff's Pitts, was used until the end of the 19th century around Hazles Cross.

There was one other coal works in Kingsley at this time. In 1741 the Overseer for the poor in the village was expected to find work for the paupers and their children to relieve the rates from the burden of providing them with food and clothing. The rates had risen since the responsibility had been placed with the vestry meeting, equivalent to our parish councils, in the Elizabethan period. The entry in the accounts:

"*1741 Spent with Sinion Waterhowe about taking Hackwood into the pit 2d*"

Waterhouse was a Kingsley name, indeed, John was a Churchwarden. Hackwood left his name at the lodge at Hazles Cross and the expenses suggest that a visit with Simon to the ale house made persuasion easier and took 1s. 6d. per week off the rates.

As miners began to go deeper and wider or further from the base of the shaft, they began to find that, at times the coal they were digging disappeared and they were forced to search for another layer. These irregularities, the miner learned, were faults in not merely the coal layers but all the measures of rock, shales and clay they dug through.

Barrow gave the impression that this small coalfield had slightly more than its fair share of faulting which, of course, added greatly to the difficulties of mining especially in the lower seams. Some idea of the difficulties created can be obtained by imagining ruck of crocks receiving a sharp heavy blow on the top layer, the shock of which reaches and cracks all through the heap, some cracks splitting the crocks in one or two ways so that they are no longer complete. In fact the shock has come from below but the effect is much the same for the miner since he has often lost his seam by a hundred feet or more. Barrow does, however, quote a case where faulting has been of benefit to a locality. A bore hole for water was put down north of Foxt near the end of the nineteenth century but struck the water carrying grit stone near a fault which had brought the lower grits near the same level, so that the bore drew from both water-carrying layers in such quantities as to be able to supply Kingsley for many years.

Barrow's geological map indicates the more important of the faults. That running east-west from Hales Hall to north of Dilhorne affected all workings in that region. A second in that direction runs from the Churnet Valley by Kingsley Holt to the Haslewall district. There are three major faults running north-south, one from the Churnet Valley, half a mile north of Froghall running south to join the east-west fault under Hales Hall; a second from Ipstones south to the Valley under Froghall continuing to Lockwood and a third from Ipstones Park, south to run under Froghall Wharf to join the Valley and continue to Eastwall. Only in a few areas do faults under the coalfield show evidence near the surface. Searching for evidence of the presence of red ironstone along the Kingsley Banks some thirty years ago, I found a good two foot outcrop of the seam had been left for support, outcropping low down in Hazlewood where many foot-rills had been made to win the stone. Whereas the stone could be found at much the same altitude across the valley in Booths Wood, along to the area between Hill House and Riddings, it had been thrown up to the top of Ruelow Wood by a fault coming from Belmont toward Booth then down into the Churnet Valley. The Cherry Eye mine, operating until

1923, had used footrills where the outside ground was blood red and near two hundred feet above the altitude in Hazlewood.

In many cases during the nineteenth century coalmining had been halted by miners coming across such formidable obstacles and much coal was then left for later men to work.

## Coals to Lode Mill, Milldale

According to one of the Cheadle Brass and Copper Company's first account books a large amount of Cheadle coal was being taken into Derbyshire to calcine the Calamine (zinc carbonate), and do away with the transport of rubbish to the Cheadle smelting furnaces. This process got rid of 8 cwt. of unwanted material from every ton of raised zinc ore, most important for Cheadle transport arrangements which was carriage on pony backs. To help cut wastage the Cheadle company had employed a builder at Alstonfield to erect a calcining furnace at the northern end of Mill Dale. it is now called Lode Mill and dealt with the calamine from Ecton Mine and other neighbouring mines. (See also *The Copper and Lead Mines around the Manifold Valley, N. Staffs*, p.244).

From 1737 the company was using Woodhead coal from the first Woodhead seam at Cheadle, but by 1750 an entry records:

> *"John Brassington, J. Smith, Salt, Alkins for coals by them D.d. to the Cally House at Mill Dale 12T 16 Cwt.*
> *£6 - 8s."*

and shortly after:

> *"Pd W. Crompton for 17 Rucks of Cheadle Moor Coal at the Mill at 4/8."*

This was the only mention of the Cheadle Moor colliery which Barrow identified when he marked the site of four shafts and found them partly filled and fenced. It is the Silverstone housing estate and the shafts are shown reaching three hundred yards from Oakamoor Road and some sixty to one hundred yards from Moor Lane. The owners of the colliery were not named, but it would not be surprising to find that the Gilberts of Cotton Hall had some part in the ownership.

# THE PARTNERSHIPS

4

By the middle of the eighteenth Century we had found a few cases of small groups, in twos or threes, often including a mining man, joining together to mine coal where it was not too deep. The old fashioned method of dealing with water underground by soughing was commonplace to the mining man who was regarded as expert by those in the group merely there to provide cash for early expenses.

By the middle of the Century, however, we were also to see the emergence of more important groups who were to form partnerships, some of which were passed from father to son with the accumulated know how to enable these groups to be active for around a century.

## The Dilhorne District

One such started in 1753, not surprisingly in the Dilhorne district, by gentry who had been dabbling singly for some considerable time before. An indenture or agreement was made between Simon Mountfort of Beamhurst Hall and Edward Bamford of Summerhill, near Bank Top, Dilhorne. The agreement was set out in a perfectly legal manner by Randle Wilbraham who was acting as solicitor to an arbitrator should he be needed. The Mountforts had already started to mine in the Newclosefields area and Edward Bamford, who knew this area well, wanted that business joined with his own nearer Dilhorne; probably because he expected to put a sough down in his workings which would also lay Mountfort's coal dry.

Bamford, at this early period, was a highly respected name. In the seventeenth Century his ancestors had occupied the old Park Hall, the ancient manorial Hall of Cheadle, but in the possession of the Banks family, previously mentioned. The earliest record of the Bamfords is in 1625 when the impoverished James I of England came from Scotland and demanded that everyone with property exceeding £40 in value should accept a knighthood. Thomas Bamford refused and, with others, was fined £10. Widow Bamford occupied the Hall in 1679 and paid Banks a Chief Rent of £20 per annum, the highest figure by far of any tenancies in Cheadle. In 1686 her son, Samuel, paid that rent but, since the building was probably of the half-timbered construction surrounded by moat, its deterioration may have been the cause of the Bamfords move to Tickhill Lane to build themselves, (according to Pitt, writing in 1817), a most *handsome mansion* at Summerhill. It may have retained some of its outer walling but its stone gate posts were of a class that would add to that very pleasant name.

The 1753 indenture pointed out that the lands, under which both parties mined, were divided, but both depended on liberties used by the other party. They, therefore, mutually agreed that all profit from any part of New Close land should be equally shared; that Bamford should inspect all accounts, be allowed to dig any loose (sic), sough or drain and should allow Mountfort all such facilities. We do not, however, have any record of any such accounts, though the partnership must have worked satisfactorily as the Mountforts retained their working interests with Bamfords for the following eighty years.

## The Kingsley District

An indenture of 1758 transfers our attention to the Kingsley district. It concerned John Richardson, William Bostock, Edward Coyney of Weston Coyney Hall and William Chawner and the two Smiths, father and son, probably of Whiston and related to the mining of coals in the latter's estates in Kingsley. It is followed by another agreement by Bostock for mining in 1759 and again refers to the Kingsley area. The three papers referring to these workings are comparatively small, two of which could be called scraps, but the partners named are certainly, by this time, recognised as of the highest reputation. There are involved Charles Gilbert, witnessed for by his brother, William, who had come into the Cotton area, and were in the 1737 venture with Robert Bill; John Holmes, whose family were in mining and were working from Delphouse, and Edward Chawner, one of the draper-mercer line in High Street, Cheadle, whose son's death was reported in the May, 1795 editions of the *Staffordshire Advertiser*, and he as *"an eminent mercer and draper in that town"*. The Chawners appeared to be sleeping partners at this period and Edward had merely signed the agreement on behalf of the working company, Wm. Bostock and Company. The document is not legally or carefully written but reads as follows:

> *"1759 Agreement between Charles Gilbert to get remaining coals in Bentley's field that are upon ye Level and enquire leave to have a sough through Gilberts Land. Wm Bostock & Company to get coles and slack in lands in Kingsley (with Chas. Gilbert)."*

A further clause seems to be added some eighteen months later:

> *"12 Jan.1761 Paying ninepence a doz at every four shillings worth of coles and slack getting all Corves of and leviling the land in a proper maner and not to damage the barn, if hurt to make it good and not to damage the fences and to pay all trespass whatever in a little time.*
> *Witness Wm Gilbert        my hand        Charles Gilbert X his mark*
> *Jn° Holmes        Edw^d Chawner"*

The most interesting point is that this again must have been in the Hazles Cross district where the talk is about ye level and the digging of a *"sough through Gilbert Land"*.

It is likely that this enterprise continued for quite some years for a Vestry Meeting entry reports in 1773 of the examination of an applicant for outdoor relief being out of work. The fact was that if he could not prove that he was a Kingsley man with a legal settlement in the Parish then he did not qualify for relief:

> *"1773. From Exam Papers. George Oliver was hired by Wm Bostock to work in the Coalpits in Kingsley."*

## The Gilbert Lease

The next lease, which turned out to be one of the most important for this period and, indeed, for the whole coalfield was signed by the brothers, Thomas and John Gilbert of Cotton with the land holder, Mr. Whitehall, on 8th May, 1759. It was for *"his coal and other mines on the south westside of the Churnet in the Parishes of Cheadle and Kingsley for a period of 31 years"* paying for the lease one eighth of the coal a Duty. At this time the Whitehall land stretched from the Booth Farm lane joining the Cheadle, Kingsley

Holt road to the Woodhead square. It became important because the Gilberts doubted the ability of a sough in any direction to drain a pit dry with a difference of less than one hundred feet from site of the mine to the brook through Woodhead district. They had decided to sink just off the road opposite the most northerly houses in the Hammersley Hayes area. Some forty yards to the west two small pit lows, now grass covered, can easily be seen, the one, clear in the upper field, the other, partly hidden under the tree, in the hedgerow which was probably planted during the Enclosure of Kingsley Parish about the beginning of the nineteenth century.

The Gilberts were as progressive in coalmining as in their other enterprises and here they decided to instal a water engine to pump out water and lift the coal to the surface and do away with the need for a sough or windlass. The track to the mine left the road at a point where the bus shelter now stands, fifty yards beyond the Miners' Rest Public House and made its way up to the pitlows. The cartographer surveying shortly after this date to prepare for the Yates map of the area published in 1775 was taken by surprise to such an extent that he marked ENGIN on the map, the only one in north east Staffordshire at that time. This became the Engin Pit by 1760 and around 1975, in talking to Jack Fallows, whose family had worked the Booths for nearly a century, about mining near the farm, he explained the lows by saying that his father always called them top engin and bottom engin. Both Cobble coal at fifteen yards and Woodhead around thirty-five and forty yards were mined at Engin Pit.

There was only one first class millwright and engineer in North Staffordshire. James Brindley at this period, the 1750s, was concerned with both watermill maintenance and a new company in steam engines. He had also met the Gilberts probably while on a visit to Cheadle to buy brass in 1758. A further note in his diary gives *"May 7, 1759 on Wednesday Night Mr. Brindley to be at Gilberts to go to Ecton the next morning"*. This was not surprising as the 1734 details (above) illustrate the variety of interests the Gilberts had. On May 17 1759 a short but most important diary entry reads *"Cheadle. Mobile Water ENGIN. May 17. 1 Day"*. The ENGIN could not have been Mobile in the current sense of the word. it must have been a large permanent structure to be mapped by Yates. There would be many interested and inquisitive strollers to see this rather ugly and noisy piece of machinery, a water driven pump. There is no further record of its working in any document until the rather sad disintegration of a partnership where the engin had to be specially valued and transferred to other workings.

It was probably a horse-gin (or whim) used to draw water out of the shaft with barrels. These were common in the Derbyshire lead mining area. Where they were often called 'engines' at this time.

## The Woodhead Concern

The Leighs of Woodhead had by this time extended their coalworkings to follow as far as possible, in their own estate, the Woodhead seam which, facing the two o'clock had become increasingly difficult to win. The appearance of the water engine only half a mile from their lands under the direction of the Gilberts eventually prompted proposals for a partnership. In fact this should haw been the most sensible course for all concerned as there had developed a veritable scramble for leases of coal in the district.

The growth of the workings of the Leigh concern from Woodhead Hall are difficult to date as no lease agreements were necessary since the land belonged to them. The new Hall had been built in the early eighteenth century and was to be the ancestral home whilst the sons found themselves houses in and around Cheadle.

They dug their shafts near the Hall in what later in the nineteenth century became known as Allen's Park, but no pitlows were left to spoil the outlook from the house. Signs of workings further west, where the Allen family later levelled the ground to make a cricket pitch may still be seen. Many senior citizens will remember the posts protecting the Allen's team cricket ground and the rivalry between this and the Cheadle town team. Further away still, a shaft was sunk about a hundred yards from the Cheadle-Kingsley Holt road. When a later owner, William Bowers, built the Woodhead complex of buildings, cart sheds, stables and a row of dwellings for his men he knew nothing of that shaft, which next revealed itself by collapsing in the north east corner of the yard in the mid 1930s!

On the 10th March 1762 a lease was made between the Rev. W. Bill & a Mr. Walker and Mr. Edward Leigh which gave permission to drive a sough under the land of Lovatts in Kingsley Parish called by the name of Lower Long Lees, to convey the coal and slack or to carry

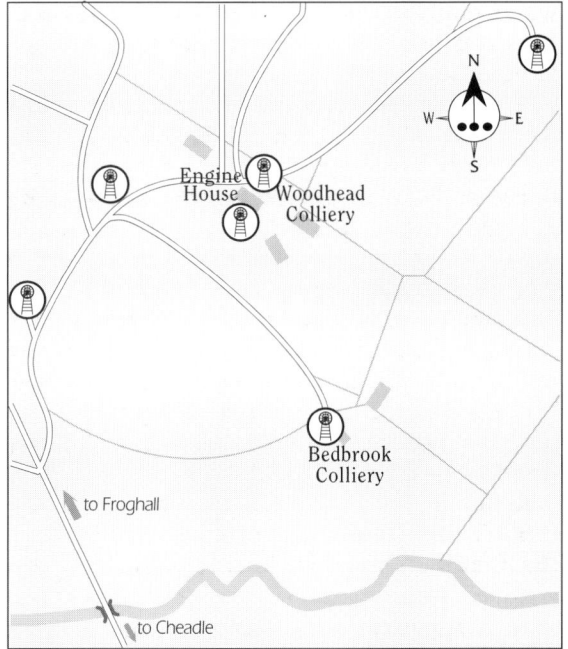

*Woodhead Colliery.*

*Woodhead Old Hall (from Plant's History of Cheadle)*

water into the sough. Lovatt's land was on the north side of Leigh's land called Long Lees and it was necessary to dig the sough to drain water as there was supposed to be large quantities of coal and slack.

A meeting of coal leaseholders and those already mining in the area on the east of the town was called and on November 2nd, 1762 they were a stronger group than could previously have been collected. When the partnership was agreed upon, all leases were to be handed in to the Gilberts to ascertain what acreage of land was available to the new company and to check the length of time each had to run.

The list of partners makes up a very heavy brigade so far as Cheadle was concerned. The Leigh family represented by the three members, Francis of Woodhead, Edward of Greenhill, which was already a mansion, and John Leigh, had much the larger share whilst the two Gilberts of Cotton, Thomas and John, very soon had much more important business to attend to. Both became closely linked with the Duke of Bridgwater and his canal enterprises and worked, together with James Brindley, around Worsley, Manchester and on the early work of the Canal. That story is admirably told and illustrated in H. Bode's *James Brindley* and Peter Lead's *Trent and Mersey Canal*.

Robert Hurst of Cheadle Grange and John Bill were minor partners, the former because he had leased land for mining to the Leigh's previously and had also joined later in the mining enterprise, whilst John Bill, the Rector of Draycott, whose sister, Lydia, three years his senior, had married into the Gilbert family, was following the tradition of an industrial connection with his in-laws.

The combined mining leases added to the Woodhead estate was by far the largest area of coal-producing land ever to be held by one concern in Cheadle. Stretching from Kingsley to the Thornbury and Hammersley Hayes district; to Woodhead and the Bedbrook and Grange land with the Whitehall land on the west side of the Kingsley Holt road running down to the present Miner's Rest, it was worked through two generations of Leigh's and one of Bowers', until the middle of the nineteenth century. The partnership itself lasted but twenty years, composed as it was of men of such strong character. The Gilberts were taken, by time, into such different streams of life and brought a critical attitude to the industry they had virtually abandoned.

There are no accounts available to show how the business thrived and the documents available threw doubt on the ability of John Leigh, who had been put in charge of the company's affairs. These papers tell the sad story of the disintegration of the largest of the Cheadle coalfield companies after the most confident beginning with this list of leases in 1762:

Leases of Colliery.
   "*18th May 1759. Mr. Whitehall lease to T. & J. Gilbert his coal and other mines on the south west side of the Churnet in the Pshs of Cheadle and Kingsley for 31 years at an 8th duty.*
   *2nd August 1762. Mr. Thornbury leases to Messrs Leigh and Robert Hurst all coal mines and other mines on his estate at Thornbury Hall for 21 yrs at the rent of £20 per annum in lieu of duty.*
   *5th November 1762. The said T. & J. Gilbert assign. said mines and Collieries so leased to them to John Leigh Thos Hurst and John Bill for the term of 27 Yrs 6 months & 10 days tendering a 6th put of the coal by way of duty. How hath the difference between a 6th & 8th been Acctd for?*
   *5th November 1762. The said Mr. Hurst & Mr. Leigh assign the Thornbury lease to the said J. Leigh, T. Hurst & J. Bill for the remainder of the term rendering the 6th Duty.*

*5th November 1762. Ed Leigh & R Hurst, as Trustees of the last will of Dr. Grosvenor dec'd payment to the former in the which lease to sd John Leigh, Thos Hurst and J Bill by the 4th put of coal and other mines in the Woodhead Estate for term of 21 Yrs rendering 3 twenth fourth parts by way of duty for all coal etc to begot.*

*Covenant from Ed Leigh & Robert Hurst to renew the lease for the benefit of the leasees for such further term or time before the expiration of the leases as they are empowered to do by & under the said lease.*

*5th November 1762. Francis Leigh leases to John Leigh T. Hurst J Bill his fourth part of the coal in the Woodhead Estate for 27 Yrs 6 mths 10 days rendering one 6th Duty with Covenant to renew.*

*5th November 1762. Robert Hurst leases in like manner the coal within his estate in Psh of Cheadle for same term and same Duty.*

*5th November 1762. Assignment from Ed Leigh to John Leigh of the Colliery lease granted to him of mines in Kingsley for the remainder of the term. All their leases declared to be in trust for the aye and benefit of Francis Leigh, T Gilbert J Gilbert, Robt Hurst & Ed. Leigh upon the terms mentioned in articles bearing equal date.*

*5th November 1762. Articles of Partnership for carrying on said mines. N.B. Mr. Francis Leigh Mr. Ed. Leigh leases were not delivered to Mr J Gilbert with others."*

Nothing is found of the accounting until some two years later when there appears to be some unorthodox interference with the book keeping department:

"23 Oct. 1764
Mr T Gilbert, Pd Mr Hurst on Acct

| | | £ | s | d |
|---|---|---|---|---|
| Woodhead & Kingsley Colliery | | £31 | 10 | |
| Acc with Mr. Henshall | | 42 | 3 | 4 |
| *Brother has a paper extracted from Mr Hursts Book* | | | | |
| Recd for coal u per Book C R | p 3 | 327 | 8 | 6 |
| Do | p 4 | 264 | 9 | 9 |
| Do | p 8 | 114 | 17 | 4 |
| Do | p 12 | 641 | 3 | 3 |
| | | 1347 | 19 | 3 |
| *Payments as per Colliery Book* | | | | |
| | p 3 | 101 | 19 | 6 |
| | p 4 | 136 | 19 | 7 |
| | p 8 | 29 | 1 | 9 |
| | p 12 | 187 | 11 | 4 |
| | | 446 | 13 | 2" |

The page of accounts, whether it represents the page of figures for the year or for the two years of the partnership, appears to show a very substantial margin of profit and is possibly the reason why no other documents are found until April 1781.

A document dealing with the affairs and accounts for 1777 had been examined by John Gilbert and he was not satisfied that the accounts were being correctly made. At a meeting called to discuss these affairs he called for the matter to be decided by a barrister. The case was set out fully with names of partners and changes since 1762 – for instance, Robert Hurst had died some four years previously and Edward Leigh, the earlier manager was now insolvent. Unfortunately, in certain transactions between these two there was a discrepancy of £150 which Gilbert felt should be in the funds of the company. The document reads:

> *"The said Robert Hurst many years since paid and recd many sums on acct of the said colliery to and from Banksmen colliers etc and also paid for different articles used by the workmen which are entered by his own hand into the ledger. But his executors cannot find many of the vouchers for the payments nor when and what quantities of coal were sold."*

It appears that later Hurst's representatives, including his son, the Rev. Thomas Hurst, brought evidence about the disputed £150, but Gilbert objected, demanding the vouchers should be shown or the matter referred to arbitration. The matter was eventually sent to a barrister, J. Mansfield, at the Temple who found in favour of Mr. Hurst on April 7th 1781.

## The end of the partnership

By 1784 a number of the leases had run out and a meeting of the partners was held at "The Star" on the 12th November to put the accounts in order. This hostelry, comparatively new at this time, standing on the new turnpike road instead of its former site on the old Cotton road, was to become quite well known by parish meetings which held a form of Civil Court, with illegitimacy examinations and to punish runaway defendants.

This meeting attended by Mr. Grosvenor, Mr. T. and J. Gilbert, Mr. Fenton on behalf of Mr. Hurst, Mr. Rupert Leigh and Mr. Hill on behalf of Mr. Edward Leigh's Creditors and Mr. Rupert Leigh on behalf of Francis Leigh, his father.

There was some small talk to do with payments of certain dividends followed by:

> *"There appeared to be a Dividend of £20-5. a/c for each and then between Mr. T. & J. Gilbert the sum of £10-2-9 ded. the value of the Enegin and working tool was transferred to Mr. Rupert Leigh."*

There was further discussion on dividends and a new lease. There was talk of finding further accounts of Mr. Hurst and Mr. Leigh when Mr. John Gilbert came into the discussion.

Extracts of part of Mr. Hursts account were produced by Mr. John Gilbert for some years after the year 1762 when the partnership commenced.

Once again there was mention of the arbitrator:

> *"Mr. Gilbert said a Bill might be filed to make the enquiry from the parties upon Oath and he thinks if they do not produce the books and accounts a Bill of Equity ought to be filed for that purpose to oblige Mr. Hurst, Mr Rupert Leigh and Mr Ed. Leigh to produce upon Oath or give the best account they can of the transactions."*

All was not sweetness and light! In fact, it was the end of the partnership and we shall see how the young John Leigh continued with the coal getting while the Gilberts spent more of their time in Canal Company work and Thomas in politics as a member for Newcastle-under-Lyme.

## *The Dilhorne Enterprise*

On the Dilhorne side of the field others had watched the progress of the Woodhead partnership increasing its output and with work and leases continuing expansion for many years.

We saw that Edward Bamford and Simon Mountfort had made the 1753 agreement but though both continued in the trade, they had not followed the Woodhead example in the next decade. We do find, however, that Edward's son, Samuel, began to take note of the trends in the industry and when he took over in 1774 he set about bringing more capital and actual mining expertise to his aid. Simon Mountfort had practically given up. He lived in Newcastle-under-Lyme and had allowed Samual to do the mining in his lands and leases in both Dilhorne and Cheadle parishes at £100 per year, so that Bamford had, during this period of growing demand, opportunities to build a coal empire. There was no Woodhead coal, as yet, available to him on the west side, but there was plenty in his area that could be mined with comparative ease.

In August 1774 he agreed, with four others, to mine in the lands he had leased. The. Agreement is as follows:

"*Between Samual Bamford, Gentleman of the 1st Part*
*Elias Goodwin, Cheadle, Chandler.*
*John Hall, Leek, Yeoman*
*Robert Benton, Cannock, Coalminer*
*Joseph Howlett, Cannock, Coalminer of the 2nd Part.*"

*Dilhorne Colliery's first "fire engine" 1778*

Bamford, it would appear, had made a wise choice in getting the services of experience with the two Cannock men. For himself, he was to be allowed:

> *"the liberty to get slack to take to lime kilns to be exchanged for lime for the improvement of their own lands, to carry away with horses carts and waggons. Also to make bricks for his own use but not for sale."*

The miners should pay a rent of £100 per year and fourpence out of every five shillings worth of coal sold (i.e. a royalty of 15%).

On the same date a regular partnership agreement was signed between these four which gave the partnership much more power. They were, for the time being, to be the only unit working:

> *"In the land of Bamford and Mountfort to put in full force a certain Coalwork or Colliery in several lands in Cheadle and Dilhorne. To take over works lately occupied by Wm Yenley, Benjamin Wolfe, George Heath, Wm Thorley, Benjamin Goodwin Charles Weywell and John Woolingscroft."*

A further clause was added stating that all partners should:

> *"share the damage and loss from the Inevitable Accident which may happen."*

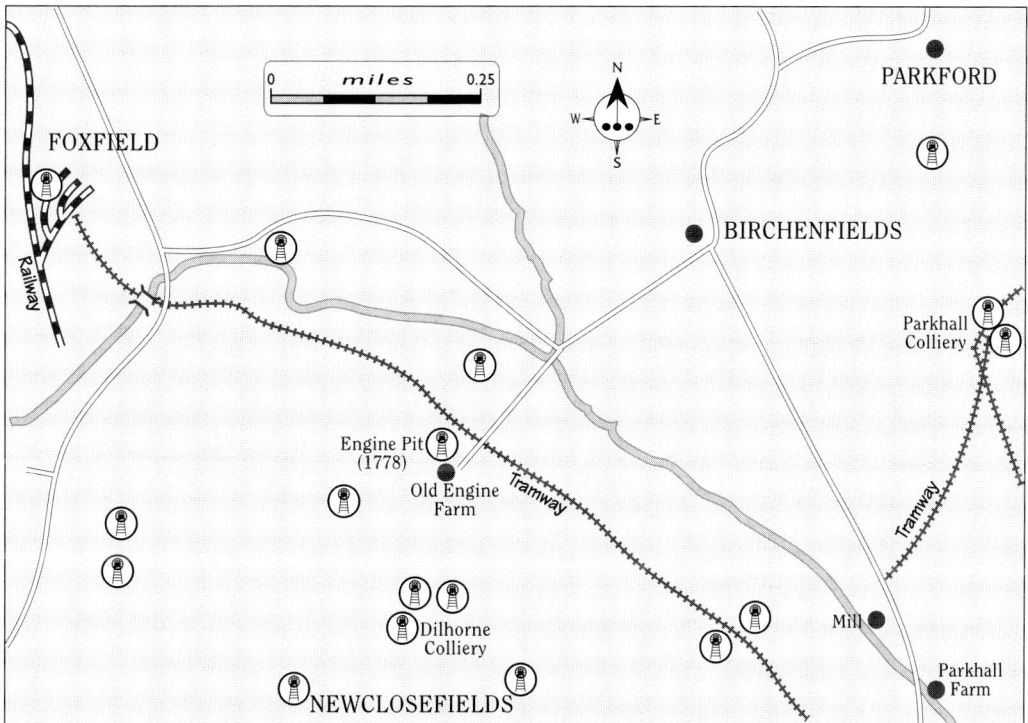

*Dilhorne Old Engine Colliery, 1770.*

Yet a further clause states:

*"That the coal which belongs to other persons which may be laid dry by the engine or engines then Samuel Bamford shall have free liberty to purchase such mines at any time so long as the agreement lasts."*

The partnership obviously felt that it would be necessary to follow the example of the Woodhead Company, especially as they were proposing to mine where soughs could not be effective.

There had obviously been progress from the beginning of the workings which had been carried on in a most business-like manner but three years later in 1777 a second agreement was made but, whether the colliers were temporarily short of cash or not, Bamford granted some relief in a most unusual manner.

*"lst July 1777 Since making and granting of the 1774 lease, the lessees have been put to great trouble and expense in erecting the TWO fire engines and finding other materials for making and carrying on work of the within mentioned Colliery. Then 1, Samuel Barnford, will release the other partners of any rent owing at my decease. My Executors will not insist on payment and at the expiration of the Term will allow a further five years and discharge of my rent."*

This was at the Dilhorne Colliery workings which from then on were known locally as the Old Engine Farm area. These engines came just too late to be included on the survey for the 1775 Yates map. These fire engines would appear to be early Newcomen type steam engines.

The Colliery continued working until 1784 when it was more than ten years old. It appears that some money troubles had accumulated which caused Bamford to call in the solicitor, John Child, who prepared a surrender document and the partnership was dissolved. A footnote was added *"Nothing written shall release or discharge the said Elias Goodwin, his executors etc from any sum of money that is due from E Goodwin to Saml Bamford"*. The document was signed by all the partners and, like John Leigh at Woodhead, Barmford was left to find new associates in the Dilhorne coal district.

## Other concerns in the coalfield

Other mining men had found places where it was comparatively easy to get coal around this period. Although there are no detailed documents, we can see from some of the earlier firms' accounts the wide area from which they could obtain fuel. The Cheadle Brass and Copper Company was now almost thirty years old and bought coal as follows:

*"Aug 1761 Beerage to Dilhorne Colly*
*3/3*
*1762 Coals from Dilhome, Shafferlong (Sleck), Shawe,*
*Litley, Mobberley and from the Ash to Alton Mills.*
*July 1763 Dilhorne*
*21T10C*
*Shawe*
*383T          10C*
*Litley*
*13T7C*

Mobberley
24T0C

In 1765 the price and cost was as follows:

*"Mobberely*                                              5/0 per ton*
*Dilhorne*                                             3/4 per ton"*

Again Shafferlong was selling Sleck and the Brass Company paid for the year £211 – 11 – 6:

*"1766 Getting coals at the Ash."* [The site of the Ash has still not been discovered.]
*"1769 Jos Flower 1616T coal £291 - 15 - 7."* [This was around 3/6 per ton.]

In 1767 John Gilbert had leased, without being partnered by a member of the Bill family, from the Earl of Shrewsbury:

*"All coal and slack mines now open or known or my be found in the Townships of Cotton and Farley. Paying 1/- for every six score horse loads."*

Although there is a possibility that he would have found some areas where the Crabtree or the sweet Coal were obtainable, he would not expect the output he was used to in the Woodhead Colliery workings. Two of the districts he may have explored are the first two mentioned in Farey in his Derbyshire list of Collieries in 1810. Among those he lists as working "Formerly" are:

*"Beelow* $^1/_4$ *m. E of Oakmoor mills and. "Carr Wood NE of Oakamoor mills 2nd Coal"*

To local folk in the district who remember seeing what appears to be a very shallow shaft mouth to the west of Beelow Hill, it must have been very distressing to think that Farey may have mistaken our local earthwork monument for a pitlow or spoilbank!

Another lease and agreement of about this time concerns the area around Crowtrees between Whiston and Oakamoor. The lease is from Dodshon and Paxton, who lived in Bristol but owned the piece of Jack Elms and a certain Thomas Mytton of Cleobury, North Salop, who also held land at Jack Elms, Whiston and Crowtrees. Only the Yates' 1775 map marks the spot just north of Crowtrees, which,within the next fifty years became Jack Stones, the settlement which disappeared under the upper British Industrial Sand quarry in the 1970s. This part of Jack Elms must have been south west away from the cover of the hard sandstone. Having dug a sough to drain his coal at his own expense around 1766, the sough would drain the neighbour's coal, hence the lease to Mytton by Dodshon and Paxton. Mytton was allowed to sink pits, airpits and dig soughs or drains and have wayleaves for horse carts etc. The accounts had to be open to the lessors who had to have a banksman paid by lessee to receive the rent monthly of one eighth part of all money from coal raised on their lands. The lessee had to fill in all disused pits to one yard above ground. They all expected this to last for a long time, but from the Kingsley Vestry Book there seems to have been some breakdown.

1773 Examination Papers in which the applicant attempts to prove that he had a Settlement in Kingsley and can claim outdoor relief state:

*"Rich. Good swears he was hired in 1766 by Thos Mitten Esq to work in his coal works in Kingsley at 9/- per week and 2 guineas a year besides and was to remain in his coalworks for life and if hurt he was to pay him the same wages during life."*

Since the lease was for 100 years it appears to have been a very good wage but unfortunately, we are not given any reason for closure.

## Joseph Bank's Visit

In 1767 Joseph Banks of Revesby Abbey, who was twenty-four years old, recently finished at University and having an interest in biology, natural history and to some extent geology, set out on a four month journey through Wales and the Western counties. His family had held property in Cheadle and Kingsley and in 1719, the manorial rights of both places. It was not surprising, therefore, that he should pay a rather more lengthy call on the manors and this is put of his account of the visit:

*"For minerals here are coals in plenty one of 6 feet called Dillen coal of which I have a little but very little upon my Estate. Its Dip is very odd laying in a half circle or rather a horseshoe open at one end the length of the horseshoe laying N & S and the dip constantly towards the middle where it has been seen but the open end dips too much under the hill to be seen.*
*Here are two other coals in Kingsleigh and the upper put of Cheadle a yard coal & a 3/4 which is called stinking and is fit only for lime [burning] which lays under the good contrary to the common method these hang to the south dipping to the noon sun and cropping to the north."*

He does not, however, talk of mining any although within three or four years is leasing land in Kingsley for that purpose. He also mentions the ironstone found *"in a wood of mine called Hazelwood"* picks up some lumps and has others collected but has a doubt about its industrial value.

He sailed on that most memorable voyage with Captain Cook a few months later and afterwards became President of the Royal Society.

# THE DUKE STAMPS HIS MARK

## 5

By the time the Cheadle district approached the end of the eighteenth century it had developed to such an extent that it could expect to be regarded as an important industrial area. We have already followed the progress of the coal industry, seen the rise and fall of a most significant iron industry (see chapters herein on the Churnet Valley iron industry), had half a century of a very important brass industry spreading to three centres, followed by an equally robust textile industry. The arrival of two much improved transport means, turnpike roads and canals, developed beyond anyone's wildest dreams to serve the limestone industry over a wide area of the Midlands. These had not only served our stable, very important and rapidly developing agricultural activities which had leaped ahead since the operation of the enclosure awards. They also gave opportunities to farmers to provide food, not only for the local populace, but also helped in the feeding of the growing urban centres.

Into this atmosphere there arrived another industrial unit under the wing of no less a person than the Duke of Devonshire whose activities for the thirty-five years from 1780 to 1815 were to provide opportunities to all from the humble labourer, to metal making men, to farmers with carts, to brickmakers and even to the well-known, now famous clockmakers, the Holmes family of Cheadle.

We read in 1758 how the engineer-millwright, James Brindley, was taken by Gilbert of Cotton Hall to Ecton where Gilbert had an interest in the copper ore working that had been tried and failed for a very long period but were now proving very profitable. Over this period, the Duke had been satisfied to lease the options for mining to various groups until Brindley's visit just about the time when prospects appeared brighter. In 1760, following the end of a two year lease, the Duke decided to go into the business on his own account with the help of a good Agent and good managers. An excellent history of this enterprise is given in Porter and Robey's *Copper and Lead Mines around the Manifold Valley,* published in 2000 after the most intensive research. The copper ore production increased to such an extent that a major change was decided upon by 1770 and this involved the local coal mining industry in the Kingsley and Foxt area.

The Whiston smelter was opened in 1770, but we have no records of the Duke's coal workings until ten years later, possibly because most of the effort came from his works at Kingsley and no records, as such, have been retained for that period. Indeed, Kingsley records are quite unsatisfactory compared with those kept for the Foxtwood project and from these we gather not only production figures but the names of both miners and carriers with wages and costs. What is known is that coal was being taken to Whiston 'from the pit' in 1770 and then taken also to Ecton Mine.

The Duke already held land in the Hazles Cross district at Kingsley and it must have stretched between the Hollins Lane and east for half a mile towards the Cross end of the village. This was next to the Breach land on the north side and only a quarter mile from where the Woodhead outcropped near the Hollins-Hazles lane. On occasion the documents refer to the Duke's Hazels Cross mine, but there is no doubt that this Kingsley Colliery was of the greatest importance in the supply of coal for the Whiston smelter. It was made up of some four shafts, the Head Pit and three in line stretching 550 yards quite near the Breach or Briches as the 1801 plan gives it. Earlier the area had been called the Birches. A level was dug to unwater the area and joined the Duke's Level to the east. The four shafts must have been sufficient to last the thirty years whilst the Foxt workings in the Third Grit coal were being replaced over the whole period. The 1801 plan does not show a fifth shaft which appeared later quite near the Hollins Lane.

The earliest one inch O.S. map of the district of 1836 does not show this colliery, but it does record another at the end of the Duke's Level. Four others, the "Woodhead", "Dilhorne", "Delphouse" and "Blake Hall" Collieries are the only ones shown over the whole field, whilst the Foxtwood workings are marked as "Coal Pits".

There is one other important feature about the Duke's Colliery. The mine needed to be drained and, with fuller accounts of the Kingsley workings, we would have read of the cost of making this most important sough. It was started in 1784 and was a major engineering feat for that period. Barrow included it on his work sheet with its title, in deference to His

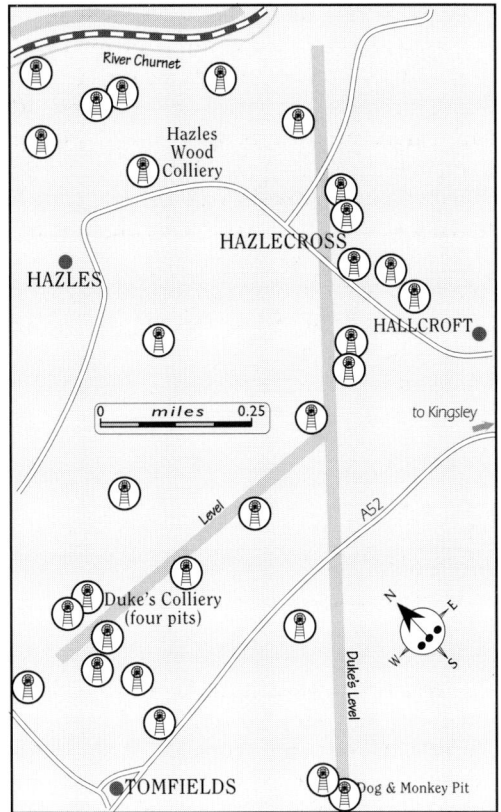

*Duke's Level.*

Grace, this was called The Duke's Level and was the longest on the coal field, running underground one and a quarter miles to the north-east, to pour its water halfway down the little streams running from Hazles Cross by Cold Ley Farm to rush into the Churnet below. It gave the Kingsley colliers both work and a talking point for the next century and had become a fable in the twentieth. This colliery was leased out after the Duke had finished smelting at Whiston and was in production until after 1850.

The whole vertically integrated industrial unit:the Ecton Copper Mine, the smelter and two coal mines, were under the Manager, Mr. Cornelius Flint, who was paid as other costs were paid, for a six-week period followed by a seven-week period to make a quarter. Flint was paid £18.15.0. per period, so that his salary was at £150 per annum, a very high figure reflecting the importance of his work. He visited regularly each unit and was seen so often in Kingsley and Foxt that the workings were called Flint's Pits and up to sixty or seventy years ago the old miners continued to use the nickname. John Heath was the clerk and had to attend both collieries. At times there was more accounting, writing and booking at Kingsley, so that he entered for the year in 1783:

> *"John Heath's Salary for his attendance upon the*
> *Kingsley Colliery due Midsommer 1783* £20 0 0
> *Ditto his attendance upon Foxwood Colliery*
> *one year* £10 0 0"

Many horses and carts were needed to carry the large amount of coal necessary to prepare the ore by calcining, getting rid of nearly fifty per cent of the weight as rubbish by heating. This process was carried out at Ecton, to reduce the volume to be carried to Whiston. This was then reduced in the Whiston furnaces with a percentage of some old slag which carried a proportion of copper. Having arrived at a stage which produced a black rough copper liquid, this was melted again with two or three passes through the furnace until the smelt had the appearance of a liquid copper. This succession of melting demanded a large quantity of the better grade of coal and usually this meant a large number of carters. These were listed in the six or seven-week period – it took both to make a quarter, with their payments for the period. It should be remembered that the costs at this time were reckoned at *"1/- per ton per mile"* and that Whiston Bank was rather more difficult than the motor surfacing of today, although the Turnpike Trusts had brought great improvements. Many of the names sound familiar because they are in use today.

| *"Thos Beard* | *Carr Coal* | | £15 | 11 | 2 |
|---|---|---|---|---|---|
| *Thos Allcock* | " | " | £16 | 18 | 11 |
| *W. Goodwin* | " | " | £7 | 18 | 6 |
| *John Ginders* | " | " | £8 | 3 | 11 |
| *George Locker* | " | " | £12 | 19 | 7 |
| *John Townsend* | | | £10 | 13 | 2"* |

The last two were certainly in Kingsley parish – Locker was in Whiston and Townsend a member of a very well-known Kingsley farming family who served their community as Churchwardens and overseers for more than two generations. One member scraped his name in the upper balustrade of the steps to the fine example of a seventeenth century house above the Smithy in High Street, Kingsley.

Each payment period included those two items which varied according to output:

| *"Expenses Foxwood Colliery* | £28 | 1 | 6 |
|---|---|---|---|
| *Expenses of Kingsley Colliery after the sale of* | | | |
| *the coal is deducted* | £80 | 9 | 0"* |

It appears that this colliery had a much larger output of Woodhead or Cobble coal than did the Foxwood of Third Grit coal.
It also appears so from one extraordinary entry in 1794:

| *"Sept 1794. Advanced to John Stivinson for the purpose* | | | |
|---|---|---|---|
| *of weekly payment of Kingsley Coaliers* | £145 | 0 | 0"* |

The payment came about because John Heath had died and his executors paid in the sum of £105 he had in hand.

## The Duke's Activities

Foxwood was really a series of very small pits whilst the Kingsley had but the four permanent shafts. Foxwood had started in the fields behind where the much later Wood-cutters Arms was to stand and worked its way further towards the north-east under small pieces of ground, a few belonging at that time to Kingsley School Trustees, and then on

Expenses for Colliery & Reckoning for 13 weeks ending Sept.r 22.
1780.

| | | | £ | s | d |
|---|---|---|---|---|---|
| John Hall | 28½ days a 14/ | | 1 | 13 | 3 |
| Ralph Leather | 20 d.o d.o | | 1 | 3 | 11 |
| Tho.s Weston | 20 d.o at d.o | | 1 | 3 | 4 |
| Joseph Jonson | 33 d.o 1¼ | | 1 | 18 | 6 |
| d.o | 12 d.o at 15/ | | | 15 | |
| Wm Johnson | 37 a 10/ | | 1 | 10 | 10 |
| John Wharton | 63 a 14/ | | 3 | 13 | 6 |
| John Shornson | 24 a 14 | | 1 | 8 | — |
| John Tatler | 16 a d.o | | | 18 | 8 |
| Joseph George Olliver | 41 a 14 | | 2 | 7 | 10 |
| William Carr | 13 14 | | | 15 | 2 |
| Tatler & Shornson 2 Lads 10 days a 1/ | | | | 10 | — |
| Hall & Bentley 2 Lads 10 d.o a 14/ | | | | 11 | 8 |
| Mary Carr Gin driver | 11 d.o a 3/ | | | 2 | 9 |
| Samuel Plant | 18 d.o a 14 | | 1 | 1 | — |
| Richard Hill | 14 d.o d.o | | | 16 | 4 |
| Richard Weston | 16 d.o d.o | | | 18 | 8 |
| Jn.o Goodwin | 22 d.o d.o | | 1 | 5 | 8 |
| Abel Carr | 17 d.o a 1/ | | | 17 | — |
| d.o Drawing Spoils & Repairing the Road | | | | 13 | 1 |
| d.o for Heading | 47 Yards a 14 d per | | 2 | 14 | 10 |
| d.o for Drawing | 18 Y.d Deep Line a 2/6 | | 2 | 5 | — |
| p.d Mr. Sherwood | 14 Loads of post Wood a 16/ | | 11 | 4 | |
| Daniel Carr Getting 757 M.l a 1/6 p Ton | | | 56 | 15 | 6 |
| W.d Faulkner Weston 118 d.o in d.o at 1/6 | | | 8 | 17 | — |
| | | | 106 | 0 | 6 |

A page from the Hazles Cross Colliery account book for September 1.780, in the hand of Cornelius Flint. It shows the number of days worked and the price per day. Note the entry for Mary Carr, Gin driver, at 3d a day. Opposite: A further page from the same accounts. Note the tonnage sent to Whiston (821 tons 17cwt 6 stones) and that just over 806 tons was available for general sale. (Devonshire Collection)

| | | | |
|---|---|---|---|
| Brought Over . . . . . . . . . . . | 106 | 0 | 0 |
| Thos Taller Glebe Land 663 a 18/ Tons | 49 | 14 | 6 |
| Td for Mendeen Heading Shallow Level at 4/ p Yard | 1 | 2 | 2 |
| Taller 9 Yards Heading Deep Level 2/6 | 1 | 2 | 6 |
| Paid for Bowing & Making Hay &c . . . . . | 1 | 1 | |
| John Braddockes Bill Post Wood | 1 | | |
| John Boltons Bill Getting & Carrying Stone . . . | | 18 | |
| Mr Dodson duty upon Coal got on Wages Dodsons Land 62 Tons | | | |
| Mr Dodsons duty of 937 Tons a 7 1/2d p Ton | 29 | 5 | 7 1/2 |
| Coal Got in Wages in the Glebe Land 28 Tons | | | |
| Tythe Coal to Mr Haywood of 691 a 5d | 14 | 7 | 11 |
| To two Pieces of Ash Repairing the Gin | | 12 | 2 |
| | 205 | 4 | 4 1/2 |

| | | | |
|---|---|---|---|
| Coals to Whiston &c Rests Ending 12 Augt | 182.16 | | |
| Do for the Rests Ending 28 Sepr Wm | | | |
| p Bill . . . . . . . . . . . | 418.1.4 | | |
| Do p Myself p Steel to Do | 116.17.6 | | |
| Do p Do to poor | 65.16.4 | | |
| Mr Gould to Cart | 38.6 | | |
| | 639.1.6 | | |
| | 821.17.6 | | |

| | | | |
|---|---|---|---|
| Totall Coal Dodsons . 937 Tons | | | |
| Do in Glebe Land 691 | | | |
| 1628 | | | |

| | | | |
|---|---|---|---|
| Mr John Heath Debtor upon the Bank Deducted | 806 . 3 . 5 | 201 | 10 | 9 |
| 1628 | 1628 | 3 | 13 | 7 1/2 |

134 . 19

to the very old track between Foxt and Ipstones. An agreement between Cornelius Flint and the Whieldon family, who were then at the Farm which now bears the family name, was reached.

At Whiston there were repeated calls for James Keates, the glazier from Cheadle, annual visits from one of the clockmaking firms, the Holmes of Cheadle; or their men, Joseph Slack or John Ashton, who charged 15/-, much less than the partner, Andrew Holmes, who charged £13. One intriguing payment was an annuity to Mrs. Jane Smith who received £20 in half-yearly instalments. She must have had some connection with the Whiston Eaves family, one of whom, George Smith, had by 1790 handed over the iron works at Oakamoor to the Cheadle Brass and Copper Company. It was a marrage settlement attached to land purchased by the Duke of Devonshire.

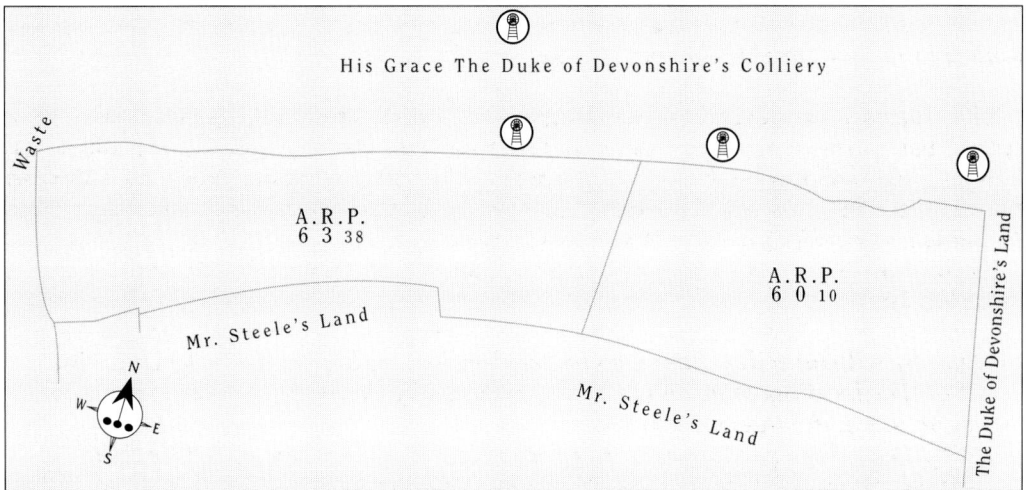

*1801 Plan of the Duke of Devonshire's Hazles Cross Colliery (see also page 56-57)*

In works of this kind there was always work for the blacksmith who could be asked to make tools of all shapes and sizes. Francis Gosling was working in his smithy at the Watt Place end of Lower Street after 1819, renamed Bank Street because a Trustee Bank was set up that year in that elegant building, now the Ex-Service Centre. The smithy continued until about 1960.

There had grown a useful trading relationship with James Beech, the new lord of the manor of Kingsley. Several timber accounts are recorded such as:

[1800]
"James Beech of oak timber                             £48        17        2
James Beech more oak timber                            £23        18        6"

Whilst at the same time the Duke had leased more land for coal to Beech adjacent to the Kingsley Colliery:

"19/7/1800 By the amount of 2A 2R 22P of coal sold to
Mr Beech at the sale, of £45 per Acre                 £118       13        9"

In 1790 the Duke had taken a further lease on the coal under that large space of Kingsley Glebe land stretching from the Brook up to Tom Fields and the Hollins:

*"To the Rev<sup>d</sup> Mr Peak for the duty of coal Got under the Glebe at Kingsley from 16/3/90-10/9/91 being 4290 Tons @ 10d per Ton       £178      15      0"*

By this time the Turnpike Trusts were taking their tolls and keeping the main roads in fair repair. It did, however, cost the industrial units a considerable amount especially in coal and lime, two heavy-weight commodities likely to put extra wear on road surfaces. It was not surprising, therefore, that industrialists looked for alternative methods of routing or carriage of loads. Most were satisfied to compound their charges at certain gates into an annual fee, for many of them held shares in the Trust and expected to receive their annual profits. To relieve the Kingsley Colliery of such excessive payment the Duke began investigation into the building of a tramway from the Colliery to Froghall:

*"25 Oct 1794 Expenses twice of different people on acct. of setting out the proposed Railway from the canal to Kingsley Colliery      £1   3   10"*

This tramway was never built, but Flint saw the possibilities of using the empty wagon system being drawn from the canal at Froghall, past the Whiston smelter and when Rennie's tramway ran by the side of the smelter in 1802, it became most convenient to the coal carrying routine. The Turnpike Trust, however, objected by claiming that the *"revenue was cut by carriage of Coals in the Reelway"*.

By this time we begin to hear of deaths in coal mines. In Kingsley Parish Registers is recorded for 1782-3:

*"Jan 14 William Hill Collier who by accident lost his life in one of the Coal Pitts at the Hazles Cross Mine on Jan 11th was buried by Coroners Warrant. A subita et improvisa morte libera nos Domine.*
*1783 Dec 27. John Moss who by accident lost his life in one of the Coalpits at Shaw mine on the 17th and was buried by Coroners Warrant.*
*Dec 22 Thomas Salt who by accident lost his life as above."*

It is surprising that with all this activity in coal, the Bailey's Directory for Cheadle of 1784 mentions only one person in coal "Bamford Samuel Coal Merchant".

The Cheadle Parish Accounts tell of some unfortunate pitmen:

*"Aug 7 1795 That Thos Hollins of Lane End Collier be allowed 5 shills.*
*Feb 1796 Benjamin Barker sent to the House of Correction refusing to go to work in Dilhorne Cole Pits.*
*May 1796 Thomas Plant allowed 4/- out of work last winter being drowned out of coal works."*

The Staffordshire Advertiser of March 19 1796 displayed:

*"To be sold by Private Contract Two Closes Dilhorne 12 Acres. Occupation of Joseph Chell under which there is a valuable mine of Coal".*

The Foxtwood Colliery had records of mining and distribution from 1780 to 1815. When the accounts started the first note read:
*"Measure of the field which the Coal has been got in Foxtwood Old Working is 2A 1R 32P."*

By 1781 the Colliery was usually paying £55 per acre.

*From the opening of these workings the names of the butties in charge of coal getting or other work were entered in the ledger:*

| "1780 Wm Foard & Co | 75T | 15H 5S @ 1/10 per ton |
| Delivered to Ecton | 3T | 7H |
| to Pen (High Moor) | 74T | 16H |
| 1781 Wm Plant & Co | 80T | 16H @ 1/11 |
| 1782 Aron Beardmore | 172T | @ 1/9 p Ton." |

There followed additional names such as:

*"Jno Currier & Co, John Archer & Co. John Ferneyhough*
*Thos Shipley & Co for getting slack by bargain 1/10 per ton.*

| *Wm Stevenson & Co.* | *100 Ton at 1/8 p Ton* |
| *1794 Samuel Bostock & Co* | *120 Ton @ 2/-* |
| *1798 Abel Carr & C.* | *114 Tons @ 2/3* |
| *1801 Jonathon Stevenson & Co* | *60T at 2/5* |
| *1804 John Carr & Co* | *112T @ 2/6* |
| *1810 Jonathon Fernihough* | *81T @ 2/9* |
| *1811 ditto* | *45T @ 3/6* |
| *1811 ditto* | *25T @ 3/6"* |

The French Wars had brought a rise in the price of coal, as it had in all rates.

The accounts give a good picture of how much coal was extracted and who were the customers. Unlike the Kingsley coal which appeared to be used mainly by the smelter, this poorer grade was sold out for lime kiln work as in the case of the 1793 production:

| *"To Hemingslow Kilns* | *469T* | *14H* |
| *To Different Persons* | *305T* | |
| *To Whiston* | *7T* | *14H* |
| *To Ecton* | *22T* | *9H* |
| *With other sundries Total* | *829T* | *10H"* |

This gave a total profit of £10 7s 3d. The following year gave what was probably the best production of 1176 Tons with a profit of £63 3s 4d while Ferneyhough and Co. were mining this at about 1/8d. per ton. There were, however, periods when the works were at a standstill as in 1800:

*"1803 Production Nil. Loss £93 Wm Stevenson and John Carr employed repairing and cleansing the Deep Level. Only 42 Tons sold off the Bank.*
*1807 395 Tons. Loss £34 Jonathon Stevenson and Co at 2/6 p Ton. No coal got Nov-April."*

There is also an early mention of concessionary coal:

*"1781 Burn coal Chas Whewell 18 weeks at 4d.        6s.        0d."*

A very large amount of detail is included in the accounts, but we get the impression that there is a rapid succession of shaft sinkings and headings in different directions that the work expended did not repay with a sufficient quantity of coal or slack.

There were sunk nine shafts in that comparatively small area, which were given names that could be changed at the wish of any of the sinkers. In 1781 there were worked the Old Pit and the New Pit. Within the following two or three years, there were the Level Pit, the New Level Coal Pits, the Old Works, the New Colliery and the Slack Shaft. Moving further north-east, there were sunk the Stockings and the Nagors with the Rice or Rise Pit and the Deep Pit.

By 1793 the workings were approaching that Foxt-Ipstones track above Ipstones Park where the land belonged to the Whieldon family. The farm had the name Whieldons during the iron ore mining period in the 1860s. The accounts record the agreement made for the coal in that area:

> *"Expenses at Foxt and Kingsley when Settling with John Whieldon   6s    8d."*

The cost was worth some three or four tons of his coal but it was no dry settlement. Earlier, the brothers John and Joseph Whieldon leased 1rood 25perches of coal in the New Work called the Stocking, also the last of the coal at the Old Works 1R 3P for £37 2s 6d. From 1812 mining finished at Foxtwood and work such as retrieving bricks, fencing shafts and levelling continued. By 1814 we find:

> *"1815 Paid to Joseph Whieldon for Damages of nine Pit Lows*
> *which had not been removed by Lady Day 1815                £100*
> *20 Sept 1815 Paid Ditto      Do                                    £43   10   3"*

One other new feature of the mining here was the erecting of Fleaks over the shaft. This was a large cover over the shaft opening designed to protect the man operating the windlass to draw up the coal and prevent rain from going down the shaft. A fleak was made of straw bought in thraves, thatched and erected as follows:

> *"1784 2 Fleak; 1787 3 Fleaks + 2 fleaks making; 1788 2 Fleaks; 1792 3 Fleaks to*
> *shade the pits with; 1794 2 Fleaks, 1 Thrave of straw for thatching Fleaks; 1806*
> *Making Fleaks (2) to shade the pits."*

This was the beginning of the pit head gear!

The men also were protected from the wet in these mines. Regular orders were recorded for material to make a form of jacket:

> *"1790 Pd Mr Simon Chawner for 3 yds Flannel at 1/4 per Yd for the wet work."*

This order was repeated nearly every year and Mr. Chawner, the mercer of Cheadle, must have been satisfied with the deal. His son, Reuben Chawner, was to figure in a take-over of the Kingsley Colliery in 1819.

In 1796 *"John Swindal for Boys Gearing"*. This was the leather strapping the ten year old boys wore over their shoulders to pull the corves or trucks of coal in a crouching position to the pit bottom. John Swindells was the Saddler in Cheadle, but the increase in coal mining gave him as much of this work as saddlery for horses.

## *Turnpike Roads*

Most of the local industries had taken shares in the Turnpike Trusts, both as a sound profitable investment and to procure improved transport for their own goods. The Trusts

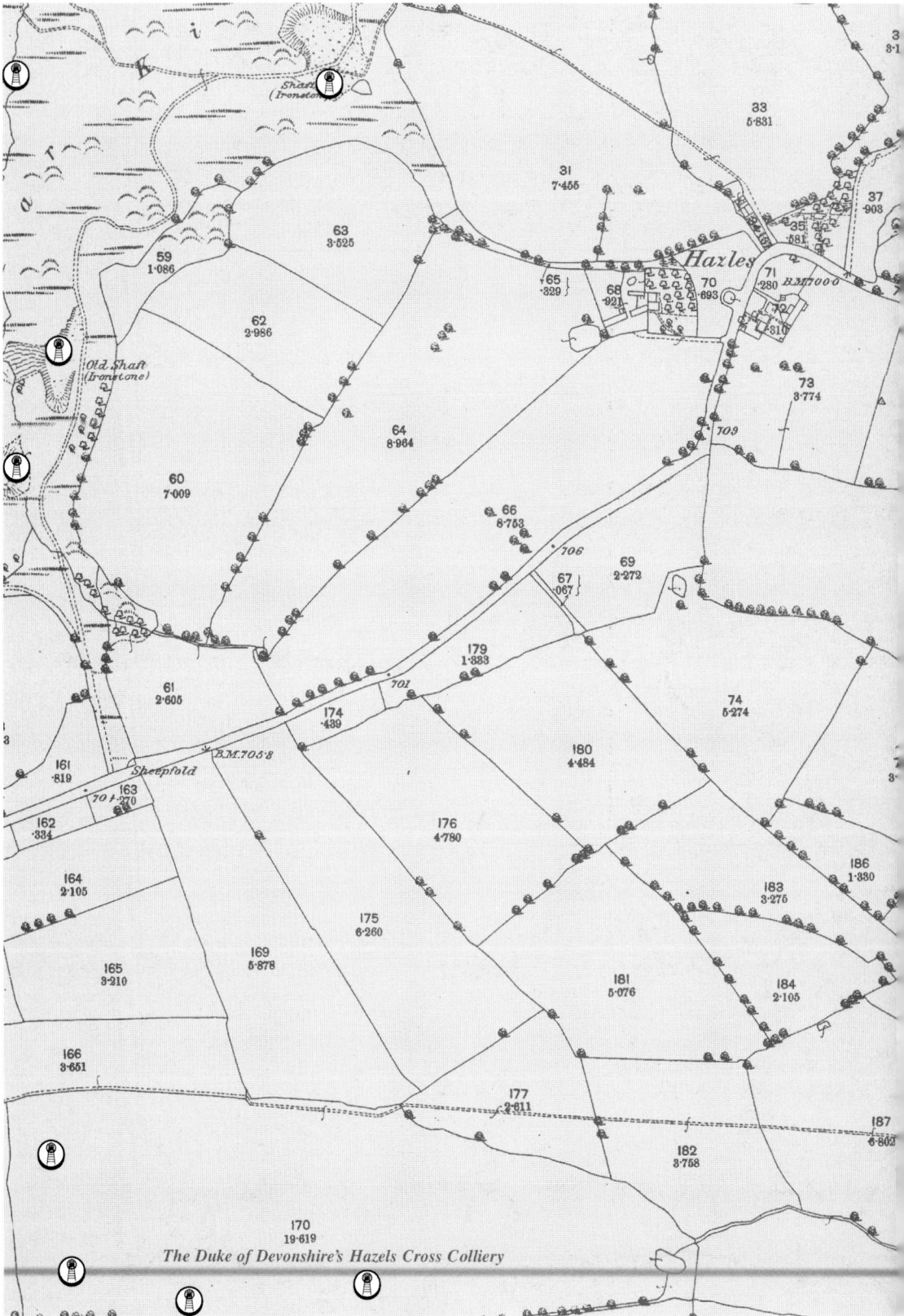

The map contains the following labels and numbers:

Shaft (Ironstone)

33
5·831

31
7·455

3
3·1

63
3·525

Hazles

37
·903

35
·581

59
1·086

65
·329

68
·921

70
·693

71
·280

B.M.700·0

72
·810

62
2·986

Old Shaft (Ironstone)

64
8·964

73
3·774

703

60
7·009

66
8·753

706

69
2·272

67
·067

61
2·605

701

179
1·333

74
5·274

174
·439

B.M.705·8

Sheepfold

180
4·484

161
·819

163
·370

701

162
·334

176
4·780

186
1·330

164
2·105

183
3·275

175
6·260

165
3·210

169
5·878

181
5·076

184
2·105

166
3·651

177
2·811

187
6·802

182
3·758

170
19·619

The Duke of Devonshire's Hazels Cross Colliery

*Mines in the Hollins-Hazles Cross area 1879*

- 56 -

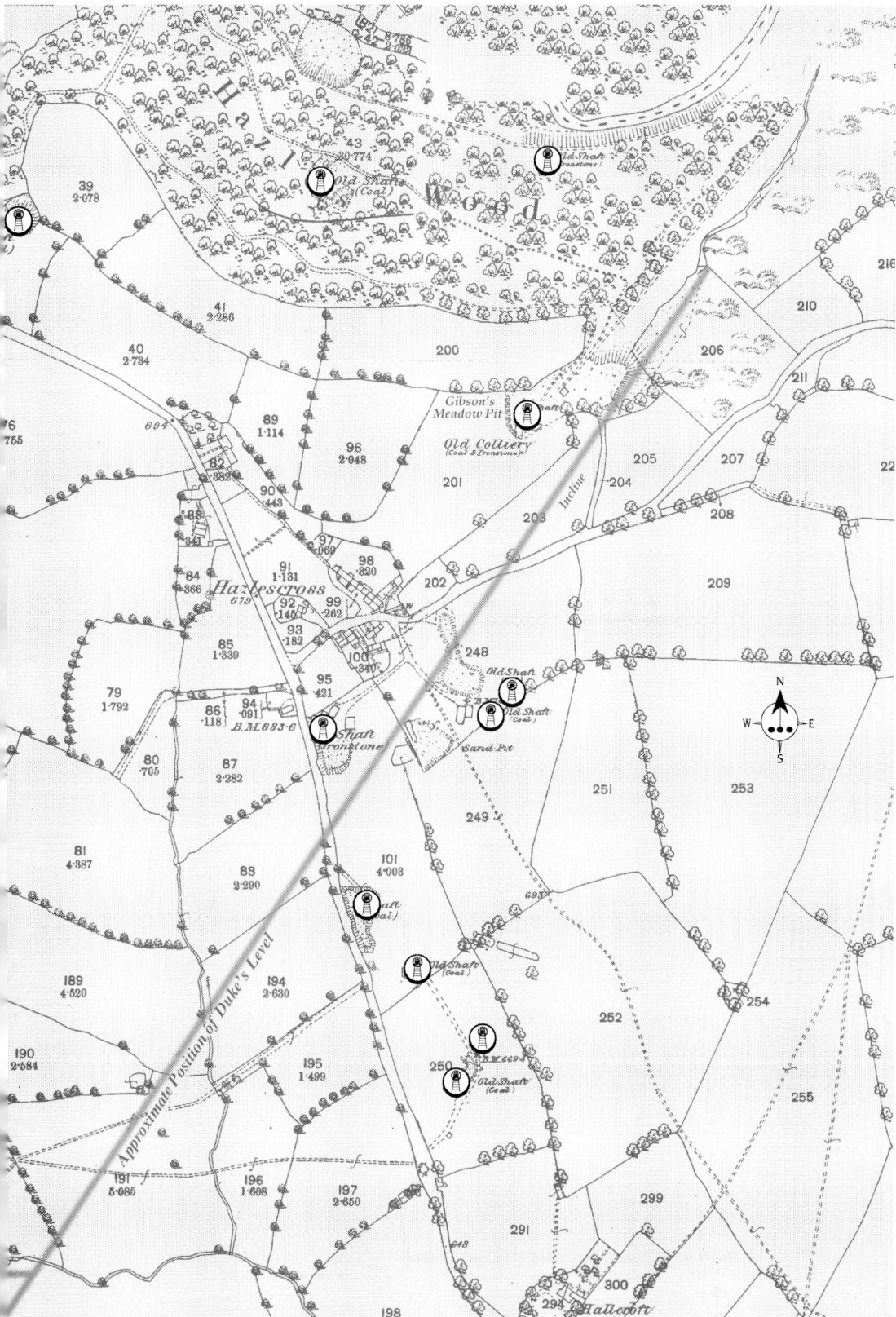

Ha[z]l

Wood

39
2·078

43
20·774

Old Shaft
(Coal)

Old Shaft
(Ironstone)

216

41
2·286

210

40
2·734

200

206

211

694

Gibson's
Meadow Pit

Old Colliery
(Coal & Ironstone)

204

89
1·114

96
2·048

205

207

22

76
·755

82
·883

201

208

203

209

88
·341

90
·443

97
·069

98
·820

202

Incline

84
·366

91
1·131

99
·262

Hazlescross
679

92
·145

93
·182

85
1·339

100
·341

248

Old Shaft

79
1·792

95
·421

94
·091

Old Shaft
(Coal)

86
·118

B.M.683·6

Shaft
Ironstone

251

253

80
·705

87
2·282

Sand Pit

249

81
4·387

88
2·290

101
4·003

Shaft
(Coal)

189
4·520

194
2·630

Old Shaft
(Coal)

693

252

254

190
2·584

195
1·499

250

B.M.660

Old Shaft
(Coal)

255

Approximate Position of Duke's Level

191
5·085

196
1·608

197
2·650

299

291

648

198

294

Hallcroft

300

N
W    E
S

often had to chide their own members for using unorthodox routes for their own purposes, as in the case of Mr. Harris of Consall Old Hall, who found a track across the valley at the Forge and saved tolls on the main roads.

Smith and Kniveton, the iron manufacturers at Oakamoor were accused of using the Dimminsdale track, though they attended the Trusts meetings at the 'Wheatsheaf'. By 1802 the Duke's Agent, after the abandonment of the Kingsley-Froghall tramway scheme carted the Kingsley coal, mainly used for the smelter, to the bottom of the new line of the Caldon Tramway, where it was loaded to be hauled up to the Whiston incline half way up which a siding ran the loaded wagons on to the works' site. The Trust viewed this unofficial use of the Railway not only as a breach of the rules, but as another new Toll dodging scheme.

By 1818 the smelter had passed the peak of copper production so that the Duke prepared to withdraw all activities from the area. Although the number of copper workers had halved, there had been very large numbers employed in mining and more especially in carting. The Turnpike from Blythe Bridge to Ashbourne had joined Cheadle, Oakamoor, Calton cross roads and Blore to cross into Derbyshire over that monumental bridge below Coldwall Farm. Since 1830 when a new Mayfield road was constructed to meet Hanging Bridge, the original Coldwall Bridge was disused for wagons and Stage Coaches. The Turnpike Milestone, however, is there to proclaim that Cheadle is eleven miles from the bridge and local senior citizens still call the road The Old Coal Road, reminding us of the distances the carts of the Cheadle Coalfields travelled. The industries also had to pay their share when the Parish Vestry Meeting was fined by the Quarter Sessions for paying insufficient attention to the local roads. Of course, the vestry tended to blame such heavy traffic as coal carts so that it was not surprising to find:

> *"1781 Turnpike gate at Tom End Brassworks Co. may compound there for Coals to their works only.*
> *1784 Trustees hoped the Duke of Devonshire would give to repair road of Kingsley Banks (Coal) Hazles Cross.*

| | | | |
|---|---|---|---|
| *1792 Expenses of the Indictment of the roads in Grindon and* | | | |
| *Butterton as per account* | *£95* | *7* | *0* |
| *1807 Expenses in Rebuilding Bridge across the Manyfold at* | | | |
| *Wetton with an enlargement* | *£184* | *6* | *11"* |

This was a voluntary effort as this was used to carry copper ore one way to Whiston and coal the other to the Ecton furnaces"

| | | | |
|---|---|---|---|
| *"1808 John Redfern's Bill of Expenses respecting the* | | | |
| *Indictment of of the Roads in the Parish of Kingsley* | | | |
| *(Stafford Sessions)* | *£30* | *0* | *4"* |

Kingsley had at one time been fined £100!

By this time mines had recently been included in the rateable property and in 1809 it is recorded in the Chatsworth Records for Ecton Mine:

| | | | |
|---|---|---|---|
| *"5th Oct 1809 Paid the Expenses of Mr Shaw and C Flint at Cheadle when the* | | | |
| *appeal against the assessment of the Colliery* | | | |
| *was agreed to be postponed.* | *£1* | *13* | *2"* |

1818 was a bad year for the district. There was already much distress and rates and relief had quadrupled. The closing of the smelter and the collieries was a bitter blow. Although Foxtwood finished completely, it was three years before the smelter reopened on a small scale and Kingsley Colliery was leased the following year to continue for a further twenty years.

# THE WOODHEAD COLLIERY

6

Following the dissolution of the Woodhead partnership of 1784, the working of the remaining pits on the Woodhead estate was left to John Leigh, who was still living on the Estate. The industry in the district was growing along with the country's population which was to double in a space of some twenty years despite the French Wars. Examples of added interest in coal mining are seen in the new ventures opening in the area. The Duke's coal enterprises had led other outsiders to enquire into the possiblities of mining and even small fields were offered to lease. In September, 1790, Mrs. Sarah Tomlinson leased, to John Sparrow, a Potteries mining man, coals at Kingsley and several other pieces of small acreage in Cheadle, such as Lower Town Field, Common Way Dale, some near the Gorbus, with Monkhouse Dale and Foden's Field, totalling not more than twenty acres.

In addition, the price of coal was rising with other commodities, so that good coal sold well. The Brass & Copper Company's accounts show:

*"1796 Company paid 5/6 per Ton of Coal at 22 cwts per Ton."*

## Disposal of Sir Joseph Bank's estate

By far the most important event in 1790 was the sale by Sir Joseph Banks of Revesby Abbey, Lincolnshire of all his properties and Manorial Rights in Cheadle and Kingsley. This family had been landlords from the middle of the seventeenth Century, later acquiring the manorial rights in the next century. In all the correspondence between Banks' London lawyers, John Steel, his Cheadle agent, and John Child, who was to be his legal advisor in this district, there is no reason given for the sale. The country was, however, involved in preparations should the revolutionary spirit across the Channel spread to our shores, but no mention was made of any fear of trouble from the time arrangements started in August for the next three months to the sale.

The sale of some ninety lots included, in Cheadle, some seven farms and five smallholdings in the fifty-five lots, whilst in Kingsley there were two farms and two smallholdings in the forty-five lots offered. John Steel, who had been responsible for collecting all rents and therefore knew all the tenants was, in August, offered the job as Agent at Revesby at £60 per year, when his duties at Cheadle were over after the sale. Both Sir Joseph and his agents agreed that the presence of coal under any of the land would enhance its value and on the two important farms, Park Hall Farm and another at Kingsley, it was proposed that borings should be made to prove both quantity and quality of coals found. By the end of October all was ready for the printing of large catalogues to do with this sale which was to affect the lives of probably a hundred families. The cover of the catalogue announces particulars of farms within *"the Manors or Lordships of Cheadle and Kingsley"* eventually mentions conditions *"besides which advantages, large Quantities of COALS will be found under most of the respective farms of superior value to the surface"* and continues *"the Wastes whereof abound in COALS"*.

**"TO BE SOLD BY AUCTION**
*on Monday the 8th. Tuesday the 9th. Wednesday the 10th. and Thursday the 11th*
*November 1790.*
*At the HOUSE of Mary Tomlinson*
*Known by the SIGN of the*
**ROYAL OAK, *in CHEADLE.*"**

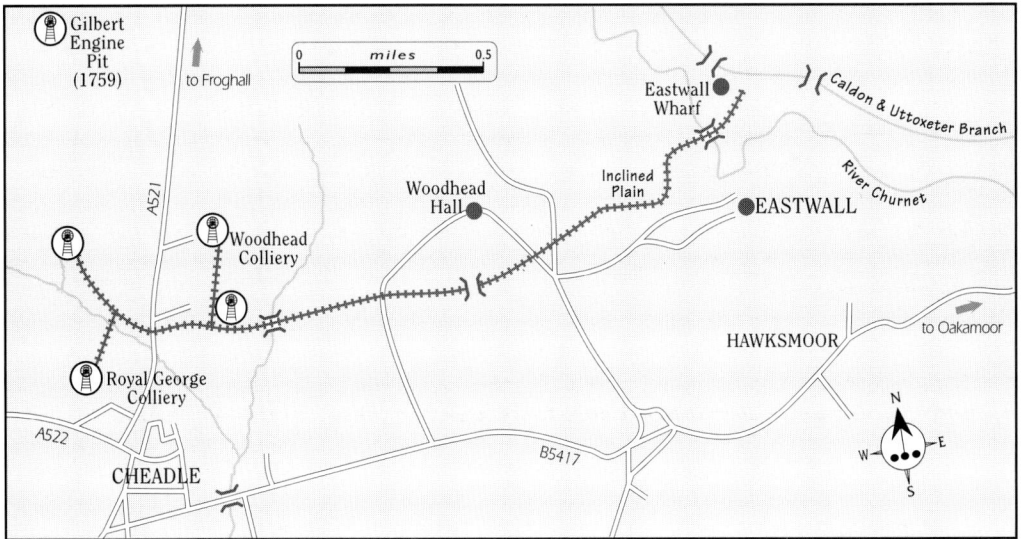

*Woodhead Tramway, 1836.*

Most of the tenants managed to retain their holdings with the help of Agents for example: John Child (33 lots), Blagg (18 lots) and a Bowers (7 lots), Sherrat (13 lots) and Joseph Bainbride (4 lots).

The most important sales were those including the manorial rights and these were sold, in the case of Cheadle, to the Lord of the Manor of Dilhorne, John Holliday at £4,400 and Kingsley to James Beech at £3,300 against the expectations of the Banks' Agents.

A letter from Mr. Steel to Revesby Abbey on the 4th mentions the business of boring for coal:

> *"as it would take some time to bore one hole down to the coal to prove the quality, and then to bore to the Rider or top of the coal measures only to know the quantity. Mr Beeche purpose's to purchase the manor of Kingsley with any or all the farms in both manors if the terms suits, a few days ago he spoke about boring for the coal."*

Steel then reverts to the political situation:

> *"I really think you have nothing to fear from the situation of state affairs/I mean peace or war/in this remote part, cheese is the only thing that rules here, and which is now*

*advanced from 28/s & 30/s to 40s/ 42s/ & upwards p. cwt & likely to continue for next years cheese."*

How gratified would be the people of Cheadle and Kingsley to read this assessment of their qualities!

Mr. John Holliday of Dilhorne Hall was certainly a progressive landlord. He had planted some hundred thousand trees around his manor and received an Arts and Manufactures Society medal for the achievement and was interested in the advance of coal mining. He died just eleven years later, in 1801, leaving the estate to his two year old grandson. His widow and daughter, Mrs. Buller, managed the estate until he came of age.

James Beech, on the other hand, had the greatest difficulty in finding the money to settle the sale price and for two or three years he was writing to Banks explaining why he could only offer £1,000 on account. In fact, there was no settlement until 1793 when Sir Joseph threatened to cancel the sale. Beech probably had other money difficulties at home. His father, John, married into the Stubbs' family, one member of which, Henry Stubbs, had taken the Shawe, Kingsley, after the Civil War and had also endowed the Monkhouse School at Cheadle in 1685 to teach six of the poorest children in both Cheadle and Kingsley. Beech also had his money troubles around the village as is demonstrated the following year 1791.

At a Vestry Meeting at which he was not present on May 5th, it was decided:

*"to consider the speediest method of obtaining valuation of all lands, woods, Tythes, mines, works and other things liable to be assessed for the relief of the Poor."*

*In 1836, Donkey Lane may have appeared like this*

Now mines had never before been rated to pay with houses and farms but times were getting desperate in this inflationary period. It was no longer possible to keep the Kingsley workhouse accounts down to those of fifty years before. Some prices prevailing were: Beef 1½ d, butter 4½ lb, Sugar 4d, a loaf 5d, Peck of Potatoes 5d, Brown loaf 3d, meal 7d, peck Cheese 3d, Ale chn not being well 2d, Turnips 3d, peck Salt 1½ lb, Soap 1d, Pair calves plucks 4d. neck Veal 4d Quarter Peas 2d, Peck of Beans 1/-, 6lbs Bacon 2/-, 10 ½ 1bs Pork 1/5.

Kingsley Registers show:

> "1765. *James, Son of Mr. John Beech and Hannah. h.w. Bapt.*
> *1787. Oct. 20. John Beech of the Shaw Sqier, Bur."*

In September, 1791, the Vestry minutes read as follows:

> *"We whose names are here under are well satisfied that there is no just reason whatsoever to alter in any way the present poor assessment and that it is the opinion not only of this vestry meeting but of the parish in general."*

The first signature was 'James Beech' and this was followed by an entirely different set of inhabitants! There appeared to be two schools of thought!

The meeting of the Vestry on February 22nd in 1794 had the record written in Mr. Beech's own handwriting. He had completed the monetary transactions after the Banks' sale and was then Lord of the Manor and contemplating an increase in his mining activities.

> *"At a meeting respecting Land Tax resolved that John Stevenson and Thos Alcock is appointed to ease Mr Beech's payments of the Land Tax, and such others as are materially over assessed, and lay it on such cottages and other places which are underassessed – or if this plan is thought improper by the Freeholders the above John Stevenson and Thos Alcock shall make such other alterations which they may think most just and equal.*
>
> James Beech"

Beech must have started mining operations before 1800, but unfortunately, with the exception of the Duke of Devonshire, he conducted the working on his own land. No documents are available to show dates or managers, miners and tonnages. We can make out a case for mining into the nineteenth century as it was possible for Barrow to get information from older miners on depth of some mines and seams worked. Shawe Hall would appear to be built in the early part of the century, a red brick building probably about the time he was building farmhouses and buildings on his estate following the Enclosure Act of 1809 and completed award of 1815.

To celebrate both the Battle of Waterloo and the award of vey large areas of Kingsley from the changed circumstances much new planning was started. The Banks' Old Hall had been occupied by Ladkins, who were in trouble during the Civil War, and followed by the Stubbs, who probably saw the last of the house most likely built of that yellowish Kingsley sandstone of which there are still samples in and around the village. The old Manor House on Hazles Cross road, surrounded by its moats, was quoted by the parson in the Terriers, or list of Church buildings and land, through the seventeenth and eighteenth centuries. From here he could overlook that great stretch of Church or Glebe land extending up to the Hollins. Its replacement was Glebe House occupied by the

Tideswells and their transport garage, and from that 1790 dispersal the new red brick Shawe Hall became the manorial seat.

There are some eighteen shafts sunk within a quarter mile circle of the Hall. Barrow's informants estimated that the Cobble coal would be found at thirty yards deep and the Woodhead at eighty yards. To unwater these mines a level was driven some two thirds of a mile long to run into the Kingsley Brook some one hundred and seventy yards to the east of Mill Pool Flat Bridge under Bradbury's Sunny Hayes Farm. A second was driven three quarter mile south to empty into Harewood Brooke, east of the Park.

At about this time, in the 1790s, landowners were using the interest in mining to improve the sale and prices paid for small pieces of land. At the Eaves, Cheadle in 1797, nine acres of land were offered with "*valuable mines of Coal and Slack*" whilst in 1799 at the Swan there were offered "*27 Acres round the Harwood. There is a valuable mine of Coal in the Estate*". Both advertisements appeared in the Staffordshire Advertiser.

## Developments at Woodhead

In 1784 we saw what appeared to be the break up of that most important of the coal partnerships. The Gilberts not only left the Woodhead consortium but seemed to transfer the remainder of their interests from Cheadle to Worsley where both became completely engrossed in canal engineering, where the Duke of Bridgwater's projects were expanding. John Leigh, whose parents were in Woodhead Hall, occupied Barlow's Farm, on part of the estate and continued working Woodhead and a small area under William Hurst which I believe to be the Bedbrook Farm. By 1800 Leigh and Hurst had a complex of buildings on what is now the site of the Little Hayes farm buildings. The plan shows that site just off the small road leaving the Froghall Road in much the same position as today's Donkey Lane; there was a swing to the left as did the road until recently into what was known as the W.A.A.F. camp. Here the road ended to be extended by tracks to the centre buildings near to which was probably the most important shaft and weighing machine.

A second shaft was sunk, but thirty yards to the west of Bedbrook Farm buildings. A third shaft was sunk in the field behind the Little Hayes Farm buildings. The approach to this was parallel to the fence adjoining a later tramway, but after some hundred yards the track turned right to the shaft thirty yards into the field. Some time before the plan was made a shaft was sunk seventy yards to the east of the road. When Bowers built the Square he was obviously unaware of the presence of the old shaft, as the dwelling houses were erected just behind it. The shaft revealed itself by collapsing just a yard or so outside a front garden in the 1930s.

## Other partnerships

By 1798 John Leigh had agreed with Edward Smith Grosvenor to the transfer of the Lawns, Gibridding Field and Wood along with three-fourth puts of the Reckoning House and fields with the outhouses, stables and barns. No coal was mentioned and the agreement could not have lasted for many years. Neither party understood how important this particular small piece of property was to be ten years later. Perhaps John Leigh's imagination, having followed the progress of work done by the canal at Froghall, dreamed of a further extension. In fact, the partners in that agreement, by 1804, had agreed that Leigh should have:

*"³/₄ parts or shares of coal, slack lying under the two Gibridding Woods and the Lawns in the Manor of Hound's Cheadle for 21 years".* Leigh was to pay 1/- for every 8/- worth of coal sold.

There are certain interesting addenda inserted by Leigh such as:

*"Lumps of Ironstone are frequently found in the materials about this coal but I conceive nothing like sufficient to be worth getting for sale. J.L."* and *"although canal is a species of coal there is no impropriety in inserting the word here. J.L."* Also: *"The Gibridding Woods and the Lawns now in the several tenures of the said E.S.G., J.L.",* and *"John Higgs or within or under any of them of the same kind or quality as the Sulpherous Coals which have been discovered to be under the top of the Gibridding Wood of the said J. Leigh."*

John Leigh apparently did not know that the ironstone was that which was so important to the mediaeval bloomsmithy down at Eastwall Furn, less than a mile away and that his sulphurous coal was the Crabtree, rarely found in this area west of the Churnet.

After the partnership had been dissolved in 1784 an agreement was made in 1792 between E.S. Grosvenor, Richard Smith and Rupert Leigh, and the owners of the Broad Haye Farm, Peter Whitehall Davies and his wife, for the coal and slack under that farm. Rupert Leigh had been a partner in the Cheadle Brass and Copper Company since 1788 and when part of the wire drawing mill at Alton transferred to Oakamoor, Leigh was allowed a shield over the great door of the new mill inscribed R L & Co 1792.

When both the Davies and Leigh were deceased (before 1809) a further lease was agreed including the Rev. W. W. Davies for the owners who were from Broughton Hall, Flint and John Leigh and Richard Smith of Cheadle. This included a considerable area of land, the whole of Broad Haye totalling eighty-seven acres, with permission to lay railway, use soughs, levels, buildings already made. The lease was for twenty-one years at a rent of £400 p.a. or one eighth of the said coal in value.

The *Staffordshire Advertiser* of 16th October, 1802 announced:

*"PARTNERSHIP DISSOLVED*
*Notice is hereby given, that the Partnership lately subsisting between John Blagg and John Leigh, both of Cheadle, in the County of Stafford, Attornies at Law, was this day dissolved by mutual consent -*
*Witness their hands this 11th day of October 1802 - J. Blagg*
                                                        *John Leigh"*

It seems that Blagg felt that, after the troubles of the Woodhead Colliery partnership, he would be better without too strong ties with Leigh. He did, however, continue to act for him.

Trouble was soon to occur after the last lease was safely signed and it came from the Leigh side of the agreement. There is no doubt that there were more small coal workings in the Cheadle district, but the Davies partners insisted on the Leigh's side paying the agreed rents punctually. In fact, they went to the lawyer which in turn forced Leighs to approach Mr. Blagg, who asked for Counsel's opinion.

The Davies claims, in many fewer words, that:

*"It is, however, notorious, and the leasees cannot deny the fact that ever since the commencement of their lease they have worked and still continue to work another*

colliery in lands adjoining the lessees belonging to a different owner (Mr Hurst) from whence they have constantly raised and sold considerable quantities of coal" sometimes at 5d and more per cwt."

They claimed also that, instead of mining the Broad Haye coal, the lessees:

*"have expended large sums of money in constructing a Rail way from the Colliery to the Canal."*

To entitle themselves to an abatement the lessees should have raised coals from the Lessor's lands to the exclusion of coals from another person:

*"The lessees have no just claim to cut the £400 rent."*

This was the Davies' lawyer's opinion.
The Leighs claimed:

*"that they had the expense of the fire Engine installed near the lands of the lessors to enable them to raise their coals and, in fact, several payments of £400 had been paid, but, although the coal had been got, had it been sold there would be sufficient to pay the rent, but in consequence of a deficiency of sale (from several other coal mines having been lately opened in the neighbourhood of the colliery in question) the lessees have been under the necessity of making a Railway at a very considerable expense from the above Colliery to the Canal between Froghall and Uttoxeter to increase sales and hoped this increase will enable to full £400 payment."*

The Counsel's opinion came through Mr. Blagg to the Leighs dated October, 1811:

*"I am of the opinion they are not in any way intitled to be repaid or reimbursed any part of the mine rents which were claimed and paid up to Lady day last. J Bulgay, Duffield, Oct. 12 1811."*

The decision did not upset working arrangements among the parties, despite the fact that the Leighs' party had openly shown that they were short of money. A further agreement or lease was signed late in 1812 for the coals under the six acres by Hammersley Hayes. The *Staffordshire Advertiser* for the 20th June, 1812 carried the following advertisement on page 4:

*"WOODHEAD RAIL ROAD.*
*To be sold, one half of the above railroad, leading between the Woodhead Colliery and Uttoxeter Canal, with wagons and business annexed thereto. Applications to be made to Pipe and Blair, Uttoxeter. N.B. the purchaser or purchasers may be accommodated with money at interest, on security being given."*

The fact of the matter was that the line was nowhere near complete and since there were no takers, remained unfinished for another fifteen years.
The canal was completed in 1811. The provision of coal wharves at Oakamoor, Alton, Denstone, Rocester and Uttoxeter would have made sales to a wider area much simpler, but this was not in operation until 1827. It meant continued trouble with the Turnpike

Trustees over obstruction by horses and carts on their road just beyond that rather narrow twisting bridge over the brook at the bottom of Froghall Road. Here the cuts queued to turn right along what is now called Donkey Lane to load and get weighed at Woodhead Colliery on Little Hayes ground.

## FAREY'S SURVEY

It would seem difficult to believe Leigh's statement that *"several other coal mines having been lately opened in the neighbourhood"* had much substance. This was, however, the case and it was amply demonstrated by John Farey who, after research, wrote his *General View of the Agriculture and Minerals of Derbyshire*. Luckily for us, he crossed the River Dove to find out and list places from which the folk in the limestone district of west Derbyshire managed to get their coal.

He published his first work in London in 1810 and called it *"Extracts from a list of collieries in Derbyshire, and in such adjacent puts of its seven adjacent counties"*. He satisfied himself with examining the Cheadle Coalfield, and listed the collieries or workings in Volume 1 on pages 188-215. He repeats Staffordshire in each case but it is here deleted:

| | |
|---|---|
| *"BEE LOW* | $^3/_4$*m. E of Oakamoor Mills, near Alveton, 1st Coal (formerly)* |
| *CARR WOOD* | *N.E. of Oakamoor Mills 1st Coal (formerly)* |
| *CLOUGH-HEAD* | $^2/_3$*m. W. of Foxton (or Foxt) 2nd Coal* |
| *CROWGUTTER* | $^3/_4$*m. E. of Ipstone, 1st Coal* |
| *CROWN-POINT* | *1m. S.W. of Cheddleton, 2nd Coal* |
| *CONSAL-WOOD* | *2$^1/_2$. S.W. of Cheddleton, 1 st Coal* |
| *DELPH-HOUSE* | *1 m. W. of Cheadle, 2nd Coal* |
| *DILHORN* | $^3/_4$*m. N.N.E. of the Town near Cheadle, 2nd Coal* |
| *EAST-WALL* | *2m. N.E. of Cheadle, 1st Coal* |
| *EAVES* | *S. of Cheadle* |
| *FOXTON-WOOD* | $^1/_2$*m. W. of the Town Nr Froghall, 1st Coal* |
| *FROGHALL* | $^1/_4$*m S.E. of the Wharf, in Kingsley, 1st Coal (formerly)* |
| *GARSTONE* | $^2/_3$*m. E. of Whiston Copper Works in Kingsley 2nd Coal (lately)* |
| *HAY HOUSE* | $^3/_4$*m. S.W. of Ipstone, 1st Coal (formerly)* |
| *HAZLE-CROSS* | *1m. W. of Kingsley, 2nd Coal* |
| *HODGE HAY* | $^2/_3$*m. S.E. of Whiston Copper Works in Kingsley, 2nd Coal (lately)* |
| *JACK ELM* | *1m. S.E. of Whiston Copper Works in Kingsley, 1st Coal (formerly)* |
| *IPSTONE* | $^1/_4$*m. S. of the Church, 1st Coal (formerly)* |
| *KINGSLEY-BANK* | $^3/_4$*m. N.N.W. of Kingsley, 1st Coal* |
| *LEES* | *Round the Village 1$^1/_4$ m. E.N.E. of Kingsley 1st Coal (formerly)* |
| *MOBERLEY* | *S.S.E. of Cheadle* |
| *NETHERFIELD* | $^1/_2$*m. E.S.E. of Ipstone* |
| *NEWSTEAD* | *1m. S.S.W. of Cheddleton, 1st Coal* |
| *PARSONS-FIELD* | *(Wolfs) $^1/_4$ m. N. of Dilhorne 2nd Coal* |
| *RAKE EDGE* | *S. of Lees $^1/_4$m. S.E. of Kingsley, 1st Coal* |
| *ROSS BANK* | $^3/_4$*m. S. of Lees, in Kingsley First Coal* |
| *SHAFFERLONG* | $^3/_4$*m. S.S.W. of Cheddleton, 2nd Coal* |
| *SHAW (ORSHAM)* | *1m. W. of Cheadle in Kingsley, 2nd Coal* |
| *SWETLEY (Lowe's)* | $^3/_4$*m. N.N.E. of Dilhorn* |
| *WETLEY-MOOR* | *(or Handley Ease) 2$^3/_4$m. S.W. of Cheddleton* |
| *WOODHEAD* | *(Mr. Lee's) $^3/_4$m. N.E. of Cheadle."* |

There are a few items difficult to interpret. His use of the terms 1st Coal and 2nd Coal belong to the period before the geologists set the coalfield seams in the twentieth century pattern and there are a few items quite confused, such as Shaw and Sham. Also the three workings to the south west of Cheddleton do not strictly belong to the Cheadle Coalfield. The list shows the reason for Leigh's concern, for the nineteen workings operating at that time covered the whole area from Dilhorne across the Churnet Valley to Ipstones, Foxt and Whiston to supply the increasing population and to compete for the 'export' trade of fifteen or twenty miles away to the east.

## Activities in the 19th century

The *Staffordshire Advertiser* in 1801 announced:

> "Freehold Estate to be sold and Coal Mines to Let
> By Auction
> By Mr. Henshaw
> At the Royal Oak, in Cheadle in the County of Stafford, on Friday the 9th day of January, 1801, between the hours of 4 and 6 o'clock in the afternoon.
> Also, to be Let, and entered upon at Lady-Day next, subject to conditions a wry extensive Colliery, consisting of several good and valuable Mines or Rows of Coal, lying and being under the Delph-House Estate, near Cheadle aforesaid.
> Valuable Coal Mine
> To be Let by Auction
> By Mr. Henshaw
> At Mr. Steel's, the Castle Inn, in Lane End, in the County of Stafford, on Monday the 8th day of March, 1802, between the hours of 4 and 5 in the afternoon, subject to such Conditions as will then be produced:
> All those very extensive and valuable Mines or Rows of Coal, now lying and being under the Delph House Estate, near Cheadle, in the County of Stafford, with the great conveniences of runaways, turnpike roads through the Estate, and an easy distance from the Staffordshire Potteries and other good markets."

The Delph-house and the Sham must refer to the same Company working. The Sham was operated by the early Delph-house company and is found with its spoil bank just beyond the Festival field. It took the nickname Sham at about this time and used it until well into the century. The following appeared in the *Staffordshire Advertiser* on 25th March, 1820:

> "Newsharn Colliery near the Cheadle Brass Works. The beneficial interest of a lease (of which about 40 years unexpired) of above colliery to be disposed of by private contract: apply to the office of Mr. Brandon."

On 9th December, 1820:

> "Coals of good quality are now selling at the Sham Colliery near the Cheadle Brass Works at 6s 8d per ton."

The Eaves Colliery was started in 1806 and would be working to capacity by the time Farey found it. Both the Hazels Cross and Foxtwood were the Duke's workings. The Jack Elms we saw had closed some years before Farey's visit.

The Mobberley was a continuation of the Eaves mining we shall consider later. At Parsons field the 'Wolf' mentioned was the Reverend Woolfe of Dilhorne, later joined by his son, who. we shall meet again in 1820.

The *Staffordshire Advertiser* of 7th October, 1815, gave notice of sale of the undermentioned property:

> *"DWELLING HOUSE, Land and Colliery, in Kingsley Parish.*
> *To be sold by Auction, by Mr. C. Barnes At the house of Mr. Thomas Hopkinson, known by the sign of the Horse Shoe, at Lees, in the Parish of Kingsley, in the County of Stafford, on Saturday the 28th day of October, 1815, situated at Rake-Edge being now in possession of Mr. Benjamin Bentley. There are considerable Mines of Coal under this property, nearly the whole of which is already laid dry, and capable of being gotten at a very small expence, the owner having lately, with a view to working the Mines himself, erected a Smithy, and provided every other appendage that can be desired for a Colliery undertaking."*

In fact, the Lees Colliery had worked the Crabtree Coal since 1753 and left a large spoil bank.

Both Rake Edge and Ross Banks were heavily mined after this sale, the former having eight shafts in a comparatively small acreage, while the latter worked until the pit lows had to be cleared to open the road when the railway had built Ross Bridge across the Churnet. The Froghall Colliery Farey found just cast of the Canal Wharf was probably as important as any of the others. Its site is easily distinguished on that tough little bank on the left of Whiston Bank where spoil banks can be seen and cart roads can be followed from the Foxt road up the steep hill. There is no doubt that this Crabtree Slack taken from three shafts was to be used for the earliest lime kilns on the canal basin.

The Woodhead and Dilhorne concerns will be recognised as belonging to the Partnerships. The latter had been worked from the 1760s.

The Leigh-Davies misunderstanding of 1809 had made great play over the laying of the railroad and in 1812 Leigh tried to raise money by selling a half share in the construction which was not half finished. He had been forced to sell some half dozen farming properties away from Cheadle in 1796 when they were advertised in the *Staffordshire Advertiser* and this resulted in a long delay in completing.

By the end of 1812 a John Clarke, a Tanner of Alton, leased more land to Leigh and Smith:

> *"Lease of Coals under two Closes of six acres at Hammersley Hayes by Mr. John Clarke of Alton, Tanner to Messrs Leigh and Smith Copartners in the Colliery called Woodhead or Broadhay Colliery."*

The rent was to be 1/- for every 8/- worth of coal raised. John Clarke was to have a Banksman to inspect and take account of all coal slack got and be paid by John Leigh and Richard Smith who shall not break the surface. This was for a term of twenty-one years.

## Completion of the Woodhead Tramway

After the Lease agreed with E. S. Grosvenor in 1804 to do with the Woodlands Lawns and Gibridding and the Reckoning House lands, the area had been sold to Thomas Honeybourne who had probably come to reside in the Woodhouse. In 1810 John Leigh agreed a new lease with Honeybourne for the coal under that land for seventeen years paying 3d. for every 8/- worth of coal sold excepting "*that used for engines, colliers and workmen*". This appeared to be another example of concessionary coal. However, a further agreement, made on the same day, gives Leigh:

> "*the liberty to make use of the present Railway from the Colliery in Gibridding Wood to the Canal now making from Froghall to Uttoxeter.*"

This agreement meant that Leigh had to abandon the plans he had made to take his railway down through Eastwall and continuing south easterly on the flatter ground to cross the Churnet and meet the proposed canal nearer Oakamoor. He could now plan to cross the corner of the Woodhouse donkey field, the hiding embankment is still plainly seen, cross the Holt Lane and travel on a low embankment across Gibridding Field to the top of the wood. By this time the Canal had made a siding for wagons, two loading basins with a lock, California Lock, between them.

The tramway at Gibridding started with an incline from top to bottom of the wood, a raised embankment to meet a new bridge across the Churnet and a long flat line to meet and run alongside the newly constructed waterway. The Canal was completed to Uttoxeter by 1811. There were great celebrations when the two boatloads of gentry, Directors and officials arrived from Uttoxeter at the marquees erected at Crumpwood for the feast and jollifications. It was introduced by the tenor, who sang a specially composed tribute to the canal builders set to the tune of '*Britannia rules the Waves*'. John Leigh was still busy ordering stone sleepers and three foot flanged iron rails. The Woodhead Colliery had by this time a further shaft in the field below Hammersley Hayes and when eventually it was worked out it was covered by distinguishing brick-built beehive shaped capping.

The tramway operated by mules and ponies, would run from Colliery buildings with its Engine to the straight length between the Bedbrook land and Hammersley Hayes, later Little Hayes land. This straight stretch was embanked by coal spoil and widened to take double lines near the small bridge over the Kingsley Brook. It was planned to continue by Woodhead Farm, cross the track to Woodhead Hall and continue around the Woodhead estate in a cutting well hidden until it joined the Woodhouse section.

The railway would cost a considerable sum but the full working meant there was enough money to meet demands. Five new coal wharves selling to the surrounding country would cut the carriage cost and increase sales.

## Other Activities

In the account book for Alton Lodge (now Alton Towers) for the years 1804 to 1808 there is a reference which must belong to the early working in Carr Wood mentioned by Farey. After noting in 1806 Coals from Woodhead the book continues:

> "*1808 July 16 to Sept 24*
> *Payments to Jos Bradshaw 3/6 per day or £1-1 p week.*"

In August Bradshaw was joined by Dan Warrington at the same payments "*for boring for Coal at Oakamoor*". Four of these shafts may have been the work of Warrington for he was paid weekly "*for boring*" at Oakamoor until September 24th. Barrow noted these shafts just as did Sam Berrisford, though R. W. Bowen, who was also a native of Oakamoor, could only remember three of them. "*One on the fringe of wood near the New Houses called Churnetside.*"

The Thos Wilson Patten deeds and Cheadle Brassworks Accounts record:

*"Jan 28 1809 Carriage on Coals 5T 3C 3Q*
*Woodhead to Wooton Lodge*                                          £2        11        6
*April 3 1810 39 Tons Coal. Shaw to Brassworks*                   £2        18        10"*

Wilson Patten was living at the Lodge:

Note the greater carriage rates between the two destinations.
The *Staffordshire Advertiser* of 10th November, 1810 announced the sale of:

*"Coals*
*To be sold by auction by Mr. Cook, at the Royal Oak Inn, in Cheadle, in the*
*County of Stafford, Friday the 21st of December, 1810, if not previously disposed*
*of by private contract, of which due notice will be given, all the mines, beds or*
*wins of coal and slack, in and under an estate called Kingsley Moor Farm, in the*
*Parish of Kingsley."*

This farm shortly joined the Shawe Estate and the coal was mined under the Beech - Bowers agreement of 1853.  The land on the north-west, and north belonged to Bowers when the Kingsley Moor New Sinkings 1859-1875 were started, and two shafts were sunk to the north to work this Colliery and become part of the Woodhead Colliery concern.  The *Staffordshire Advertiser* of 12th April, 1817 announced the following, an item which was to cause Robert Plant so much trouble fifty or sixty years later:

*"To be sold by auction - at the house of Mr. Waiters Wheat Sheaf Inn, Cheadle, 18*
*April 1817 6 - 7 p.m., all the mines and coal under several pieces of land called*
*the Birches, close to Cheadle adjoining the Cheadle to Uttoxeter Turnpike Road*
*which are in full work, with engine, engine house, ane, buckets and other imple-*
*ments: to view colliery apply to Simon Plant; Brandon and Brown, Solicitors,*
*Cheadle."*

John Leigh was by now anxious to find a residence of more standing than his second class house near Woodhead.  He took Belmont for a year until Consall New Hall across the Valley was ready for him to occupy.  The *Staffordshire Advertiser*, 12th January, 1811 reads:

*"Belmont, Staffordshire.*
*To be let.*
*Belmont is a healthy and pleasant situation, about an equal distance of five miles*
*each from the market towns of Leek and Cheadle; about 3 miles from coals and*
*lime, and only half a mile from the River Churnett and the Canal, and is now in*
*the possession of John Leigh Esq."*

The next advertisement indicates that Leigh had moved. Staffordshire Advertiser, September, 26th, 1812:

*"Belmont, Staffordshire. To be let."*

# The Dilhorne Colliery

## 7

After 1784, Bamford was left to build another organisation to dominate coal mining on the Dilhorne side of the Coalfield. This was not to be difficult since he was a man of both character and substance; indeed, other members of the family had done service of a different kind in the community. In 1769 Charles Bamford had been Cheadle's overseer for some years, but by 1800 he had come upon hard times. The Vestry account for that January reads:

That Chas. Bamford, former farmer of this parish very respectable be allowed a load of Coals at the Pit. Mr Harvey of Pounton to give him carriage.

In July of the same year it is recorded that *"Ed. Sherratt and wife allowed to buy weights and scales to sell coal at Uttoxeter"* and in November *"Wm Moss allowed load of Coals at the Pit as is usual"*.

We saw in about 1777, well before the dissolution some seven years later, that there were real fire engines at Dilhorne. I think it likely that Bamford continued to work these to some extent, but by 1787 both the Colliery and "several fire engines at work" were up for sale. The farm near the colliery was, by 1800, known by the name *'Old Engine Farm'* and since then its neighbouring farm has become *'Little Old Engine'*. There has been some confusion about the Engineer responsible for the erection of this, a long time after Brindley's death. It was, however, a very expensive piece of mining expansion and it is my belief that the machinery, instead of being lost to the district, was kept in Bamford's possession and maybe transferred to other local working centres which attracted Bamford's attention during the next thirty years.

There had been a certain amount of mining, much along the same seam areas as the Dilhorne Colliery district, nearer to Cheadle at Newclosefields and nearer the main road at Brookhouses, the mine which by 1800 was known as Sham. In fact, a tramway was laid between the Newclose Wharf through the Dilhorne Colliery (Old Engine) site to its Wharf on the Dilhorne road above the Godley Brook Chapel. Half a century later, when the Foxfield line was completed the tramway crossed the road to connect with the lower end of the Foxfield railway line.

There is a small note-book among other coal documents, dealing with the sale of postwood and both pits, called the Newclosefield Colliery Postwood Account:

| | | | |
|---|---|---|---|
| *"1800 Dec To allowed in Sham Postwood Acct* | £38 | 10 | 0 |
| *Stopped out of Coals sold Aug - Dec 27 1800* | £38 | 10 | 0 |
| *Dec 1801 To allowed in Sham Postwood Acct for Postwood* | | | |
| *used at Newclosefields Colliery this year* | £139 | 0 | 0 |
| *Stopped out of Postwood sold* | | | |
| *(at about £3 10 per week Jan - Dec 1801* | £139 | 0 | 0 |
| *Dec 1802 To allowed Sham Postwood Acct for Postwood* | | | |
| *Used at Newclosefields Colliery this year* | £141 | 12 | 0 |
| *Stopt out of coals for year (weekly approx £2)* | £141 | 12 | 0 |

For 1803 Postwood stopped        £166    6    1"
The book finishes in January, 1804 with *"Used £10 - £12"*

By the following year, 1805, more coal had been leased for mining by the Dilhorne Hall Holliday family. The widowed Mrs. Holliday continued to promote as much interest as possible in this valuable mineral which could help the finances of this large estate. This lease was concerned with a piece of land near Godley brook where the Two Yard coal cropped out, but Barrow found signs of only one shaft near the road and the present white railings.

Bamford was, however, much more interested in the activities of the following year when he was joined by three strong partners:

*"7th July 1806. Between Wm Holmes of Cheadle Eaves of the frst part. Samuel Bamford, Summerhill, Gent, William Ingleby, Cheadle Gent, Richard Whitehurst of Whitehurst, Yeoman and Wm Deaville, Croxden, Yeoman."*

William Ingleby, something of a businessman, was connected with the Inglebys of Woodbank, Oakamoor. The Whitehursts we have known of since the sixteenth century; only Deaville was the new partner. Holmes leased to them all coals under Cheadle Eaves in his possession. The Eaves house was probably newly built shortly before this date. It gives the impression of a later Queen Anne style and Holmes was concerned for the structure by insisting that miners should not work the coal to within twenty yards of the buildings of Cheadle Eaves. The term was for twenty-one years and the rent was to be £151 4s per acre mined and twenty tons of coal per acre free.

There soon appeared steam engines and other machinery, probably the equipment offered for sale at Dilhorne Colliery, and four shafts were working between the Eaves and Mobberley, the lower being down to fifty yards. There was no doubt that this was a successful enterprise as, in less than one year, the agreement was extended from May, 1807 for a term of twenty-one years *"now that coal of 33 inches in thickness has been found at 28 yds, 43 yds and 66 yds 2 ft"*.

Barrow was careful to mark out the shafts and some of the information on the coal which. he probably gathered from local old miners. For instance, he could show where the engine operated and where the Cobble coal was obtained at a thickness of 1ft 6in - 2ft 0in with a slaty roof and fair floor at 60 yds deep. The new rent was £136 - 4s per acre paid half-yearly and Holmes was to have ten tons of coal half-yearly with three tons at the pithead at any time:

*"If it should degenerate in thickness or not average over 100 sq yds at 30 inches at least, or if it shall be found to be Stinking Coals and no good coals discovered then the agreement shall be terminated."*

The same year on 24th June, 1807, a similar lease was signed with Thomas Morrey of Tenford by the partnership for coal under *"closes in psh of Cheadle commonly called The Breaches.....those found by boring in the Eaves Estate"*. The conditions were similar to those of the Eaves. This agreement must have been successful since it worked for thirteen years until November, 1819 and only closed following a Deed of Surrender which could only state that one partner, Wm Ingleby, had died. (His will was dated 8/8/1817). Wm Holmes, the lessor, agreed to purchase *"all engines, machines, coals got and stacked for £260"*. Shortly after this deal, Mr. Holmes moved from the Eaves to live at Doveridge and Bamford and Co., now with a new partner named Thomas Ward, returned to Dilhorne

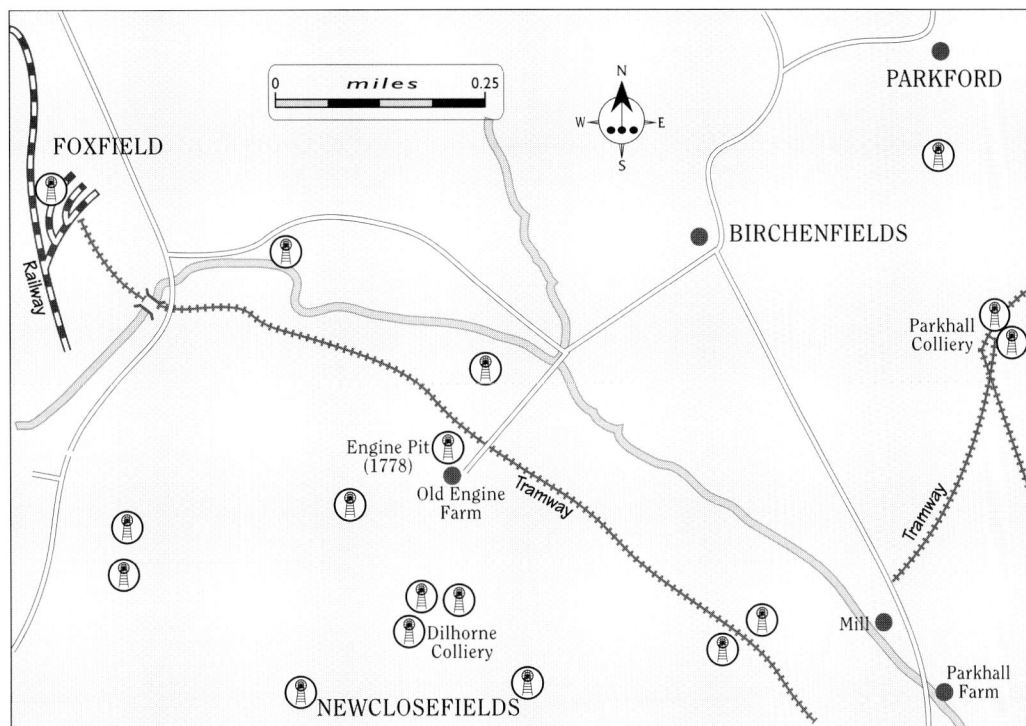

*Dilhorne Old Engine Colliery, 1770.*

for further prospecting. Someone must have partnered William Holmes for the remainder of the term, a matter of ten years, and the machinery must have been good for Holmes to purchase, but no details are available until in the *Staffordshire Advertiser* edition of March, 1829 we read:

"*STEAM ENGINE*
*To be sold by Public Auction at the House of Mrs. Munton, Royal Oak Hotel on 27th March, 1829.*
*All that recently erected and complete 'STEAM ENGINE' of 14 HORSE POWER together with about 57 Yards of 10 inch PUMP TREES and cast iron CISTERN 700 GALLONS in the ENGINE PIT. CYLINDER measures $20^1/_2$ inches in DIAMETER. All in very good condition. Situated at Huntley Colliery Near Cheadle.*
*For Particulars to view Apply Mr. Holmes at Eaves Colliery.*
*Feb. 26. 1829.*"

We saw that Mr. Holliday, Lord of the Manor of Dilhorne, purchased the manorial rights of Cheadle at the Bank's sale in 1790. Mr. Holliday had married into the Dilhorne rights and the Hall when he married the daughter of Thomas Harrison, who had succeeded to those rights from Copwood Hollin. Now that Mrs. Holliday was widowed, she began to show a more businesslike attitude to the mining of coal under the manorial property. In 1806 she had approached Mr. Bamford with a view to clarifying the position before she was likely to start making leases of certain stretches of coal under her lands. She pointed out to Mr. Bamford the fact of an old partition of Madgedales through the above succession gave her a third share of all coals whenever got in those lands.  She continued *"Mr Bamford will notice that the claim of this share of Madgedale coal was given to Mr Glover in 1806"*.  There does not appear to be any evidence to prove that Mr. Glover took advantage of this, but Mrs. Holliday was anxious to put herself in control of what mineral was available.  She repeated queries to do with Madgedale and about her land next to Hazlewall with what coal there was under it.

There was, however, something of a lull in coal getting in the Dilhorne area shown by the decrease in the tolls taken by the turnpike in the area.  Mrs. Holliday's note to Mr. Blagg in February, 1808 reads as though she had taken a lease of the Dilhorne Toll Gate.  She complains that at that Gate *"the money received has been much decreased for want of coals being got as it was expected they would have been when the Gate was taken last year"*.  The new Dilhorne Turnpike had been taken over between 1794-5 and local gentry were invited both to subscribe and often to become Trustees so that from 1795 onwards we find entries in the Bamford accounts such as:

*"Received Decr 4th 1795 of Mr Thos Steele Twenty Pounds on Acct of the new Dillorn Turnpike Road £20 For Mess Bamford & Co.*

*Issac Milner*

*2nd of January 1798 Recd of Thos Steel twentey Pounds on account of Intrist Due from Dilhorn Turnpike Road.*
*Rec'd by me Sam Bamford.*
*1808 Recd for S B & Co by Josh Ingleby.*
*1809 Recd for Bamford & Co        £10                by W. Ingleby."*

From this it is clear that Thomas Steele does not appear to have left Cheadle to accept the position of Banks' Agent at Revesby.  One of the most interesting changes made by the new Turnpike from Blythe Bridge to Cheadle can be seen when it came to cross Dilhorne Common at what we now call Boundary.  In the last two hundred yards approaching the cross roads from Forsbrook, the remains of the old road move away in the field on the right until, at the brow, it turns right to cross the lane by the side of the Red Lion, zig-zags down through the woodland, passes to the west of the Elms and reappears some two hundred yards further down the hill where two old yew trees once stood by its side just before it finds that the new Turnpike has usurped its place.

Many will remember the old barn catching fire some in the 1930s.  It had probably served the two Bull Engine pits of the Delphouse group recently completely filled, and may even have been part of the Old Delphouse which stood near that spot until the Turnpike took its place.  It would not have been such a striking change as one planned in 1833 for the approach to the town, when it was discovered that the section up to and past Rosehill was making problems for horses in snow and frost before reaching the Town End Tollgate.  The road Engineer, Hamilton, recommended that the Turnpike should turn right at the Beer House called the Waterloo into the Majors Barn and continue up to another public house called the Fighting Cocks on Lead Lane. From there it could enter the main street by the Tythe Barn (near Watt Place).

At about this period Mrs. Holliday was willing to enter into coal dealing with Bamford in a quite unusual way, since he was suggesting that she should buy some pieces of land from him so that later, when he needed the coal, she could lease it to his company.  However, he did not always find the lady in the most generous frame of mind, as in 1811 when she replied:

*"Mrs H cannot possibly advance £100 on a new account before Michs next. If that time should suit Mr Bamford Mrs H will be glad to have the business laid before her before Lady Day next."*

On another occasion the following year, in the writing to Mr. Blagg in December, 1812 about purchase of land and coal under it from Mr. Bamford:

*"Loss of income she must submit to until this new purchased mine begins to be regularly worked which cannot be till Mr Whitehurst has completed his present engagement with her. She will send for Mr Heath to give his opinion of the coal. Pay £2000 in 1813."*

Again in February, 1813 certain land deals with coal leases were made by Bamford with his partners Whitehurst and Ingleby. Business other than coal was critically viewed by Mrs. Holliday as in the following – Lady Buller to Blagg:

*"She has written Messrs Bamford, Jos. Ingleby & Mr Askin to refrain from sporting on her land. She was having a gamekeeper, a servant and a labourer in Dilhorne Woods and Plantations."*

Within twelve months the ladies wished to emphasize the above warning by ejecting Barnford from property adjoining the woods. They informed Mr. Blagg, their solicitor *"Sending notice to Bamford to quit the Fox Fields.' He rents three fields.'* The 'Fox Fields' were to be much better known than for gaming a century later.

In her earlier correspondence with Mr. Blagg she tells of her proposals:

*"to buy land from Bamford by paying £1000 Lady Day 1813, £1000 mid-July 1813 and the remainder at midsummer, 1814"* and sometime later she is:

*"pleased to finish purchase of one field and agreeing to let coals in it also coals in the Broomhurst expecting it to be mined by Bamford Ingleby and Whitehurst."*

However, the firm now T. Patten & Co. decided to close the works in 1830 and since the Pit was worked by John Keates, the Company declined an offer of £6,000 for land and coal by Mr. Buller (Holliday's grandson) as being less than their valuation.

The Cheadle Brass and Copper Co. had been buying considerable amounts of coal for their furnace work at Cheadle, Alton and Oakamoor. They kept account of the costs and had been forced to build a slag block wall around the Cheadle works *"to prevent pilferage of coal."* They decided to sink their own Pit and Barrow has marked it between the site of the Brass Works and the later Gas Works. It was replaced by another below Delphouse called Deepmoor, by 1824 work at Cheadle was running down.

At about this period a few interesting items from Alton deal with colliery working:

*"Shrewsbury Papers.*
*Sept. 1812 A wagon load of Coals from Mobberley Colliery and expenses*
*(mainly carriage)* £1 3 8
*Dec. 1812 James Daken for 2 large buckets with iron grids for drawing water from coal shaft at Oakamoor Baddaley & Co for 3T 10C of Cannel Coal at 20/-Leigh & Co. Coal merchants* £69 16 8$^{1}/_{2}$
*Grid handles for drawing water from coal shaft at Oakamoor Mar. 1815 Woodhead*

| | | | |
|---|---|---|---|
| Colliery Co for coals | 1 | 1 | 7 |
| Xmas 1823 Woodhead Colliery Co for coals | £175 | 8 | 10" |

In 1817 Pitt published his *History of Staffordshire* and among his list of Subscribers were the following local gentry:

> "Thomas Chawner, Cheadle (A surgeon)
> Mr. R. Godwin, Hazlewall (Coal owner)
> Mr. J. Ingleby, Cheadle (Manager, Brass & Copper)
> Mr. J. Leigh, Consall Wood, Cheadle (Coal owner)
> Mr. Edward Milner, Cheadle."

Mr. Chawner was related to the Mercers and Drapers in Cheadle. Mr. Leigh moved to Consall Hall about this time though his Woodhead company continued in Cheadle. Mr. Milner's family became more involved in coal into the last half of the century. Mr. Ingleby had many interests both in industry, vestry meetings and Turnpike Trusts.

Pitt gives some descriptions of various areas of Cheadle. Of Cheadle Park he says:

> *"It is now in cultivation and abounds in mines of coal of great value."* The town is *"three miles in circumference and contains 33 enclosures. Here are some valuable Coal mines".* Of Dilhorne and the Holliday Estate: *"there are also excellent Coal mines in this estate. But the most valuable Coalmines hitherto discovered in this parish are those in the estate of Samuel Bamford Esq who has a handsome mansion near the village of Dilhorne with extensive pleasure grounds."*

## Elsewhere in the coalfield

Away from the Woodhead and Dilhorne activities, the most important event of 1819 was the re-opening of the Duke of Devonshire's coal mine in Kingsley. It had been standing for a year since Cornelius Flint, the Duke's Agent, bid goodbye to the village and much less was heard of Flint's pits. There was no doubt that this venture was worked well and the Duke's level kept the whole area dry so that it was not surprising that some folk in the locality saw a worth while venture waiting to be restarted. On the 20th March, 1819 the Duke leased Kingsley Colliery to Reuben Chawner and Richard Godwin for twenty-one years to 1840. Reuben Chawner belonged to the Mercer establishment, but now farmed at Hanbury, whilst Godwin lived and farmed Hazlewall but was termed 'Gent'. The lease referred to:

> *"All those Mines Beds or Delphes of coal already opened under all that tract of land in the Coy of Derby……by the name of the Kingsley Colliery."*

The Duke's solicitor's clerk had lost his way and the final reading of the agreement had not corrected the geography!

The Chawner - Godwin copy remained in Mr. Blagg's office for nearly one hundred and fifty years when it was necessary to discard it in place of a new century of documentation! The rent and royalties were quite heavy being £360 per year and £180 per acre of coal mined. In addition, by 1821 the mine was assessed for Kingsley Rates at £130.

The Vestry Meeting agreed Messrs Chawner and Godwins Colliery to be valued to the Poor Levies at £130 but should the mine improve to be adjudged again.

The Colliery continued to serve the village workhouse, school and church, in addition to normal sales, until 1861.

In 1820 Bamford was involved in an Assignment of Leases of the New Sham Colliery and machinery. This was an extension of an 1809 lease by the Rev. John Wolfe with the consent of Bamford and Mountfort to the following working partnership: Messrs. Whitehurst of Whitehurst, Yeoman; Edward Milner, Gentleman of Cheadle; John Keates, Brassworks, Yeoman; Thomas Howlett, Cheadle, Yeoman. They were to take all 4 ft coal from under the Old Engine Field and several other closes to the Brookhouse corner. In addition, they were to mine the Litley Coal in Bamford's land at Dilhorne. The lease was to last for fifty years, but no charges were mentioned except that there should be six waggon loads of Coal annually sent to Mountfort at Beamhurst.

The working, however, lasted but ten years as will be seen in 1830, when Bamford and Mountfort were forced to terminate the agreement as:

> *"the four miners in the 1st Part had not been working the 4 ft, $^1/_2$ yd or Litley Coals as they should have done. They had also trespassed in driving and making pits, shafts, levels and ways in other of Mountforts lands. The miners then surrendered the mines to Henry Mountfort to work for himself. They shall make good the land and fill up any pits and shafts left."*

This was the end of an agreement among what appeared a good group of trustworthy coal masters who were expected to work on the lease in a straight-forward manner without being led astray by any one or other of them. These men continued in coal and were prospecting in the Harplow and Litley with the exception of Whitehurst, who rejoined with Bamford.

We have already noticed the concern of Mrs. Holliday to do with the effect of Turnpike tolls on the sale and carriage of coals. It was not possible to collect coal by cart from either Woodhead, the Eaves, Kingsley or Dilhorne without using Toll roads and if the purchaser from the south or west of the town wished to buy from Woodhead then he must be prepared to be charged at two or even three toll houses, gates or chains. The Trusts were keen to collect as much money as possible, as they could justly claim that coal carting, in some places, put a greater burden on the roads and, therefore, increased the cost of their repairs. One writer discussing roads around Dilhorne, reported on the proposal for a Turnpike through the village. He mentions:

> *"the Legislature for a Turnpike Road through the Parish which met with opposition by some persons interested in the mines in the neighbourhood. But one of our brave Admirals, who was in Parliament, having with his Lady made a visit to Dilhorn, declared that he would rather be in the Bay of Biscay, in a Storm, than upon one of the Dillorn Coal Roads in Carriage."*

The opposition died awayand the Bill passed into a Law.
The notes continue:

> *"These Mines are in such Reputation as to be sought after, by Land Carriage, twelve and fifteen Miles round, altho' the expense of Land Carriage is nearly One Shilling per mile for every Ton of Coals."*

By 1820, the Turnpike Trust had discussed a complaint to do with the Woodhead road near the Colliery situated in the field where later Little Hayes farm buildings were erected.

Solicitor Brandon had been directed to write to the coal men, John Leigh and his Agent, W. Bowers:

*"Steps must be taken to remove the nuisance near Bedbrook occasioned by the carts and waggons standing in the Road near Mr Leigh's Colliery."*

This was the first we had heard of the Bowers family, but they were to figure and lead in the coal industry for the next ninety years.

Bamford also had trouble with the Turnpike Trusts. It was not that there was any complaint of nuisance, but that the Trust by 1820, was determined to erect a Toll house at Forsbrook on the corner of the Dilhorne road. Bamford and Thomas Holmes of Delphouse, where small mines were working, combined to object. They employed John Blagg, the solicitor, whose premises were on the site still using his name by the Church-yard, to circularise the Trustees with an appeal against such action.

*"This measure is strongly objected to by the creditors on the Dilhorne Turnpike Road, by Messrs Bamford, Ingleby and Whitehurst as Proprietors of the Dilhorne Colliery*

*Con: Inhabitants of Forsbrook would have to pay toll on two roads i.e. Oakamoor Turn-pike and Dilhorne Turnpike to travel to Dilhorne Colliery and would drive Teams to some other works. The Colliery is now maintaining a large proportion of the poor families resident in or near Dilhorne. The Colliery would be turning away many hands and fami-lies on the Public for support.*

*Case for.: "Are not the Cheadle People equally taxed by payment of half toll for coals from Woodhead, Delphouse and Sham? Is not the greatest part of the repairs caused by Coals and Carriage to the Brassworks ?"*

The argument continued for the next nine years until in 1829 an agreement was made between the three parties:

*"1 . Thos Holmes of Cheadle*
*2. Samuel Bamford, Surnmerhill, Jos Ingleby, Cheadle and Richard Whitehurst of Whitehurst.*
*3. Trustees of the Turnpike.*
*Thos Holmes is lessee or Proprietor of a Colliery at Delphouse in Cheadle and Bamford, Ingleby, Whitehurst are proprietors of another Colliery at Dilhorne, and Toll Gate at Dilhome Lane end would injure persons using collieries so No 1 and 2 will pay sum of £40 p.a. to prevent erection of Toll Gate to be paid for 7 years and order to be paid made Holmes £175 at £25 p.a. Bamford & Co £105 at £15 p.a."*

The agreement was signed at the Trusts' solicitors, Brandon and Cattlow, Cheadle by Holmes, Bamford, Ingleby and Whitehurst.

The Shrewsbury Papers record the purchase of coal for this period while Alton Abbey was being extended to become Alton Towers:

| | | | |
|---|---|---|---|
| *"1825 Chawner and Goodwin Coal* | *£62* | *0* | *0* |
| *Woodhead. Coal to Xmas* | *£218* | *14* | *0* |
| *Coal John Leigh Esq* | *£113* | *2* | *0* |
| *April 1832 John Leigh for coals to Xmas 1831* | *£347* | *17* | *0* |

*John Wilson hauling coal from Alton Wharf*        £288     18     0"
The Cash Book for 1827 records lime burning work:

*"The Ribden Mining Company with Thomas Smith for Coal and Slack*

| | | | | | |
|---|---|---|---|---|---|
| *1827 to coal and Slack* | | £91-12-7 | *By Lime from the Co* | £26 8 0 | |
| *1828* | *Do Do* | £186-6-0 | *do* | £35-6-11 | |
| *1829* | *Do Do* | £170-8-6 | *do* | £34-5-10 | |
| *1830* | *D D* | £171-3-1 | | | |
| *1831 Cash* | £135."| | | | |

The Alton Steward decided that another effort should be made to cut the cost of both fuel coal and its carriage. Further prospecting was carried out in Cur Wood following the efforts by Joseph Bradshaw and Daniel Warrington some twenty years before this campaign in 1827.

Sales for the month of February read:

| | | | |
|---|---|---|---|
| *"Coal on the Bank 14 Tons at 9/2d* | £6 | 8 | 4 |
| *Slack 410 T " 5/-* | £102 | 10 | 0 |
| *Sold 7 Tons 9/2* | £3 | 4 | 2 |
| *31 Tons at 5/-* | £7 | 15 | 0 |
| *Balance Against* | £40 | 5s | 7d." |

Three months later there was a distinct increase in price:

| | | | |
|---|---|---|---|
| *"April 14th Coal on Bank 10T* | | | |
| *Slack 644T at 6/8d.* | | | |
| *Cr. to 17th March* | | | |
| *Cooper for getting 94 Tons at 2/11d.* | £13 | 14 | 2 |
| *Guy and Co. 17 Tons* | £2 | 9 | 7 |
| *Day Work for making level head banking gone, 14 yds* | £13 | 15 | 0 |
| *Heading 20 Yds at 2/6* | 2 | 0 | 0 |
| *Horse driver 17 days* | 3 | 1 | 0 |
| *483 Ton Slack 5/-* | £120 | 15 | 0 |
| *14 Ton Coal 9/2* | 6 | 8 | 4 |
| *Mr Chrystle for a months wage* | 8 | 0 | 0" |

Mr. Chrystle was the manager.

By April the Butty system, note Matthew Cooper & Co., was being worked and the operations had moved towards Cotton in the Starwood. Around 1960, Bill Bowen took me to this place to show me the hollow of the sunken Starwood shaft. The local folk called this Beardmore's Pit from the name of the farmer, he thought, at Golden Hill farm. Star Wood seems the most unlikely spot to have any connection with coal mining and the stone-arched level which runs its ferruginous drainings from the bottom of the shaft into the Dell appears quite out of place. Yet this Alton Colliery Account Book provides much more detail of working than in any other enterprise either before or after. Of course, the manpower used or output of coal could not be compared with the larger collieries already dealt with, but here we find the men's names, their specific jobs and their working places:

*"April 14th 1827*
*Mathew Cooper & Co.*                                 86T

| | | | |
|---|---|---|---|
| Wm Guy & Co | 82T | | |
| Bradshaw & Co sinking at Starwood | £10 | 10 | 0 |
| Beardmore & Co Boring 20 Yds @ 3/6 | £3 | 10 | 0 |
| 12 May Cooper & Co | 32T | | |
| Guy & Co. | 63T | | |
| Bradshaw sinking shaft Star Wood | £9 | 10 | 0 |
| Guy & Co Heading gate road and Levels 28 Yds | £2 | 16 | 0 |
| Bearmor & Co boring Oakr 18 Yds @ 8/5 | | | |
| Candles in day work 14 lbs @ 7d | | | |
| (In hnd) Coal 10T Slack 714T @ 6/8 | | | |
| 11 June Cooper & Co 108 Ton slack | | | |
| Guy & Co 69  Ton slack | | | |
| Bradshaw James & Co sinking Starwood shaft | £17 | 10 | 0 |
| Day work men and horses | £12 | 12 | 6 |
| 9th June 1827 Mat Cooper & Co 69T Guy & Co 84T | | | |
| Ball & Co getting 14 Tons" | | | |
| (New names are now recorded on extra work) | | | |
| "Beardmore sinking Shaft Oakamoor | | | |
| 5¹/₂ ft wide 17Yd deep at 7/ | £4 | 11 | 0 |
| Evans & Co sinking shaft heading securing | | | |
| 4Yds at 2/6 | | 10 | 0 |
| Smith Moses drawing as above 5Yd @ 4/- | | | |
| Culling and heading up level 10 Yds at 2/6 | £2 | 5 | 0 |
| Guy & Co cutting to water No 1 and taking coal to brick kiln | | 11 | 0 |
| Bradshaw & Co Star Wood shaft | £10 | 10 | 0 |
| 7th July Slack to Lime Kilns | | | |
| Cauldon Lowe 72T 2Cwts at 6 - 8 | | | |
| Oakamoor 58T 2 Cwt at 6 - 8 | | | |
| Coal to Brass Co. & others 14T 16 Cwt | | | |
| To Brick Kiln 5T 2 Cwts" | | | |

Many of the above names and jobs are repeated but new names and jobs are worth noting. Bill Bowen may have been mistaken. It may have been Beardmore, the shaft sinker, who named that pit:

| | | | |
|---|---|---|---|
| "Stevenson heading in fault etc. | | | |
| James Mathew sinking air pits at Oakamoor 10 Yds | £2 | 10 | 0 |
| Guy & Co boring for Air | | | |
| Heading level Head 12 Yds No 1 Pit at 2/10 Yd | | | |
| Bradshaw sinking Starwood Pit | £27 | 0 | 0 |
| 4th Aug for 1 month 1827 | | | |
| Stock building up 600 Ton @ 6/- | £1 | 10 | 0 |
| William Cooper repairing & Cleansing | | | |
| Starwood Level | | | |
| Johnson Bill for sawing 133ft timber | | 4 | 11 |
| Smith & Co for lowering shaft Top | | 7 | 0 |
| Cooper & Co getting at Starwood Level | 97T | | |
| No 2 & 3 Pits Guy & Co | 156T | | |
| James & Co Bricking No 3 shaft cleansing | £2 | 15 | 0 |
| Johnson R & Co Cleansing Level Head (Water Level) | | | |

*Cooper & Co Heading to prove coal on deep side*
*of fault Starwood Level 12 Yds @*           2     6"

The increased extent of the workings especially in Carr Wood is shown in this last Account:

"*Aug 9th Stevens & Co getting at Starwood 80T @ 3/6*
*Johnson & Co ditto No 5 Pit 25T Slack @ 4/0*
*Stevens & Co ditto No 6 Pit 20T @ 3/6*
*ditto coal 3T @ 3/6*
*Bradshaw & Co sinking No 5 Pit 11 Yds @ 6/6*
*ditto No 6 Pit 12 Yds @ 6/6*
*Bradshaw & Co heading No 5 to No 4*         £2    12     0
*Stevens & Co heading No 3 to No 6*         £7     3     0
*Slack got at Starwood 24T*
*ditto Oakamoor 9T*
*Balance against Colliery*                 £7     0     4"

The coal accounts for both Cauldon Low and Oakamoor kilns for this 1828-30 period served to give some idea of how small workings had increased all around the coalfield whilst the larger collieries had continued.

The smaller men, often on the outskirts and in the Crabtree coal, found that most or all of their output was in the form of slack. Lime kilns, therefore, were very good customers to them although the demand was not sufficient to keep all at work for the full years.

1828 Lime Kiln A/cs at Cauldon Low
| | | | | | |
|---|---|---|---|---|---|
| "*Took Slack from Mr Smith (Whiston Eaves)* | 25T @ | 9/2 | | | |
| *ditto Oakamoor* | 6T @ | 7/- | | | |
| *ditto Mr Dawson* | 10T | £3 | 6 | 0 | |
| *Aug 9th Slack Mr Smith Eaves* | 90T | 9/2 | | | |
| *Dilhorne and Cheadle* | 16T @ | 8/3 | | | |
| *Oakamoor* | 10T @ | 9/2 | | | |
| *Mr Smith* | 30T @ | 9/2 | | | |
| *Plants* | 34T | 9/2 | | | |
| *Oakamoor* | 2T | 9/- | | | |
| *9th - 27th Sept. Slack Mr Smith Eaves* | 50T @ | 7/- | | | |
| *Oakamoor* | 60T @ | 5/6 | | | |
| *Cheadle Dilhorne* | 25T | 5/6 | | | |
| *Starwood* | 17T | 6/8 | | | |
| *Woodhead* | 52T | 7/- | | | |
| *Sept - Oct 25* | | | | | |
| *Slack from Woodhead* | 17T | 7/- | | | |
| *Patten & Co (Deepmoor)* | 4T 16C | 5/6 | | | |
| *Mr Smith* | 65T | 7/- | | | |
| *Oakamoor* | 50T | 5/5 | | | |
| *Starwood* | 4T | 6/8" | | | |

1829 Lime. Kilns at Oakamoor. This was now worked by the Bottom or Botham family:

*"Slack from Mr Smith                              137T    6/10*
*Mr Leigh Consall                                  149T    7/-*
*Langley & Whitehurst                               50T    5/6"*

The day-to-day delivery of Slack from March 2nd to September 2nd i.e. six months totalled:

*"Mr Smith (Eaves)                                 266T 8C*
*John Leigh                                        359T 5C"*

Both these suppliers would be able to use the canal by loading at the Jackson Bridge basins and would deliver to the lime kilns wharf at Oakamoor. Both continued into mid-October when totals became:

*"Smith                                            377 Tons.*
*Leigh                                             418 Tons"*

This canal transport represented a great saving on cartage down to Oakamoor.

Through 1830 smaller deliveries were made from a variety of small workings over a wider area, and in most cases the coal carrier is named:

*"Charles Beard, Cotton Bank and Rakeage*
*Thos Ratcliffe, Cotton Banks, Rakeage, Foxt Wood, Rakeway*
*R Bradaley, Litley, Dilhorne*
*Mr. Appleby, Blakeway Lowe*
*Mr Smith, Cash Heath*
*Mr Riley Upper Cotton, Slack Cotton Banks*
*Mr. Draycott, Ramshorn, Cotton Banks*
*Whieldon, Foxt, Foxtwood*
*Langley, Cheadle*
*Hardell (Gorsty Croft) Foxtwood*
*Mr. Morris, Foxt*
*Mr. Baker, Newclosefields, Cheadle*
*Mr. Stevens, Ipstones Edge*
*Mr. Titley, Newclosefields*
*Mr. Tenison, Ipstone, Foxt, Cotton Banks, Foxtwood*
*Mr. Mawley, Rownall*
*Mr. Geo. Smith, Rakeage*
*Mr. Massey, Dilhorne*
*Mr. Hodgkinson, Ipstones, Foxt, Cotton Rakeage*
*Mr. Clews of Foxt, Cotton*
*Mr. Taylor of Foxt , Cotton, Revedge"*

By this date it will be seen that in addition to mining, the industry is providing a great deal of work for carters.

In the Kingsley Vestry Minutes of the period 1823 - 27 there were entries which show that the Overseer and Churchwardens knew that the depression following the French War was by no means over. Although we find that in 1823 the vestry might have felt that Mr. Beech was over-rated on his mines *"Allowed to Mr. Beech on his coalmines £5"*, they had to try to keep the rates as steady as possible, although there were additional calls for relief:

> *"1825 at the A.V.M. [Annual Vestry Meeting] Overseer Brough ordered that he do not in future relieve any of the Colliers or other persons who are well in health and able to gain a livelihood if fair wages were allowed.*
> *1826 Thos Wheawall's son Lamed in Pitt*                             3/-*
> *1827 Mr Godwin Coals to the Workhouse*               £2       0       5d"*

By 1831 it appears that Thomas Smith of Whiston Eaves, who had recently been selling a great deal of slack, was in financial trouble. The Eaves house had been built some thirty years earlier, but the documents read:

> *"6 May 1831 Sales of Eaves Ford Farm by Assignees of Thos Smith (Commission of Bankruptcy) were to sell to Joseph Locker (Occupier) for £4660 the farm of 142 acres. Except the materials of buildings made at the Old Coal Works on the farm by the Cauldon Low Company."*

Within two months of the sale of a steam engine by Mr. Holmes at the Eaves Colliery, a second was put on the market by the Dilhorne Colliery or Mr. Bamford and his associates. *"The Staffordshire Advertiser"* of the 9th May, 1829 printed the following notice of sale:

> *"Engine and materials to be sold at Dilhorne Colliery near Cheadle.*
> *One cast iron Engine Beam complete with Arches 24 feet LONG.*
> *5 Tons in weight.*
> *One round wought iron BOILER 13$\frac{1}{2}$ft in diameter nearly new.*
> *One Air Pump and Condenser complete with a Brass Working Barrel in case in the same,*
> *15 inches in Diameter.*
> *One Brass Working Barrel 8 foot long 7 ins Diameter.*
> *Also about 30 Yds of 11$\frac{1}{2}$ inches cast iron*
> *And other useful articles PUMP TREES*
> *Belonging to the Engine Business."*

There should not have been difficulty in selling such valuable machines at this time for new projects were being started. The fifty-year lease under the names of Bamford and Mountfort was terminated by 1830 when the mine owners, Whitehurst, Milner, Keates and Howlett had not complied with the terms, so that Mountfort, the owner, set about working his own teams of men around Blake Hall. This house was a second edition of the great and stylish building of the fifteenth and sixteenth centuries, which was the home of the reputable Adderley family, lost after the seventeenth century with only the mill opposite Park Hall Farm as a memorial to their existence. There is a farm lane to the site from a gate on the right, half-way up the Boundary and the four spoil banks can still be seen.

The mining party to that agreement turned their attention to the Harplow district. Working there on a smaller scale, but having a measure of success, their enterprise lasted for more than thirty years, and having a branch on the Litley land, became known as the Harplow and Litley Mining Company.

By the middle of 1831 the following notices began to appear in *"The Staffordshire Advertiser"*:

*"16th July 1831.  New Colliery. Blake Hall.*
*The public are respectfully informed that a NEW COLLIERY is now opened at Blake*
*Hall adjoining the old SHAM COLLIERY situated between Cheadle and Dilhorne within*
*a mile and a half of each place.  The YARD Coals may now be had of the FIRST*
*QUALITY.*
*N.B. The roads have lately undergone a thorough repair and are now in excellent condi-*
*tion. Blake Hall July 7th 1831."*

Another advertisement appeared a month later which indicated the increased activity
in coal at this period:

*"Wanted immediately engineers at Eaves Colliery Nr. Cheadle 6th August 1831."*

This notice probably did not attract sufficient increase in sale possibly because the
roads were not all they were supposed to be but most likely that most mines had a wharf
near a recognised road which would save time and trouble in loading a cart or waggon.
    Another notice followed in *"The Staffordshire Advertiser"* for October 8th that year:

*"NEW COLLIERY, BLAKE HALL*
*The Property of Henry MOUNTFORD of BEAMHURST HALL.*
*The public are respectfully informed that the YARD COALS of the best quality are now*
*conveyed by RAILWAY from this Colliery down to the New Sham Machine House,*
*situate close to the Cheadle Brass Works and may be had there or at the Colliery at the*
*usual price 7/6 per Ton.*
*BLAKE HALL          SEPTEMBER    29th 1831."*

Just four months later there was a change of tone.  *"The Staffordshire Advertiser"* of
25th February 1832 reads:

*"To be let for a term of years – on Lady Day next.  ALL that newly established Colliery*
*called BLAKE HALL. The Engine is a new one of 40 horse power, the Winding Engine*
*and the railroad are also new.  The Coal is of the Very best quality and only 62 Yards*
*from the Surface.  There is also another vein 18 Yds deeper of equal quality.  The roads*
*are in excellent Condition and the Coals are conveyed by railway within about a $^1/_4$*
*mile from the town of Cheadle.  The above Colliery is in an easy distance of the*
*Potteries being within 5 miles of Lane End and affords an advantageous opportunity*
*to manufacturers whose consumption of coal is considerable.*
*Applications to be made to Henry Mountford Esq. of Beamhurst Hall."*

Within a month the miners in the broken lease of 1830 had good news to proclaim in
*"The Staffordshire Advertiser"*:

*"New COLLIERY situated between Huntley and Brassworks near Cheadle.*
*The LITLEY and HARPLOW COLLIERY COMPANY respectfully inform their FRIENDS*
*and the PUBLIC that they are now prepared to raise an AMPLE supply of the YARD*
*COAL which is known to be of EXCELLENT QUALITY. 20th October 1831."*

In 1832 when Thornbury Hall was advertised for sale the following lines were added:
    *"It is supposed there is coal under the whole of this lot and the mines are open in the*
*adjoining lands."*

The last of the coal leases found among documents of the, Bamford period was one signed in 1836 under which lease Edward Buller of Dilhorne Hall granted to Samuel Bamford, Richard Whitehurst and Joseph Ingleby, all carrying on their business at Dilhorne Colliery:

> *"All that the halfyard of 2ft 3in thick and the 2Yd Coals under all Closes called Madgdales in the occupation of John Hammersley and Richard Bettany, tenants, containing 11 Acres, with authority to make Railways over Broornhurst and the Mill Birch for a term of 20 Years."*

The Lessees were to pay £200 per acre along with all rates, duties, either Parliamentary and Parochial. As usual the Lessor could inspect the dialling at any time and the lessees were to keep accounts of all coal mined. The latter was to make sure that there was no trespassing.

The fewer documents through the 1830s give the impression that Samuel was slowing down and it is not surprising to find him passing over his property by Abstract of Title on March 2nd 1839. The document recites that Samuel Bamford of Summerhill, Dilhorne gave to his trustees, John James of Summerhill, Colliery Agent, his son James Bamford and daughter, Mary Bamford and their heirs, the profits of all Colliery concerns on his Estate. However this excluded his youngest son, Samuel, if he had married Eliza Slater, but he later left him an annuity, as with his mother of £30 per annum.

He had offered to sell, with his partners, Richard Whitehurst and Joseph Ingleby, Dilhorne Colliery to a William Brooker for £10,000, but if not sold, Whitehurst and Ingleby were to continue to work the mines as they did as Bamford & Co. until the middle of the 1840s. The Bamfords had had nearly a century in coal on the south and west side of the coalfield. Samuel died in September, 1839, leaving five children, but his widow lived until 1863. John James had been Agent to the Bamfords over a long period and was especially useful to Samuel as time went on. He was taken to live at Summerhill and stayed until he died in 1862.

Richard Whitehurst was also involved in the coal industry beyond the Dilhorne Colliery. When work had started at Harplow, he had bought himself a quarter shareholding and must, with his experience, have been an asset to the management there. He first made a will in 1837, but added codicils until it was finally completed by July, 1841. He left all his farming stock to his son, John, and all household stock to Elizabeth, his daughter-in-law. The estate and colliery shares were put in the hands of John James and William Eddowes, a neighbouring farmer and butcher. J. M. Blagg signed to witness whilst John Salt of the Machine House and John Hammersley of the Old Engine Farm acted as Executors. This again was probably the end of a long line of mining Whitehursts since those early days of ironstone mining and carting in the late sixteenth century.

The Turnpike trouble in 1821 first mentioned that a William Bowers was acting Agent for Leigh at Woodhead. We saw that by 1810 Leigh had seen Honeybourne build his tramway incline through Gibridding Wood in preparation for the coming of the Froghall – Uttoxeter Canal and that when he started to construct his own much longer line, there was considerable coal rent trouble through 1811. It seems that Leigh and Bowers must have found a remedy for the Turnpike trouble and Leigh was then content to leave the general conduct of the Woodhead affairs to the Agent. He was not satisfied with his own residence and by 1816 he had bought Consall New Hall. He overlooked the very important fact that the tramway was not completed, neither had he sold that half share he had advertised. Instead, he joined with four other adventurers in a scheme to run a tramway from Consall, where lime could be burned, to a spot near Meir or Longton. Since neither had the money to pay his share of the costs they decided that one should approach the Exchequer Loan Commissioners on July 24th, 1817 for a loan of £8,000, *"To Compleat the North Stafford Railway"*.

The application was made by George Lambert Clifford of Foxearth and granted for three years, on the personal security of two Cliffords, two Coyney brothers of Weston Coyney and John Leigh of Consall Hall, and the £8,000 was granted. Now Leigh was short of money, in fact, he was again in debt. The Consall Plateway as it became locally known, instead of the glorified title of the North Stafford Railway, never looked like repaying in three years. It also served its purpose to a few other people in addition to the Consall lime burners. An old pocket account book, belonging to the Bottom family business of lime burning and brick making in Oakamoor, contained payments to the North Stafford Railway for carriage of lime and bricks through the 1830 period. A Wharf was opened on the line where it crossed the Kingsley – Cellarhead road where it rises just three hundred yards from the traffic lights. It is locally known as Lime Wharf. At the same time, a trio of kilns were built by the canal side at Consall, but the condition indicates that they were little used.

By 1824 Leigh was taking the idea of completing the Woodhead tramway more seriously and approached Honeybourne with a view to shortening his stretch by joining with the Gibridding incline instead of continuing his independent line through Eastwall. He leased a 9ft. slip of land through various fields *"to lay down, construct and use a Railway"*. He was to pay £20 per annum for the 200 year period. During the following year, 1825, Woodhead Hall was occupied by a Mr. Thomas Thompson but this did not interfere with the railway agreement which was completed by 1827. It was important that the railway should be in commission as the Broadhay Agreement was renewed after the death of John Clarke by his widow to whom Leigh paid a single fee of £204 10s to continue to 1833.

A further most imporant lease was made in 1832 by the Trustees of the late James Beech of Shawe Hall, Kingsley, with John Leigh, *"Two mines of coal called the Two Foot Coal and Woodhead Coal now in the course of working"* covering some 120 acres of the Shawe land with some on the east of the Kingsley Holt to Cheadle Road. This was for a term of 21 years at a rent of £180 per acre mined with a minimum of £500 per year. In addition, a fee of 1s. 3d. for every one thousand bricks made and one hundred tons of coal per annum at 1/- per ton for Mr. Beech, junior, at Shawe Hall. The Beech Trustees contracted not to let the privilege of building a railway from Kingsley to the canal at Froghall to any other person. Soon after this lease Leigh and Bowers planned their own alternative transport system in the form of their own horse and cart team. About 1838 a square of buildings was erected to house horses, carts, work shops, smithy and cottages for the men to operate the scheme. The planner, unfortunately, built the rectangle of buildings and enclosed the first of the disused pits, at Woodhead which was forgotten until it collapsed a century later.

This lease certainly ensured that the Woodhead Colliery had many years of mining ahead so that the Woodhead tramway was now extended to be able to reach into this area.

By the time the first One Inch O.S. map of the Cheadle area was prepared in 1836 it shows the Woodhead Tramway crossing the road at Woodhead, Cheadle and extending up to the Beech land, near to Booths Farm, where the clay pits, brick works and colliery were established. A branch turns westerly, across the brook, to a pit in the fields just off the Highfield Avenue road, today known as the Royal George field.

The slight embankment down the field to cross the brook over a small bridge can still be followed, though from the 1840s the Colliery became known as the Royal George. By 1834 White's Directory announced *"At Alton Mills. Woodhead Colliery Agent at Wharf."* This meant that the system was working as Leigh intended some twenty years before. There would be a definite improvement in sales when coal was sold from five or six wharves along the canal to Uttoxeter.

At the same time, there was bad news in the way of Pit deaths. In 1833/4 the Kingsley Registers record three deaths for the period:

> *"Paul Carr accidently lost his life. 18$\frac{1}{2}$ Yrs of age in Woodhead Coal Pit July 20 1833.*
> *George Bentley 16 Yrs of age Nov. 27th 1834*
> *George Hall 25 Yrs of age Nov. 29th 1834*
> *Accidentally lost their lives in Woodhead Coal Pitt."*

At about this time, Leigh decided to renovate the larger Flint Mill at Consall but the rumour went round that, although William Bowers was also in charge of this work, the money ran out before the floors were completely boarded and the work was suspended. It came as no surprise when the following notices appeared:

> *"Sale of Freehold of Consall and Woodhead Estates including Consall Hall. Tuesday 23rd May, 1841 by Messrs David Smith & Son at the Mint in the Bank of England. Rental and estimated value of property £7,000 per annum."*

The catalogue begins with Consall Hall:

> *"(A mansion on a small scale). 1800 acres. Inexhaustible mines of coal with a vein of ironstone. Six capital and superior lime kilns. Lawn Farm. Chase Colliery. The Flint Mill with three water wheels two lately new, 30ft in diameter and 9ft wide. The annual profit £3000 to £4000 per annum at least."*

The mention of the ironstone cannot refer to the red hydrate ore which caused such a stir twelve years later. If Leigh could have held on until 1853, he could have made the fortune which his successor at Consall Hall, Fergison Smith, made in the twenty years following. The great 30ft water wheels will be remembered by many folk who either used the Churnet Valley railway which ran in full view of these rotating monsters, or those who used the canal towpath or the Kingsley Banks paths for their Saturday or Sunday walks. [The two were known as Jack and Jill].

The last Lot was the Woodhead Colliery Estate. It gives no detail of the pits but mentions the tramway running near Mr. Beech's Colliery, the canal and the *"contemplated Grand Railroad, from Macclesfield to Derby in the Vale of the Churnet"*. It continues to describe:

> *"the present building along the line of the railway and on the Farm consists of 1st at the westward end near Cheadle, a superintendent's house, a long line shed wharf, counting home, beyond are the Colliery buildings, engine house with 45 h.p. engine, extensive stabling, cut houses, smithy and workshops sheds etc. and several cottages nearly all substantially built with brick on stone with tiled roofs. A brick ground with kilns and sheds."*

William Bowers, Leigh's Agent, managed to find the money to rent it.

From 1841 Bowers worked the Coal Complex at Woodhead as his own property. By 1850 he had an eye on the Flint Mills on which he had, with Leigh, done so much work. He was able to lease them from Leigh's creditors for a sum of £500 per annum. There were no other Leighs to follow in the coal business and nearly a century of the story was closed.

There had been national counts of population throughout the country every ten years since 1801, and this proved very useful for general statistical purposes, but by 1841 the Census, as it was now called, was much more particular in that it required to register a person's job or profession. This enabled historians to see changes in the number's working in certain trades, most important in a small community such as Cheadle. In 1841 in a total population of 4,399 there were 172 males in the coal industry. These could be men, butties, coal owners or children down to eleven years of age or less. This proportion would be very similar in the surrounding villages, for walking three or four miles to the pits meant little in the early nineteenth century. Alongside these figures, the Directories of the period help to complete the coal industry picture. The 1828 Directory named eight Collieries and the owners as follows:

> *"Bamford & Co., Dilhorne*
> *Godwin Richud, Hazel Wall (Kingsley)*
> *Holmes Thomas, Delphouse.*
> *Holmes William, Eaves.*
> *Leigh John, Woodhead.*
> *Milner, Keates & Howlett, Sham.*
> *Plant Mary, Lucks Hall.*
> *Ribden Mining Co., Oakamoor."*

The 1835 Directory named only five, omitting the following three:

> *"Holmes William of the Eaves.*
> *Plant Mary, Lucks Hall.*
> *Ribden Mining Co., Oakamoor."*

It is very likely that the lady coalmaster, Mary Plant, had something to do with a Thomas Plant, who was a collier of some thirty years of age living at the back of the town. The name Lucksall was home-made for the Cobble coal which was mined from a small working in the field now used as the Primary School playing field. The small spoil bank was levelled around 1950.

The Litley and Harplow had split from the Bamford combine and had this advertisment in the October *"The Staffordshire Advertiser"*:

> *"New Colliery situated between Huntley and Brassworks near Cheadle. The Litley and Harplow Colliery Company respectfully inform their friends and the public that they are now prepared to raise an ample supply of the Yard Coal which is known to be of excellent quality.*
> *20th October, 1831."*

The 1842 Directory named seven with four alterations and additions:

> *"Bowers William & Eli, Woodhead.*
> *Hammersley William & Co., Huntley*
> *Whitehurn William, Harplow.*
> *Milner Keates Howlett, Harplow."*

The following notice appeared in the *"The Staffordshire Advertiser"*:

> *"Colliery accident at Cheadle - 13th June, 1846. On Monday morning last at a Colliery belonging to Messrs. Howlett & Co. 3 unfortunate individuals lost their lives. An inquest was held on Monday evening at the Buck public house. The inquiry was adjourned the Talbot Inn, Cheadle the following morning."*

By 1840 the Industrial Revolution was abolishing the worst of the evils of the recession that followed the Napoleonic war. The coal industry in many parts of the country was barely able to meet the new demands to keep the new steam engines turning and the fires in the houses of the growing towns burning. This period gave greater increase in population than the country had ever seen. In many cases, children had to work at the pit top and even below to drag the coal from the working to the shaft. Also there were reports of women working underground. The stories of such scandals so stirred parliament that by 1841 they decided that commissioners should tour the whole country specifically to report on the employment of women and children especially in mines. It was entitled: *Report by Samuel S. Scriven, Esq. on the employment of Children and Young persons in the Coal Mines of North Staffordshire and on the State, Condition and Treatment of such Children and Young Persons, 1842.*

It would be impossible to repeat all that Scriven reported on the whole of his visit, but that dealing with,Cheadle mines and miners cannot be omitted. Having visited the early Mossfield Colliery just out of Longton, he was invited to descend and, although this was not Cheadle, he gives a vivid account of his underground passage which could have been anywhere underground in the 1840s:

> *"The height of these passages obliged us to grope in the semi-flexed position the whole distance of nearly half a mile so that, at the end, I had a painful difficulty in recovering myself. I cannot easily forget the scene that presented itself on my arrival at the place of operations, where about twenty men were working in their peculiar posture around the walls of the excavated chamber, assisted by the dim light of some dozen candles. Their appearance had something truly hideous and Satanic about it, prompted me to ask myself – Can these be human creatures? The*

*heat arising from the congregation of so many persons and so many candles, together with the offensive odour from their excessive perspiration, was intolerable; all were naked or nearly so.*

*The next field of my labour was at the Collieries at Cheadle where I arrived on the 18th March. Here I found the works of Mr. Bowers, 'the Woodhead Colliery', having four pits; those also of Mr. Holmes, the 'Delph-house Colliery', of four pits; of Mr. Thomas Fowell, the 'Harplow Colliery', of two pits; of Mr. Whitehurst, the 'Litley Dale Colliery': Messrs. Malkin and Hammersley, the 'Huntley Colliery'; Messrs. Bamford and Co., of the 'Dilhorne Colliery'; and the Cheadle Brass and Copper Company's Colliery and Brass Works, both at Cheadle and Oakamoor; from each of which I took more or less evidence.*

*I descended the Dilhorn Pit and had to stoop, my hands supporting the body upon my knees the whole distance. This position the boys acquire when young, and like the sitting posture of the "pickers' who rest upon their heels, becomes habitual to them. Pass these men in an idle hour, and it is ten to one but you will find that they are resting themselves in this way."* Shades of Fred Hullah !!

Scriven continues with a paragraph which even historians will find difficulty in giving credence. This is the period of the Industrial Revolution which some historians called the Hungry Forties but such was the impression gathered by the researcher, both from the masters and men and boys, that the account belies most histories. Because the report deals with Cheadle and its people, I have felt compelled to give the results of his interviews as they appear in the report to the Commissioners, for most of them could have been our grandfathers of five generations ago:

*"CHEADLE WOODHEAD COLLIERY, rented by Mr. Bowers*

No. 14. *Mr Bowers*, aged 33. Examined March 19:

*I am the superintendent of my father's colliery, at Woodhead; I always make up the account of wages, and transfer the amount to the machine man. We have eight pits, in which we employ about 50 persons above 18 years of age, and about 30 under; out of this number there are 13 butties, who employ and pay all the rest. The usual time of work is 10 hours a day. The characters of the boys are various, some good, some bad, but I am of opinion that they are generally good; many of them read and write, but this depends a good deal upon their parents who, if ignorant themselves, keep their children in ignorance. I have not observed any very material difference between those who have been well educated and those who have not , both make at times very good workmen, and good and honest members of society; but if I had to chose of two boys, one that could read and write, the other that could not, I should certainly take the first into my service, lest I should want him for any confidential or particular duty. We have had no accidents either from fire-damp, black-damp, or machinery, within the last two years.*

(Signed)  ELI BOWERS.

No. 15. *John Goodwin*, aged 34. Examined March 19:

*I attend the weighing machine of the whole colliery, and keep the weekly accounts of the people; I also pay them on Saturday night – always in cash at so much per ton. I pay the butties, they pay the men and young people whom they employ; We have nothing to do with either the pay or engagement of the latter. We have three deep pits of about 100 yards, and five others of from 15 to 26 yards, in each of these we have, at a rough guess, from 10 to 20 persons of all ages; there are no women or girls. They all go to work at six in the morning and come up when they have done their work, which is generally between four and five; they have to get about 12 rucks or 108 skiffs. They take their dinners always below, and get their breakfasts, and tea, or supper before and after they come up. About four descend together in chain tackles, very seldom in corves, master will not suffer it on account of their greater liability to accidents. Our tackle is made of flat rope ; there is a bailiff whose duty it is to go down he pits, and look after the work and tackle; we have also a superior engineer, who works one engine, and if anything should be the matter with another he is called to that; the same number (four) come up together. I have been here between five and six years; I have never known a rope to break in that time, or known any accident by the carelessness of the engineer. I have known of one accident from black damp, in which eight hands were killed; on that occasion two men, who had been to work at night, lighted a fire at four in the morning at about the middle of the road, which created the obnoxious gas and killed them; six others descended at the usual time in the morning to their work, they died likewise before any assistance could be rendered; I have known of nothing of the sort since. We have no machinery below; the boys draw the skiffs on the rails; in some cases horses do it, that is only in one pit. I think the youngest child we have employed is 10 or 11, the weight of the skiffs they drive is 500; they run them from the workings to the bottom of the pit in pairs; they never draw with the girdle, at least not many, most of them push or drive.*

(Signed)  JOHN GOODWIN

No. 16. *John Hammond*. Examined March 19 :

*I don't know how old I am, I was baptized 22ⁿᵈ last October – 14 years. I went to school at Kingsley before I came to work; I have been to work more than four years. I go to Chapel Sunday-school at Kingsley where I live, about two miles off. I can read but cannot write; I have got no mother or father; I live with Thomas Stephenson and his wife Ellen Stephenson, they sent me to school and paid one penny a week for books and that like. I always go to chapel every Sunday with them, they are Wesleyans. I work in the slack-pit with three men who undertake the work; they pay me my wages, 7s. a week; I give it to Thomas Stephenson, who looks after me, he finds me everything, and is very good and kind to me and my two brothers, who live there too; both of them work in pits; one gets 9s. a week, the other 4s. When I'm in pit I draw coals with a pair of byatts over my shoulders that come down my back; I keep my waistcoat on, but take my shirt and jacket off; I keep my boots and stockings on, and put a little cap top on my head: all the other boys do the same in the small pits; the passages from the workings to the pit's mouth is fifty yards, and about three quarters of a yard high; I am obliged to stoop very low to draw the corves on, or I should knock my head. I can't always tell how heavy thet are; some is little ones, some is big ones, they weigh from 100 to 200 weight. I leave home at Kingsley at a quarter to six, and get to the pit about a quarter past, and go down, I come up about seven. I get my dinner down in pit, am allowed no particular time for it, get it as fast as I can, I generally eat it in a quarter of an hour; I get meat pies, sometimes bacon and cheese with bread; the butties behave very well to me, I have never known other lads beaten, if they were to beat us master would soon stop that and make them fine a shilling. I like the work pretty well, it is hard sometimes; I get very tired when I get home.*

(Signed)  JOHN HAMMOND

No. 17. Edward Edwards, *aged 41. Examined March 9:*

*I am one of the Charter-masters of the Woodhead mine, belonging to Mr. Bowers. I employ 12 men and eight lads under 18, the youngest is between 13 and 14. I undertake the work by the ton, and pay the men and boys daily wages; the men receive 2s. 8d., some 3s. the difference is occasioned by the difference in the kind of work – the hardest workers, as those who pick and load too, and get slack out; they continue to work a little later. The boys are paid in the same way, some receiving 1s. 8d. and 1s. a day, depending upon their age and strength and activity; their employment is to push the waggons or skips upon the rail in pairs, if one cannot do it another is put on; the weight comes to about 400, and the number they draw from the workings to the pit mouth is 108 or 109 rucks. We have no horse in the pit, the waggon-ways being level; they (the boys) work in their waistcoats, but without coats or shirts, and with a girdle over their shoulders. I do not remember any accident that has happened within these few years from damp or machinery; about four go down and come up together; there are no bonnets to the tackle; I do not remember a rope breaking with men on; our machinery is in good order, I never saw better. I have been a buttie about 17 years; I do not think that children are over worked; or ill-treated, when they come first they have light work do; they are broken in by degrees. I do not think their health suffers from the work or from the place they work in ; they seldom complain. I was never educated in youth, that I have always considered a drawback to me; I should have stood a better chance if I could have read, and wrote.*

(Signed)   EDW. EDWARDS

No. 18. Ralph Hammond, *aged 16. Examined March 19 :*

*I pust waggons along at Woodhead bottom-coal Colliery for Edwards the butty. I went to Kingsley day school, and learnt to read and write, both of which I can do well; I attend the Wesleyan Chapel Sunday-school every Sunday. I came to work when I was 10 years old, and get now 9s. a week; I give it to Thomas Stephens, who looks after me and my brothers. I come to work at a little before six in the morning, and leave at four or five sometimes later, that depends upon how I get on; the passages in which I work be of pretty good fettle (repair) and I can walk easy, they are four feet high, some places are less; 'tis harder work sometimes than at others, the roads are heavier; I get tired when I get home, but I have to walk two miles; I get my breakfast afore I come from home, and my supper when I go back; my dinner always in the pit, the time allowed me to get it is uncertain, I do not take many minutes, because I should be longer afore I came up if I did. I never had any injury in this pit, I had at another where th top was not so high, I got my head cut open there: that stopped me from work about a week; another time the chain fell down the shaft and cut my head. I have seen fire-damp come out of the seams of coal, and have put a candle to it to burn; it never did me any harm, I only wanted to try it.*

(Signed) RALPH HAMMOND

No. 19. *Thomas Cooper*, aged 14, and *Thomas Barker*, aged 16. Examined March 19:

*We draw waggons in the bottom-coal pit for Edward Edwards, the butty; we draw in byats or shoulder-straps that come down over our backs, and is made fast by a hook to the front of the waggon; the distance we have to draw is about 300 yards, the height of the waggon-way four feet – there is plenty of air in the passages; I carry a candle with me, sometimes it goes out with the draft. We have no fires below to make drafts, there is plenty without; we are warm enough without fires. The men behave very well to us, they give us a lick in the back if we are not sharp enough, not very often, we have nothing to complain of in that. The work is very healthy for us, we can always sleep at night, and eat out suppers, breakfasts, and dinners, I believe we can; we get meat in the morning, bread and cheese for dinner, and potatoes and bacon, or that sort of supper. We go to school on Sundays at the Church Free School, and both of us can read, and write a little. I, Thomas Cooper, get 6s. a week, and I, Thomas Barker, get 10s. in full work; we would rather be colliers than sailors, or anything else; we like the work, it was never too much for us, all the boys in our colliery are strong and well.*

*(Signed)* THOMAS COOPER
THOMAS BARKER

THE CHEADLE BRASS AND COPPER COMPANY'S WORKS - *(Coal Pits).*

No. 20. *Simon Robinson*, aged 16. Examined March 20:

*I have worked at the Delph-house pits six months, at Harplow, before that 7 months, at Litley Dale 12 months, and here one week. I went to the day-school at Cheadle three or four years; I go to Sunday-school now, and can read, and write. I draw the skips in this pit for John Barnes, and get 8s. a week. I strip my jacket and shirt, put the waistcoat on again a top o'my bare hide, always work in byats; the distance from the workings to the pit's bottom is not far yet, we have only just begun to head. At Delph-house it was 400 yards and very hard work, up-hill and down. I got the same wages there, 1s. 4d. a day, while other boys had the same work, and 1s. 6d. a day, that made me leave. We have but two pits here, one water, the other coal; it is a very wet pit, I work in water up to my knees, it is a very cold pit just yet, because we are only 18 yards deep. I have come to work at four o'clock in the morning this week, and have left at four in the afternoon. I come so early because we are sinking three turns (or sets) of eight hours each, night and day; I then worked upon bank. I never met with more than one accident, that was coal falling on my foot and squeezed it. I was never burnt; I am always in good health. The work agrees with me very well, but I should like anything else better.*

*(Signed)* SIMON ROBINSON

DELPH HOUSE COLLIERY

No. 21. *Mr. Thomas Holmes*, aged 50, Occupier. Examined March 20:

*I was first employed in these collieries as clerk, under Thomas Swinnerton, Esq., for 12 years; I then became the proprietor, and have continued so for 21 years; I have three pits now at work and one engine or water-pit, and from 80 to 100 men and boys employed – no women: if I could not carry on my work without women I would drop the colliery, because I do not think it right to stow women and men together in such places, it would be both degrading and demoralizing to do so ; there are no pits, to my knowledge, in this neighbourhood in which they are so employed, in the south I believe they are. The boys are engaged generally in waggoning, pushing, and pulling; they pull their jacket, waistcoat, and shirt off and put on a flannel donkin (under flannel jacket) and draw in byats (two pieces of leather over the shoulders, falling down over the back and terminating in a chain and hook) which they attach, to the skips or waggons - they work singly, unless one is poorly or weak, then they work in pairs; the heights of our waggon-ways are four feet or four and a half, so that there is not much stooping in the draw-roads; there is in the workings, where the men work in the flexed position, to which they become so used that if you see a number together in a high-ways of a pit it is ten to one but that they will take it to relieve themselves. We are not subject to fire-damps in this neighbourhood, but are very subject to choke or black damp, which we take care to get rid of by ventilation; I have never lost a man or boy since I have had the management here, now 33 years, or any accidents with machinery. As it regards the educational condition of the lads that work here, you shall go to the pits, examine them all, and not find one that cannot read or write; they all attend the Sunday-school, and have attended in their youth day-schools, a great many of them now attend the evening school after work to learn (as they call it) to sum, it is their own choice, not by my positive desire, although I am glad to know it; the parents wish it and doubtless insist upon it; the moral conduct of my men and boys is really good, if there is one scabby sheep amongst them he leaves of his own accord, the rest are too much for him; I have not had occasion to discharge a butty for misconduct since I have been here, or the butty to discharge a man but very rarely. I do not allow any punishments to be inflicted by men upon the boys. I believe the boys are very healthy, very happy, and always willing to work; if upon any special occasion I wanted overwork done they would willingly and cheerfully give it; you will find the same at Harplow.*

(Signed)  THOMAS HOLMES

No. 22. *Joseph Salt*, aged 54. Examined March 20:

*I am a buttie collier; have worked in Delph House 12 years and more for Mr. Holmes; I contract for the "Old Sawny" and the "Litley" pits; I employ about a score men and near 10 boys in the two pits; the youngest is about 12, I cannot say exactly. I engage to deliver coals on the bank to the rnaster, at 3s. a ton, sometimes it is more, never less; 12 or 13 years ago it was but 2s. 10d. The price rises or falls proportionate to the amount of the men's wages, which wages are regulated by the demand for labour; it has, however, been almost a regular price for the last 30 years : I have never known vary more than 4d. a day, and that only for a short time. We are now drawing nine to ten ton a day, before now I have drawn 20 tons and more than that. The men under me are paid day wage, but they have to draw a number of corves per day each man, the quantity of corves depending upon the number of men employed; the average of men's wages is 3s. per day; the boys are paid in like manner, they having to draw or drive so many corves; their wages vary from 8d. to 2s. 6d. per day, according to their strength and age, from 10 years to 18. They draw or drive on rails; the bottom is soft and slushy; the height of out mainways varies from three to four feet, but it is always changing, as the earth is constantly rising. I have seen the mainways hove up clean full, stopping up air and everything in a few weeks. I have never known any fire-damp, wildfire, or sulphur in the pits. We get plenty of choke-damp or black-damp, which we get rid of by good circulation, by lighting big fires at the bottoms of the up-cast shafts, or if that should not be enough, we pump water down the down-cast shaft and create a draft through the roads or addits. I have never known any death result from either foul air, or machinery, or defective ropes. About four years ago a little boy fell down the pit from the top by handling a corve which he had no business to do: he was killed: he was no pit lad. I began to work when I was seven years old; had no other education but at night and Sunday-school, where I learnt to read and write, which I have found of great use to me in every respect as a collier and a Christian. Having seen and known these advantages myself, I am a great advocate for the education of our youths now-a-day. As it regards those who work in our colliery, I am glad to say that they have been very well looked to; all of them can read and most of them can write; every one of them attend Sunday-school; if there is an exception I do not know it. They work the same number of hours with the men, that is, from six or seven to three or four, very seldom 12 hours. There are night sets occasionally, from six at night till two or three in the morning. This is the result of circumstances; at times there may be choke-damp, or machinery may be out of order: it is not a regular thing to work at night. I think they enjoy as good health as any boys, very different to factory children; they are never punished, or suffered to be by anybody. The men behave well towards them. I have been, as I said, 12 years at work here, and if I were required to be put on my oath I could say, that I had never seen one of our men stop a day's work from drunkenness: it is not the practice for them to swear or be disorderly.*

*(Signed)  JOSEPH SALT*

No. 23. *David Carr*, aged 16. Examined March 20:

*I work in "Old Sawny" pit for Joseph Salt the buttie. I came up from pit this after-noon, went home and put clean clothes on because 't was Saturday night; I always do the same, and so do the other boys in a general way. I went to day-school, go to Sunday-school now at the Independent Chapel. I can read (very well) and can write. I go to work betwixt five and six, come up at different times, sometimes three or four, four or five, five or six. All of us get our breakfast before we go down and our tea when we come up; we get our dinners down in pit, and take it as fast as we can; we take half an hour, and rest when we feel to want it. I never met with any accident in the mainways by waggons. I sometimes drive, sometimes pull with a girdle; I strip, and put on a flannel donkey or one of moleskin; when we push we push with our hands, just as it wants; we push with our heads when the comes run heavy. I like the work pretty middling; I think I should like some things better. I shut off at four mostly: 'tis my own fault if I do not go to evening-school; I mostly attend chapel of week nights; my father is a member of the Independent.*

*(Signed)  DAVID CARR*

No. 24. *Elijah Lownds*, aged 17. Examined March 20:

*I have worked at the "Sawny Pit" for Joseph Salt now seven years; went to school before I came, and go now to Sunday-school; can read well (very) and can write a little; I always go to chapel Sundays. In he seven years that I have worked I had only one accident - a coal fell on my head; I did not remember anything about it at the time, but I was a fortnight in bed; it was down the shaft when I was going up - I never heard of one of this kind before or since. I draw the corves with a byat round my shoulders, the weight of the corve is about 400. The distance from the workings to pit's bottom 150 yards, some is 500, some less. I go all the length and return with empty corves; I draw about 12, or 13, or 14 a day. I am mostly very tired at the end of my day's work; it agrees with my health very well; I was never sick from that cause; can always sleep, and get my meals with a good appetite, I have never any punishment inflicted either on myself or other boys by the men or butties. I get 9s. a week in full work; I average about 7s. 6d. all the year round; I give it to my mother, she finds me all that I have for it, she gives me 6d. out sometimes. I have no regular holidays, I get too many of them, as I only work four days in the week at times, and then get only 6s. I would rather work six days than four; I like the work pretty well; I'd rather be collier than upon farm, I would not swop – if I began again I would be a collier.*

(Signed) ELIJAH LOWNDS

No. 25. *Joseph Coates*, aged 54. Examined March 20:

*I am a banksman at Mr. Holmes's "Old Sawny" pit, and have been employed there upwards of 40 years; I am the oldest upon the ground. When first I began men had 2s. 6d. a day, then 2s. 8d., and latterly 3s., then 3s. 4d., and now back again to 3s. The amount of our wages depends upon the demand for coal and labour. I am paid by the day, 2s. 2d., and in addition a little for loading carts, &c., which makes up 3s. The characters of the men and children in former times were not so good as now. There were no Sabbath-schools or chapels in Cheadle; there are now many, and to that source I attribute the better state of the children: they used too to drink more, and neglected their persons, their work, and their families. I think they did not work so hard for their money as what they do now. I speak of the men – the boys worked harder, because things below were not so well managed as now that we have rails and our workings are higher. The machinery is now better (the steam). I formerly went down and came up by hand first, and then by a "gin", now by steam and better gear, but I never remember any accident that has occurred from bad gear; if that should be, it would be our own faults, as master never wishes us to get into danger. Most if not all the boys in our colliery can read, and many write – they attend the Sunday-schools and evening-schools to learn. My opinion is, as a collier and the father of a large family (12 children), that it would be a great deal better for the next or present generation of children if they were required to read and write, and be 12 years old before they came to work. I think they would be more enlightened, better men, and better Christians; there would be less drunkenness in the country, less rioting. I am no scholar, although I can read well, and learnt to do so after I came to work at eight years old, but I know enough to be satisfied that if he next generation is better informed, that there will be many more loyal, well-disposed, and honest men. I received a letter with the "Staffordshire Advertiser" at the time of the potters', strike, in which we were advised to strike, and fix our own wages and time for working, which I and many others thought unjust, and we refused to join. Things were doing very well, and have continued to do, without our meddling with politics. None of us are great politicians; have no rioting or turns out, or anything else of that sort. Some of our colliers at our works are very clever men, and many of the boys too; two of the men are capital arithmeticians, and can work any problem in Euclid; that man you have examined is one; he is a good land-measurer, and is a deal employed for that purpose when there are disputes about land; both are self-taught like myself. I cannot write now at all, my eye-sight fails me; I never could write much, which I have had reason to regret. I believe all the children live well and clothe well: if you go to Sunday-school to-morrow you will find them all respectful, clean, and well-behaved. All the chapels have Sunday-schools; I go to all of them when there is a sermon preached for them, and give my mite to all.*

No. 26. *Charles James*, aged 16. Examined March 20:

*I draw corves in the "Old Sawny" pit for John Lowndes the buttie. I went to day-school before I went to work and go to Sunday-school now at Bethel Chapel; I always attend worship Sundays and sometimes on week nights; I can read (well) and can write a little; don't know anything about summing. I go to evening-school to learn to write; my father is a collier at Delph House, he is a member of Bethel Chapel; he makes us all go to school; he cannot read much himself, but he knows its value to us, and teaches us to value education. I go to work like all the rest of the boys at six o'clock, and return from pit at four or five; but we have so much to do, and the time we come up depends on how we do it, whether quickly or otherwise. I get milk and bread for breakfast, bread and cheese, sometimes flesh meat for dinner, and potatoes and bacon for supper, always enough; I am never sick or ill; the work agrees with me very well and I like it. I'd rather be a collier than a farmer's servant. I feel very tired when I get to bed, but I can sleep, eat, and drink as well as any boy. I am very happy at home and in the pit, so are all the other boys for what I know: I get a bit of play with them sometimes upon bank at marbles, balls and prisoners' base, when we have done work at evenings.*

(Signed)  CHARLES JAMES

No. 27. *George Plant, aged 15. Examined March 20:*

*I am a drawer of corves for John Lowndes the buttie. I have been to work six years; went to school before I came to work at day school; go now to Sunday-school at Bethel Chapel; I always attend the chapel worship. I can read (well) and can write a little. My work has always agreed with me; I have never had more than a fortnight's illness in my life, then I caught a cold above ground; I strip below ground, and put on a donkey (a waistcoat with sleeves), and wear a pair of byats over my shoulders. I am not obliged to stoop much in the mainway, it is three or four feet high. I give my head a bit of a knock sometimes, or scratch my back, but not enough to hurt me much. I never had accident; was never beaten by the men or butties: if I neglect my work my wages would not be so good; I am not punished in any other way. I am tired when I get home at night, but have never found the work too much for me; I have never known other boys complain of it; sometimes we meet together to eat our dinners in the pit in a dry place. We are all pretty hearty and eat out meals with good appetite; we are all happy enough. I do not get much play, am too tired for that, and I am bit too old for that. I would rather be a collier than anything else that I know of that is, as I am to work.*

(Signed)  GEORGE PLANT

*RICHARD WHITEHURST AND CO'S LITLEY AND HARPLOW COLLIERY*

No. 28. *William Flewit, aged 14. Examined March 22:*

*I drive corves and waggons for George Day the buttie. I went to day-school afore I worked in the pit and I go to Sunday-school now; I learn to read in Bible to get my soul saved; I go regular every Sunday unless I am poorly; I can read (very well) and write but very little; I am learning now into a copy-book at home; I am too late to get Monday night's lessons or I should go. I go to pit about quarter afore six, leave home quarter past five; on Saturdays I go a little earlier because we all like to knock off earlier in the afternoon. I have a mother but no father – I never had one that I knew. Every other but Saturday I go from pit at six or seven o'clock; the time, however, depends upon the quantity of coals got out; we have to work so much a day; some-times 'tis near the pit's bottom, sometimes away off; when 'tis away off, master puts another lad on push or pull. We all strip when we go down, and put on a short flannel donkey and a pair of byats; we could not work in shirts or jackets, 'twould be too warm, and we should sweat desperately. I am very tired when I come up at night; I do nightwork in winter, when people want more coals, but I do not work night and day* too, we have turn and turn. I like the work pretty well, I'd rather work than be idle; I would rather be collier than a farmer's lad at plough. I don't often meet with accidents; was once hurt in the leg by hitting it against the corve, and was bad 14 weeks.

No. 29. Elijah Weston, aged 11. Examined March 22:

I have been to work in the "Cross Pit" at the Litley Colliery, 12 months. I went to day-school at Huntley before that for two years. I go to Sunday-school now, I can read (very well), but cannot write, I push waggons down in pit upon rails, the distance from the works to pit's mouth is two score yards or more; I am obliged to stoop, the waggon ways are about four feet more or less high. I go down about six o'clock, and come up between five and six, or six and seven. When I have done my work I have drawn six rucks a day, there being 12 corves in a ruck; the weight of every corve with waggon is 500 and a half. I get my dinner down in pit, and take half an hour to eat it, I get sometimes bacon and tatees, I get breakfast before I go down and tea or supper when I come up; I always get as much as I can eat; I earn 4s. if I work six days; I give it to my mother, I got a father but don't live with him (illegitimate). I like the work very well, I am tired when I've done, and go home and get to bed; I can sleep very well, eat and drink very well, and am in very good health. I'd rather be a collier than a farmer's lad. I don't work every day, and when I don t I get a bit of play at marbles.

No. 30. Mr. Howlett,  :

I have been, and continue to be the agent, and one of the principals in the frm of Whitehurst and Co. Colliers, and work the Litley, and Harplow pit. We have one pit at each place; at Litley there 10 men and eight boys under 18, at Harplow there are nine men and six boys. I have been engaged in the colliery all my life; the mode of working is very different and much easier than it was years ago, because we have now steam power to draw the coals instead of the common barrel or winder that was used – and because the boys draw and push corves on rails instead of drawing them upon slips there is quite as much room in our mainways as there used to be. We employed boys at that time as young as we do now, as it regards the moral state of the men and boys as compared with those of the present it was far different and much worse. There were no schools, Sundays or week days, or chapels; there was one church and that was all; there was a deal more vice, profligacy, and drunkenness; the boys and men do now attend the chapels and schools, and have profited by it; I can see vast difference in the characters, though there are some here and there that are bad still and will not receive instruction when they may. We were never subject to wild-fire or chokedamp in our pits, at least but very seldom, our seams are narrow and therefore not so liable to accumulate gases. The weather influences the state of our pits in a great measure; when the wind is high, or when rain is indicated by the barometer, the circulation is not so free as it should be; then the choke-damp collects, the candles go out, and we take the precaution of lighting fires at the bottom of the up-cast shaft or part way down it; this speedily gets rid of it and the candles burn again. We have no Davy lamps, or ever had occasion to use them, we never had an explosion or the symptoms of one. We have had no accident with machinery, or ropes, the ropes are renewed as often as we think it necessary, we have no general rule for renewing them.

(Signed)  THOMAS HOWLETT

## MR. WHITEHURST'S COLLIERY, LITLEY DALE, CHEADLE

No. 31. *Thomas Weaver, aged 14. Examined March 22:*

*I have worked at Litley Dale pit five years, as a drawer of corves; I never went to day-school, but go to Sunday-school every Sunday at Zion Chapel. I can read, but cannot write. I go to work at six o' clock in the morning, and leave at six at night, if I make a day's work. I go down in the slings with corve and all, sometimes two and sometimes three others go down with me, never more than three; the same numbers come up together, but never more than four. When I get down I strip my jacket and shirt and waistcoat, I put my waistcoat on again, and a pair of byats over that (a leather strap with chain at the end). The distance of the workings from the bottom of the shaft is 90 yards; the rail does not extend all the way, about 30 yards short, the run is downhill, the weight of the corve is 400; another boy helps me then by pushing or drawing, the height of the way up to the rail is about three-quarters of a yard I reckon. We are obliged to stoop and get on, I draw 30 corves a day; 'tis middling hard, but I like being a collier, I would full as leave be a collier as farmer. The work agrees with me, I am very well in health, I am never sick or ever sorry except when I've got no work to do. I can eat and drink and sleep very well, and get enough of it.*

No. 32. *Samson Day, aged 11. Examined March 22:*

*I have been to work in Litley Dale Colliery about one year and a half, drawing corves for George Day the buttie, he's my father. I went to day-school before to work at Cheadle, I go to Sunday-school now; I can read and write. I go down in pit at five or six in, the morning with father, and come up when he does. I never met with any very serious accidents sometime dirt falls on us, and hurts our legs. I do not remember that I ever laid by a day from sickness, or accident; I do not find the work too much for me, I do not always work six days a week, sometimes only two and a half days in three; other days I fetch water and do odd things at home for mother, and work in garden little bit with father. All the men down in pit behave very well to me, I never get flogged, I have seen other boys slapped upon the back with the bare hand if they are lazy; never hurt much. I am tired when I get home, get my supper and go to bed; I have enough to eat and drink.*

*(Signed) SAMSON DAY*

No. 33. *Mr Thomas Fowell, aged 44. Examined March 22:*

*I am the owner of the Harplow Colliery; employing five men and three boys. I reside in Birmingham, and am well acquainted with the neighbourhoods of Dudley, Wolverhampton, and Bilston; the people there who work in the collieries are better paid, but are more improvident and much less civilised than in this place, the boys are certainly not so well provided or cared for, either physically morally. The educations condition of the children here is half a century before them. I believe most of ours can read and write, and attend regularly places of public worship in this place; we have no sources of political excitement, I never heard of such a thing as a radical meeting, nor do I believe the people know even what is meant by Chartism, Socialism, or any thing of that kind; they are generally speaking a sober, honest, hardworking, industrious, and loyal class of men, I should say in an extreme degree. I am, and have been for some years in the habit of holding conversations with the labouring colliers, agents, and masters, and have never heard any compliants made by one party or the other ill-usage. It is very rare that I hear of accidents in pits, either from choke-damp, sulphur or wild-fire, machinery, or gear; there are occasional cases of choke-damp, but never wild-fire. Our seams of coal vary in thickness from 20 inches to three feet; the gases cannot accumulate in them. We always look after our machinery; if the men were to complain of its ill condition it would be immediately rectified. I do not remember any case of accident, except that of a boy falling down a shaft who had no business there. We have no system of rewards or punishment for boys. I do not ever hear of punishments being inflected by the men, they are generally too indulgent to them; the men are of a very religious character.*

(Signed)  THOMAS FOWELL, Principal.

No. 34. *Simeon Wheaver, aged 17. Examined March 21:*

*I draw waggons for Thomas Flowett the Buttie. I never went to day-school, but go to school on Sundays: can read, and can write a little. Father is a collier, and works at Litley Dale; I get 11s. a week if I work full time; I only work about four days, upon the average, in the winter and less in summer, I never work at night, go to pit at six and leave at six; the work agrees with me very well, I like it middling ; I don't mind what work I do as long as I get enough to eat. I give my money to father, who has to support a large family; I have eight brothers and sisters, three of us work, the rest are too young. I get bacon and tatees for dinner, and supping for supper, (milk or broth). I am always in good health.*

(Signed)  SIMEON WHEAVER

*March 24th – Descended the Dilham Colliery with John James the Agent, found the men had ceased working, and had to come up. Took no evidence. The bottoms were very wet; and all the drawing was done by boys. Mainways too low for ponies. This was the pit that was to have supplied London, and contains coal enough for about a month's consumption or less."*

These were, in general, very good reports on Cheadle colliers. In the Potteries, however, the Chartist movement had roused them to a measure of violence and in July 1842, Pugin, the Earl of Shrewsbury's Architect, wrote in his diary:

*"The house fortified against Colliers. As I came through the Potteries I was told the Colliers had gone to Macclesfield where they were turned back. The Earl must keep vigilance at his house."*

The Woodhead Colliery had been taken over by William Bowers with plenty of scope for extending its activities and Bowers was the type to see that it worked the way he intended it to grow. The Woodhead Tramway, which had taken so long to complete, had completed twenty years' service, but the steam railway had overtaken the canal and scores of proposals were made to cover the country with a network of lines to improve both goods and passenger transport. The North Staffordshire Railway Company was incorporated in 1847/8 defeating the half-dozen other proposals. Unfortunately the Manchester – Derby branch was to use the Churnet Valley and in 1849 had to be built on the Froghall – Uttoxeter Canal. The Woodhead Company lost its valley coal wharves and its tramway was finished.

By 1849 the Kingsley Vestry Book refers to Bower's plea for reduced rates on the Coal ground he was working on the Beech's Shawe ground:

*"At the V.M. agreed to reduce his rate to £100 per year for the Woodhead Colliery occupied by Mn Wm. Bowers Esq. for one Book only."*

During that year there was reported an accident in Consall Colliery, the Chase Colliery mentioned in the Leigh sale catalogue of 1841. *"The Annals of Coalmining"* tells how Joseph Foxall was severely burned and died. Much more was heard of this mine when it mined deeper for ironstone some five years later.

By 1850 Bowers had continued with the Leigh customers such as the Shrewsbury account:

*"1850 Wm. Bowers Coal*                                               *£3000        0        0"*

In addition to the Collieries on the 1842 Scriven list, there should be remembered the Kingsley Colliery of Chawner and Godwin which still had many years to run.

If we check on the 1851 Census we find a considerable increase in the number of men and boys involved in the industry. The 1841 count had given 173 boys and men so employed in Cheadle, but ten years later there were 194 as colliers including a boy of just over nine years of age, whilst there were 22 who called themselves higlers or carriers and 17 were engine men. This made a total of 233. This figure compared with the 139 men or women in the textile mills. In the village of Kingsley at this time there were 56 colliers of whom only five were not native, and at Ipstones there were 16 men in the mines around that village. These figures indicate the necessity to retain the coal mining for the benefit of other industries; even the Arkwright textile mill at Rocester would some day need to change from water power to steam power.

The 1851 Census gives names and addresses of certain coal masters and Agents. William Bowers, the Younger, who was Superintendent of his father's Woodhead Colliery in Scriven's 1842 report is, in 1851, registered as Wm. Bowers, 35, Coalmaster, Lodger with Rupert Bowers, Farmer, Oakamoor Road. In fact, he was at Parkfields Farm. Thomas Plant, Collier, and his family at the Back of Town registered his children, of whom the boy, Robert, ten years old will be the subject of a later chapter.

One of the most important events of the middle of the nineteenth century concerned William Bowers, Senior. The 1832 lease under which the Trustees of the late James Beech of the Shawe at Kingsley granted to John Leigh, for twenty-one years, a very large acreage of coal, had now expired so that William Bowers, the Younger took a new lease with the second James Beech for another very large area of the *"two feet coal and the Woodhead coal working lying or being"* under the great area mentioned in the 1832 lease with, in addition, the Hazels Cross coal and seam above and the Shaw mine.

This lease of 1853 was for a further term of twenty-one years with coal rents of £130 per acre of Woodhead, £100 per acre of Two foot Coal, £15 per acre of Hazels Cross or Shaw mine coal. The mining must work the seams sufficient to pay £450 per annum by the second year of working. In addition, Bowers was to pay 1/3d. duty for every thousand bricks made and the Shawe Hall should have fifty tons of coal a year at 4/- per ton as long as the lease lasted.

It will be noted that the coals were given the names of the place where they were first mined, but there is no doubt that the most expensive were the Woodhead and the Cobble. The lease was drawn up in the office of John Michael Blagg who was, within the following years, to keep both himself and his staff very busy and equally well paid when the legal work on coal was joined the next year by the work on the ironstone mining industry.

Since most of the coal on the east side of the Woodhead centre had been mined, Bowers now looked to the new lease to keep his machine working to capacity. The Woodhead tramway was shown to have crossed the Froghall Road, the A521, at Woodhead yard and by 1836 that first Ordnance Survey map shows it heading to the northwest.

There was, however, a branch to serve a new colliery to the west. It turned at right angles to the main line, crossed the brook by a brick bridge and proceeded some one hundred and fifty yards up the fields to the colliery which became the Royal George. From nearer Cheadle a cart track was made from the Froghall Road to this mine which is today Highfield Avenue. A footpath continues across the fields from which the remains of the tramway embankment may be found, though signs of the colliery site have nearly disappeared. The path continued to a six building settlement only one hundred yards from Booth's corner on Clamgoose Lane. It was called Fould.

The 1836 map also shows the tramway going only as far as the brick kiln at the southern end of the wood whilst the coal pits of that name lay some two hundred yards to the north. Further still, only three hundred yards from Booth Farm was the Red Shag mine and at both sinkings the Woodhead could be found at about seventy yards deep. This Red Shag had unhappy memories for the Fallows' family for their great grandfather, as a young man of twenty-nine years fell down the shaft and died leaving a widow to attend nine children.

The coal not used for brick making, the slack being used in the kilns, was easily loaded onto the tramway to be taken to the new wharf.

On the west of the track, two other shafts, first the Rimmons Pit, thence almost four hundred yards further on, the Remington Pit, found the Cobble at fourteen yards and Woodhead at eighty, though the latter found increasing evidence of very old workings for it was near the Crompton's workings of 1632. No information on how these two acquired their titles can be found. The Remington was but three hundred yards from Clamgoose Lane.

At this time the new wharf was the terminus. The old section was redundant since 1848 when the railway came to replace the canal and Donkey Lane was no longer used. With the loss of the canal wharves increased haulage was provided from Woodhead Yard. The enlarged wharf on the west side of the Froghall road was served by the tramway which split into three sidings, where carts could load from the trucks, and cross the road to the weigh machine, before setting off to deliver.

The wharf itself was the largest in the area at this time, advertising its presence by having huge blocks of Woodhead coal at both ends of the wharf on the roadside and in times of reduced demand Bowers undercut the prices of other collieries by a shilling a ton.

None of the last-mentioned pits lasted for long. The Royal George and the Clay Pits were the only collieries on the extended line shown on the 1836 map, but three or four of the others south of Clamgoose lane must have been counted in the Woodhead eight pits in the Scriven survey of 1842. In fact, Rimmons, Remington and Red Shag are quoted as closing by 1855. The Clay pits continued to 1865 in both coal and bricks.

Since Bowers had much more Beech land to mine further north, it is not surprising to find the tramway extending to serve new pits. The extent had to match the ambition of this second William Bowers and the last half of this nineteenth century tells the second half of the story of the Bowers' Empire.

See map on page 28 for the location of some of these pits.

Although the Woodhead and the Dilhorne collieries were the heavy weights, the leaders and maximum producers, there were others, through the nineteenth century which, when conditions were in their favour, were worthy rivals as coal suppliers. These, though working with fewer workmen and boys, made the ventures pay, whilst all the time gaining in experience of the special conditions appertaining to the Cheadle coalfield.

We have had little to say of Thomas Holmes of Delphouse and his workings with their apparently innumerable pits and disused shafts. Delphouse Colliery is first mentioned in 1802 and again by Farey in 1810, when it was implied that it was working in the 2nd Coal. The owner of the working is not named although the Holmes of Delphouse (Thomas Holmes) is nominated, with William Holmes of Cheadle Eaves as working by 1828. The 2nd Coal means nothing in the Dilhorne/Delphowe area when Barrow in 1900 gave us a full picture of the seams available in that area.

Workings were carried on in this trough of land until after the mid-century and the 1879 map was able to point the whereabouts of some eighteen shafts recognised by Barrow, who in 1900, travelled the area with old shaft sinkers like Anthony Carr, who had spent half a century covering the field. There were breaks in the workings in this district, but there was always someone to try his hand in a district where four seams, the Two Yard, Half Yard, the Yard and the Litley could provide 14ft 6in, of coal at a depth of some eight yards. The Holmes operation had finished by 1870 and it was then taken over with other mines in the same district by Bagshaw & Co. with Taylor Bagshaw of the Elms in charge for five years; thence by Sir Lionel Pilkington (who owned land in the area) for a year or two beyond the 1880s. It was at Delphouse that we first came across Stephen Offer who had left the Potteries coalfield to try his luck in Cheadle. He was one of the earliest Certificated Managers after the Certificate was instituted, but before long he had joined the Draycott Cross concerns and by early 1887, the new Cheadle Park Colliery.

Another Bowers, Alexander Bowers, living at The Grove near Leafields Farm was identified in the 1851 directory as a farmer, but the previous year, Hunt's mining statistics had him doing some mining below Above Park farm at Kingsley Moor. His workings, known as the Dilhorne Footrill were near the brook behind Above Park which runs down towards Dairy House Farm. This was worked for five or six years and although Barrow found it within a short distance from both Woodhead and Rider coal outcrops, nothing further was done until it was taken over some forty years later from Mrs. E. Brassington for protective purposes.

The Blake Hall Colliery, we last saw being offered to let in 1832, was taken over by Thomas Holmes with the Black Craft Pit and operated until 1865. It had a small branch tramway to a small pit known as the Bang up Colliery, which was half way down the Blake Hall line to the Dilhorne Road. Black Craft was a notoriously wet pit where men lay on duck boards to work while the water trickled under them. This was in spite of the fact that a sough had been cut to take the water away. It ran down in the direction of the tramway and under the Dilhorne Road to surface in the field and join the brook. At about the same period the Sham workings, by the north side of the road by the Festival fields, were re-opened as part of the Delphouse Colliery with a brick kiln and weighing machine and, according to Barrow's informants, could reach the yard coal at forty-five feet, the Litley at ninety-six and the Four Foot at one hundred and thirty-five feet.

There were plenty of people in that area of Delphouse interested in selling land as appears in the advertisement in the '*The Staffordshire Advertiser*' of Saturday, 14th January, 1937:

> "*Valuable coal mines lying under lands belonging to Mr. Chell Samuel Bamford, Esq. & others situate near to Cheadle & Dilhorn.*
> *The Yard Coal*
> *Fourfoot Coal*
> *Litley Coal.*"

At Draycott Cross the earliest venture to sink through the near-maximum depth of Bunter Sandstone was in 1845 by the Lord of the Manor of Draycott, Mr. Edward Vavasour. He knew there was a likelihood of a railway line, probably Stoke – Uttoxeter, running through the Draycott estate:

> "*It is essential, therefore, to my infant Colliery, that facilities should be secured for its produce, if ever realised, being conveyed by a tram line to the main line.*"

He relates that a "*Mr. Bond has traced out two lines*" both using the Draycott Glebe land and asks for the incumbent's support. Unfortunately, the infant Colliery died at birth and there was no produce. In another twelve years in 1857 a second attempt was made under Mr. Vavasour and taken over by the Keys' organisation, who had bought the Brass and Copper Company, the Deep Moor Colliery, and had acquired the Whiston Smelter. Their efforts ran through the 1860s and the following advert appeared:

> "*Deep Moor and Draycott Cross Colliery. Keys & Son. March 29th 1866. 10 cwt of Cobbles for 2/6.*"

The last attempt at the west end of the railway tunnel found little coal but plenty of water which is now Severn Trent property.

In 1857 the Kingsley School property at Foxt, on the north side of the road below the old Woodcutter's Arms was, leased for mining the Crabtree coal. The lessee is not known, although the School Trustees may well have given the opportunity to some well known local man. It was worked for two years and mined under most of the land. Two shafts were sunk and can easily be found by the spoil banks, one below and the other above the farm. The plan shows a third shaft, nominated 'Pattinson's Pit', which was quite near to the Woodcutter's cart track and may well have been a search for ironstone as Pattinson of Froghall was made a salesman for an ironstone firm in the year 1867. At abandonment the plan was drawn on cloth in a first class fashion, with some colouring by John Boot, a Derbyshire mineral surveyor.

The coal workings at Fernylee Colliery on the opposite side of the Foxt road, were operated by the Worthington brothers, John and Josh., who had come out of the Potteries to start here in the middle of the 1890s. They left one of their sons, George Worthington, to be the landlord of the Wheatsheaf in Cheadle for some twenty years into the late 1940s.

In 1837 a group of Potteries people, all of the Williamson family, made an agreement with the farmer at Greenhead, Kingsley Moor to sink a shaft for the Woodhead coal. It was, to be three hundred and fifty yards from the road and they laid a tramway to it. By 1839 it did not appear that progress was satisfactory. Machinery was expensive and in 1840 it is probable that the Woodhead was reached, but unfortunately, a very awkward fault passed just to the north. The fact was that the Williamsons had bankrupted themselves and disappeared. There did arrive, however, around 1940 a couple of Canadians who wished to see the pit where their grand-parents had lost all their money.

Both Madgedale and the Dale just south-east of Dilhore had been worked, although in both cases the Bunter sandstone (now called the Sherwood Sandstone Group) ridge had to be pierced – no easy matter – and at some places quite risky, being near water. Ward, the geologist, reporting in 1890, was informed of a Mr. Herbert Salt, who worked coal in 1867 at the Dale through one hundred and twenty feet of Bunter and on for a total of 268 feet to reach the Yard coal. A fault spoiled this working and a second was sunk nearby and found the Yard coal at only 240 feet deep. At Madgedale there were two old shafts which were started soon after the death of Bamford, senior, in September, 1839. A deal of responsibility was left to his Agent, John James, who began to explore in this area. The fact was that no one knew how the upper seams were re-acting in form under the Bunter. Barrow, using information from local folk, traced the supposed outcrops in a wavy line showing the difficulties in prospecting in that area.

One of the Whitehurst family sank two shafts on the Dilhorne corner of the Boundary crossroads. They are either side the footpath leading to Blake Hall. They would be hindered by the presence of three small faults, but mining continued for some fifteen years to 1865. On the opposite corner – the Red Lion corner – then a coal wharf, two shafts were sunk from one hundred and twenty yards through what was the Bunter to the Yard coal. The engine house was built between the shafts. A short tramway had been laid south-east to join the Delphouse Company's No. 3 Shaft and line to the railway. This colliery had a steam whistle to blow *Loose – it* at 4.00pm.

The Harplow Company, had workings which can easily be seen on the left of Draycott Cross road above the present New Haden site. In the following years after Bamford's dissolution of 1838, as was expected, the Harplow and Litley concern came to be known as Richard Whitehurst & Co., Litley and Harplow Colliery. Milner, Keates and Howlett still had their shares in this concern, but by 1842 there had been some changes. Milner and Keates were only shareholders and sleeping partners, and were replaced by Thomas Fowell, who claimed ownership of Harplow. Howlett was an Agent and at the same time *"one of the principals in the firm of Whitehurst & Co"* overlooking both pits. The firm prospered, probably digging further shafts. There were five on the Harplow site and two at Litley, these being in very close proximity. The man power of nineteen men and fourteen boys remained until 1860, but were reduced in the next three years as the concern closed in 1863.

The present road from Draycott Cross down to New Haden Pumps entrance is a comparatively new length. The old road can be seen only forty yards from the top of the Cross disappearing into a cutting on the right across the Harplow fields, so that it was to the south of the New Haden engine house site. It continued in its easterly direction to veer to the left where the New Haden Pumps exit emerges. It kept this curving path whilst horses and carts needed to use it, but later moved forty yards to the north to leave more room for later pits.

William Hammersley and William Malkin formed a company around 1840. Both had an interest in farming; Hammersley from Gorsty Hill and Malkin near Mobberley. Their early operation was called Malkin & Co. when they set up the Huntley Engine Pits under the Huntley Colliery Co. At about eighty yards they found the Dilhorne coal but it was shortly to be called the Huntley coal. They seem to have been working until 1867

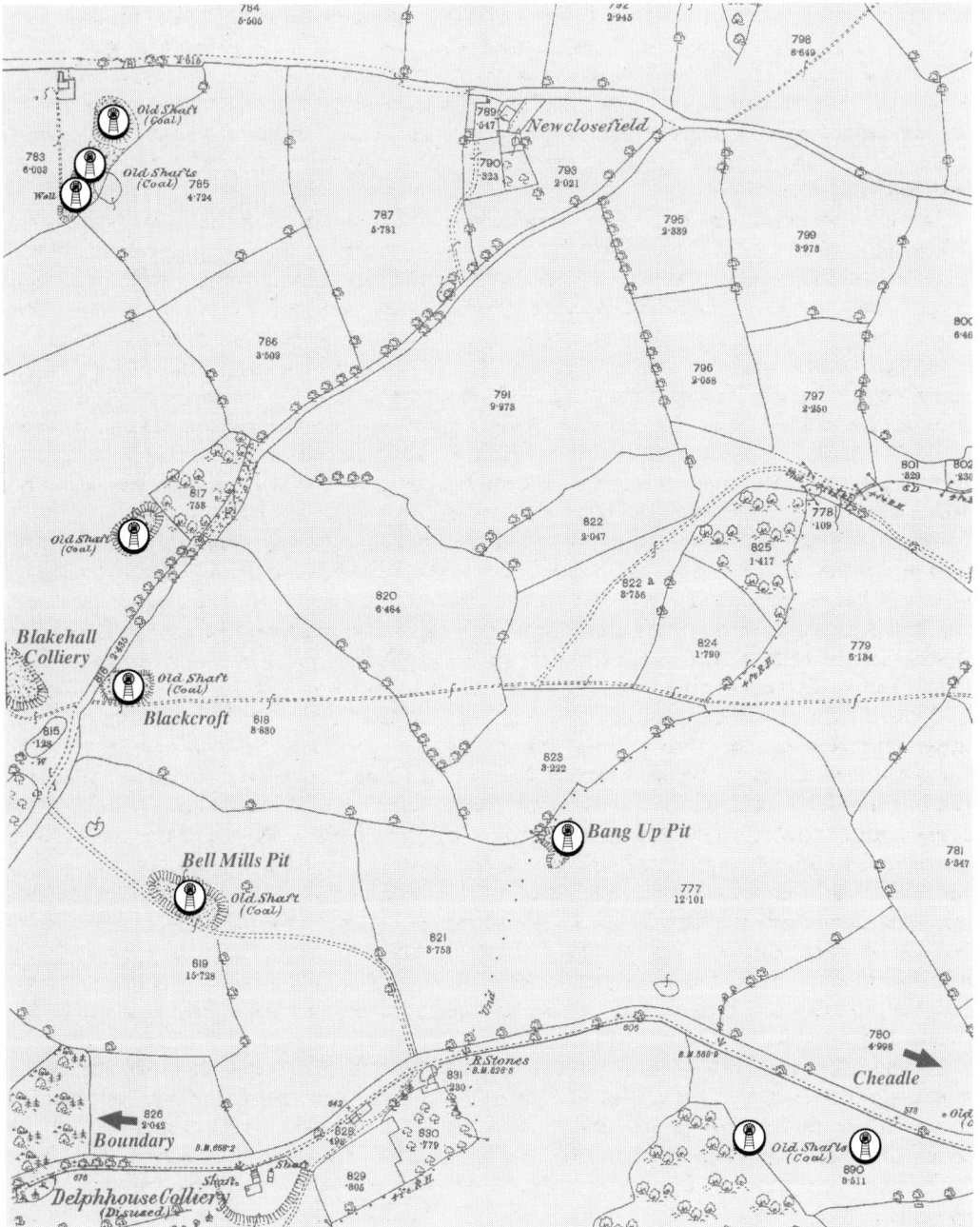

*Blakewell Colliery and other shafts northwest of Brookhouses*

while they registered as Malkin & Co. in *Blunts Mineral Statistics* of 1863. The Huntley Colliery Co. was said to have worked this coal to very near the Majors Barn fields.

The National Coal Board have among their plans of Abandoned Mines, one quite insignificant little area to the east of the canal between Cherry Eye bridge, No. 50 Bridge and the Crowgutter Mill. It is a small area opposite the main Consall Mills and now completely overgrown with sizeable trees except for a clearing for a line of High Tension cable. The wood marked as Booth's Wood shows two small spoil banks by which, since 1852, William Bishop was working. He was a Cornish man with a long experience in mining tin, lead and coal. His wife had a small-holding at Hazles Cross and he took a lease of a small piece of the wood for getting coal where it could easily be tipped into a boat down a shute over the towpath.

This tiny working was to change the character of the valley for the next thirty years. When he had completed two footrills marked on the plan as No. 3 Level and No. 4 Level, he came across a two foot seam of red iron ore which set the valley alight as though he had found gold. He contacted William Bowers and following a few further test diggings and analysing of the contents of the stone, Bowers determined to have a share of this new wealth just below their feet. Unfortunately, Bishop died in April, 1853 and his son, Thomas continued mining in that piece until 1856. Before many months the district was in a turmoil. The mining of the new product began on the Kingsley side of the valley following a lease agreement signed in 1854 between Beech and Bowers, and on the Ipstones side, another agreement between the Masseys of Paddock Farm, Ipstones and a company of iron smelters of South Staffordshire.

Bowers found the stone on the Kingsley side of the valley outcropping along the bottom of Hazles Wood. This was just where Joseph Banks picked some red ironstone in 1767. He took little notice although it was on his Estate. Bowers had ten footrills into the Two Foot seam then he sank his five shafts for ironstone around the top of Kingsley Banks. At the end of the small valley between Kingsley and Consall he sank a coal mine in the 1860s. Here he mined the Crabtree at 2 feet thick and seventy yards deep. It was 250 yards from the Hazles Cross to Hollins Lane at the Sheepfold. This ironstone mining overshadowed any other mining activity in the area so that there was no longer time for coal in the district. Within three or four years there were no coal boats seen. Three red boats and and one white, carrying the red ore and limestone, passed along the canal every hour of the ten or twelve hour day of the bargee. Men left the coal pits for the iron mines and hundreds of others invaded the district for a new living in a new land. The turmoil lasted for twenty-five years and Bishop would have been forgotten had he not left sons around Hazles Cross to carry his name for the next half century.

By 1863 *Hunt's Mining Records* state that the Churnet Valley, i.e. Froghall to Consall, dispatched more than half a million tons of iron ore, 200,000 tons by rail and nearly 300,000 tons by canal to Shelton, to South Staffordshire and South Wales annually between 1855-1868.

The middle of the nineteenth Century saw, in spite of the emergence of the ironstone mining, a tendency to an increase in the number of coal enterprises, though this tended to accelerate as the iron passed its peak after 1867. In 1856 Hunt had recorded but seven of which four belonged to the Bowers' family including Alex Bowers at Above Park, two were Plant and Company including one at Ipstones and the tailend of the Godwin concern at Kingsley. Seven years later, in 1863, *Blunt's Mineral Statistics* list some sixteen pits, many of little significance:

| | |
|---|---|
| *"Bank Top, Binns & Co.* | *Blake Hall, Thos. Holmes* |
| *Boundary, Whitehurst* | *Callow Hill, Plant & Co.* |
| *Cheadle, Chas. Haigh (Plants)* | *Clay Pits, Wm. Bowers* |
| *Delphouse, Thos. Holmes* | *Dilhorne, Dilhorne Colliery Co.* |
| *Draycott Cross, John Keys* | *Harplow, John Fowell* |
| *Hazles Cross, John Goodwin* | *Ipstones, Plant & Co.* |

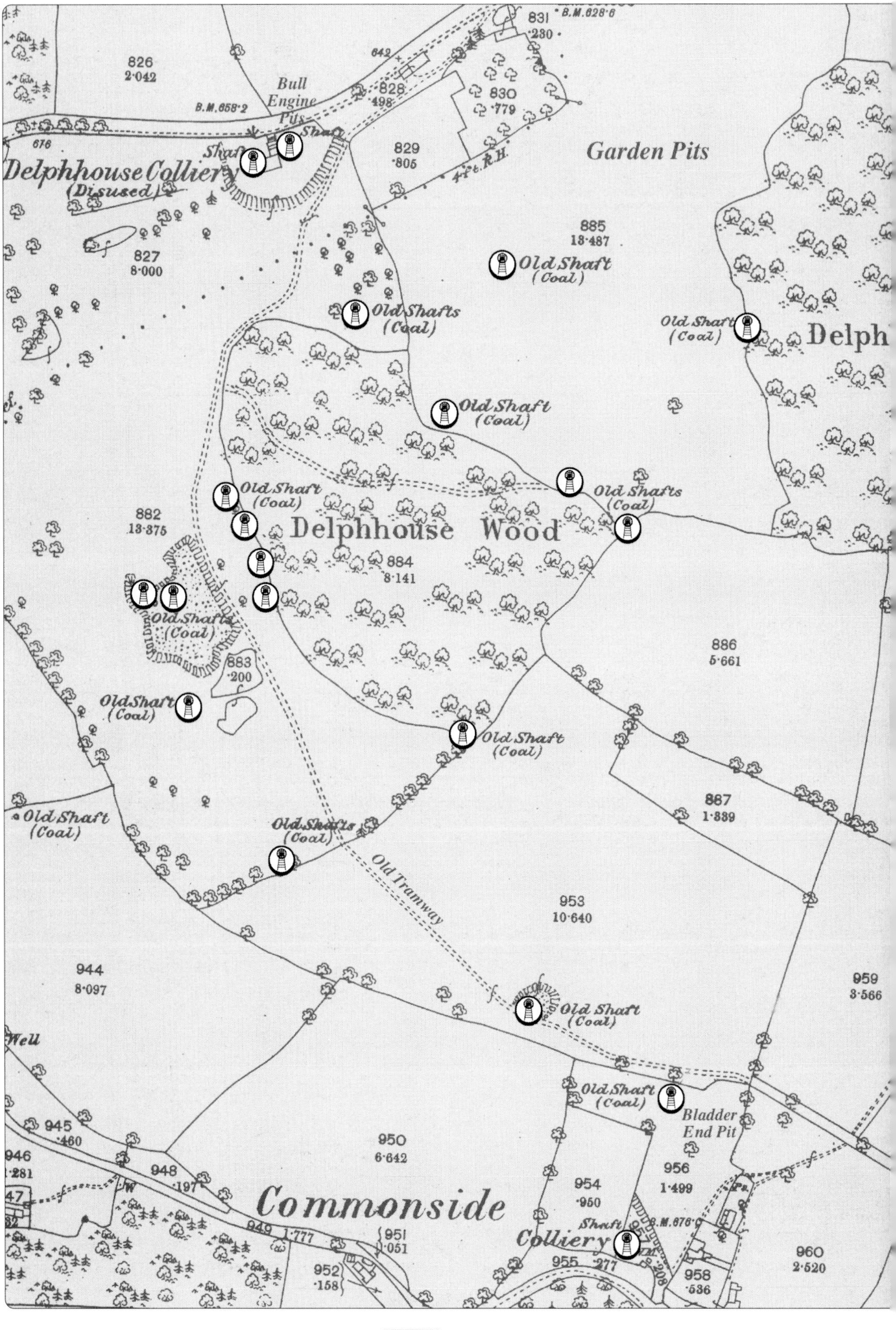
Delphhouse Colliery (Disused)
Bull Engine Pits
Shaft
Shaft
Garden Pits
Old Shaft (Coal)
Old Shafts (Coal)
Old Shaft (Coal)
Delph
Old Shaft (Coal)
Delphhouse Wood
Old Shafts (Coal)
Old Shaft (Coal)
Old Shafts (Coal)
Old Shaft (Coal)
Old Shaft (Coal)
Old Shaft (Coal)
Old Shafts (Coal)
Old Tramway
Old Shaft (Coal)
Old Shaft (Coal)
Bladder End Pit
Well
Commonside
Colliery
Shaft
826
2·042
828
·498
830
·779
831
·230
829
·805
827
8·000
885
13·487
882
13·375
884
8·141
883
·200
886
5·661
887
1·339
953
10·640
944
8·097
959
3·566
945
·460
946
1·281
948
·197
950
6·642
954
·950
956
1·499
949
1·777
951
·051
952
·158
955
·277
958
·536
960
2·520
B.M.658·2
B.M.628·6
B.M.676·

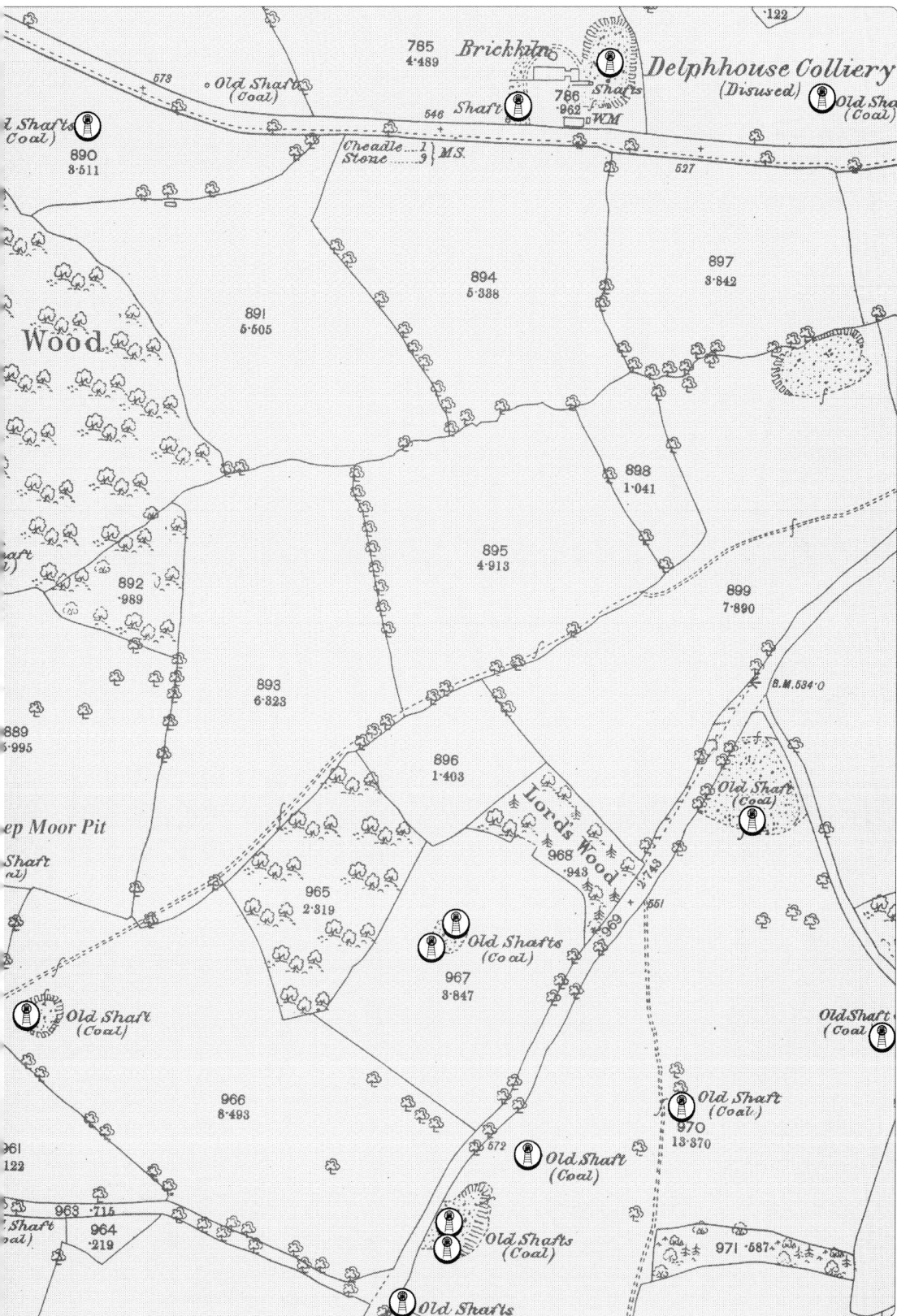

785
4·489

*Brickkiln*

*Delphhouse Colliery*
(*Disused*)

o *Old Shafts*
(*Coal*)

578

546

*Shaft*

786
·962

*Shafts*

WM

*Old Shafts*
(*Coal*)

*Old Sha*
(*Coal*)

890
3·511

*Cheadle......1*
*Stone......9* *M.S.*

+

527

897
3·842

894
5·338

891
5·505

*Wood*

898
1·041

892
·989

895
4·913

899
7·890

B.M.534·0

893
6·323

889
·995

896
1·403

*Old Shaft*
(*Coal*)

*ep Moor Pit*

*Lords Wood*

968
·943

2·749

*Shaft*
(*al*)

965
2·319

967
3·847

*Old Shafts*
(*Coal*)

·969

·551

*Old Shaft*
(*Coal*)

*Old Shaft*
(*Coal*)

*Old Shaft*
(*Coal*)

966
8·493

970
13·370

961
·122

·572

*Old Shaft*
(*Coal*)

963 ·715

964
·219

*Shaft*
(*al*)

*Old Shafts*
(*Coal*)

971 ·587

*Old Shafts*

·122

Newclosefield

to Adderley

N
W — E
S

The
Dale

Blackcraft

Blake Hall Colliery

Blake Hall

Bell Mills

Bang Up

A521

Bullpit
Engine

Garden
Pits

Delphouse
Wood

No.1

to Brookhouses

Engine House

Willow

No.2

*Tramway*

No.3

New

Pump
Station

BOUNDARY

Deep
Moor Pit

Bladder End Pit

Commonside
Colliery

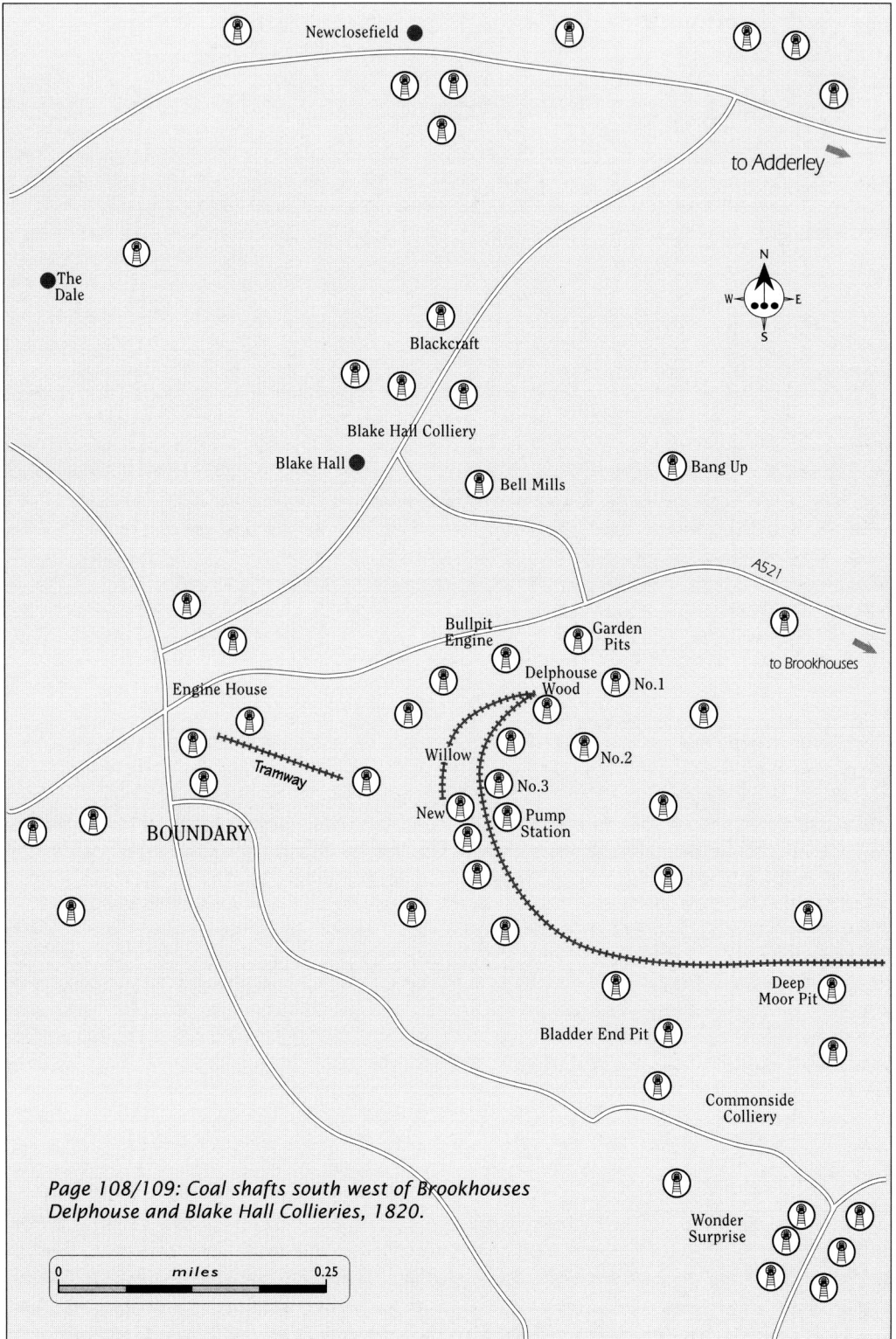

*Page 108/109: Coal shafts south west of Brookhouses
Delphouse and Blake Hall Collieries, 1820.*

Wonder
Surprise

0        *miles*        0.25

*Ladyswell, Wm. Bowers, Junr.*      *Madge Dale, John James*
*Mobberley, Malkin & Co.*      *Woodhead, Wm. Bowers, Jr."*

The Dilhorne Company, working the Old Engine Colliery, had now acquired a new nickname, *"The Flatts"*.

In 1875 J. C. Tildesley, in his report, remarks that the Cheadle Coalfield *"is one of the highest above sea level in England"* and is a coalfield in a trough. He gives the number of collieries as nine but does not name any.

## Bladder End Pit

Other mines are remembered because they took the name of the district and have remained. Two such were Commonside Colliery along the Boundary to Draycott Cross ridge, the other, Well Street Colliery near the middle of the town. Both of these were managed by Robertson but under the control of Sidney Wm. Malkin, the Accountant of Rock Cliffe, Cheadle, and were opened in 1875. Commonside was yet another of those ventures which meant tackling the Bunter Sandstone. It meant cutting through 270 feet to find the Yard Coal, but both collieries worked at intervals, for ten years. Commonside had but four to five acres and continued with a minimal staff some three or four underground and a maximum of two on the bank. Old Arthur Rushton was said to be in charge of winding, weighing and loading. The coal was sold at 6d. per barrowload which accounted for the appearance of some over-sized wheelbarrows. Once loaded with a generous 6d. worth, the women collectors could barely lift them from the ground until, round the corner, appeared their co-conspirators with their empty barrows to share the load into two barrows for 6d! This was nicknamed the Bladder End Pit!

## Well Street Colliery

This mine, the plan of which was taken from the 1879 Ordnance Survey 25in to the mile map, was nicknamed 'Old Malkins'or at other times 'Hoods Colliery' because just one hundred and fifty yards to the north, where the allotments used to be behind Queen Street, there were two shafts on what was called 'Hoods Meadow'. The shafts were sunk by J. Carr, but the coal was of little use. The Well Street Colliery would find the Cobble coal at some 65 yards, but working south, it would reach its boundary with Plant's new colliery in some 120 yards so that ten years would see the end. The weighing machine here was used by Hoods Meadow as there was a track between them. This colliery suffered demands from Robert Plant for the payment of a certain amount of coal to keep his great pumping engine at the Birches Colliery at work. He claimed that his pumping and the level he had dug from his pit to empty water into the brook under the Eaves, was unwatering all coal to the north to the Well Street Colliery. There is no evidence of an agreement being made.

## Dilhorn Common Colliery

The workings of Charles Salt can easily be seen from the Boundary – Forsbrook Road. About a hundred and fifty yards down the road on the left there is a widening for a wharf and a gate. Just around the bend one of the spoil banks, from the 4 ft. seam working, hovers over the fence. The Colliery, in 1867, was on land which belonged to Sir Lionel Pilkington who held small pieces of land from the Boundary to Cheadle. After boring through some fifty feet of sandstone the four shafts, sinking to between seventy-six and eighty yards, provided the opportunity to sample either the Yard, Litley or Four foot coals, all of which outcropped on the west side of the Bunter within half a mile. Salt worked these for some ten years, 1867-77. He also worked the Stinking Coal at Whimpney Wood, Dilhorne, from beneath the Bunter Sandstone which was some 60 yards thick. Ward, in his Geology of the Staffordshire Coalfield, used this information given by Mr. Salt's son.

## Milner's Pits

Just to the south of the Dilhorne Common shafts Barrow marked three other shafts in rough ground about one hundred and fifty yards from both the Forsbrook and the Commonside Road. These were the Milner's Pits working between the 1860s and 1870s and mining the Yard coal. Elisha Beardmore was born in 1856 at the Lamb Inn at Daisy Bank on the Commonside and at the age of five years took his father's dinner to these pits. The owners must have had some connection with the Milner who had been a partner in the Harplow concern through the 1840s.

## Callow Hill Pit

As the mining fraternity learned by practice some of the geology of the area, they decided that since the upper seams came up to outcrop as at Salt's Dilhorne Common on the west of the Boundary sandstone ridge, so must that much sought after Woodhead seam. An attempt to find it was made on the Callow Hill estate some six hundred yards to the west of the Farm. The small spoil bank can best be seen from halfway along the Forsbrook – Dilhorne road where the bank is but two hundred and fifty yards to the east. This attempt was registered as made by a Plant company who sank to fifty yards, but though the Woodhead was found, it had so deteriorated that little was taken away. Three generations of the Carr family had succeeded in making a reputation as the best of shaft sinkers or well sinkers. Anthony took up residence at the Miners' Rest after a spell at the Swan. Dan Bridget, Kingsley Holt, was his assistant.

## Other ventures

Following into the twentieth century, there were a dozen or so small ventures, outcropping in small areas where the Woodhead seam came to the surface and providing gainful labour for a year or two for two or three men. Because none were of any significance in terms of output or working time, they did provide a dozen sparks where all but four or five of the major lamps were extinguished. None of these operations expected to spread for any distance from the original shaft or more often, footrill, more especially when the Mines Department began to demand an excessive (for the twenties and thirties) licence fee of £50. At Kingsley the Woodhead outcrop was worked near the Brook by the Carrs and partners in 1923 and later at Kingsley No. 1 and 2 in 1941. Behind Kingsley Holt, down what was usually known as the Limey Grounds, Stephen Johnson of Lockwood had the Coleman brothers of Chesterton mining for the Woodhead, in both No. 1 working through 1938/9 and in No. 2 for a couple of years to 1942.

The Consall Mining Company led by Mr. Jebb were also chasing the Woodhead at Windy House, Kingsley Moor, behind the Blakeley Farm. This lasted for nearly a year, using two footrills, but was abandoned by January, 1924 as unprofitable.

## The Whiston Area

At Whiston Eaves Mine the Crabtree coal was worked from a 46 feet deep shaft, but soon ran into the old workings of 1877 and further north-west to much older workings. Messrs. A. and J. B. Stanway of Whiston turned to the east where they worked until April 1930. Barrow had, in 1900, listed Whiston Eaves as a popular area for old men workings in the Crabtree:

*"Over all this area the Crabtree has been worked some distance in from the out-crop. A shaft 500 yards south of Eaves Ford passed through three seams of coal below the Crabtree."*

They were probably not worth mining at that period.

Another group of four workings are found at Whiston around the Mount Pleasant area where the Crabtree could be worked but not without difficulty, as a fault ran in a south-easterly direction and one of the shafts was to the west of it. Since there are no documents on these workings and they are not named on any nineteenth century lists of collieries including Farey's 1810 list, we may expect that they were later and not of much consequence, expect to the copper smelters. There must, however, have been some hope of making the pits pay, for the miners had unwatered the area by digging a sough to take the water under Harston and opened it at the bottom of Harston Wood to join the Shirley Brook. The coal from the Mount Pleasant area was used at the Whiston copper smelter after the Sneyd company had passed it on to the Keys company, who were also running the Cheadle Brass Works, in 1846.

## Consall and Foxt Wood

In Booth's Wood near Consall the Froghall Mines Limited under R. W. F. Mayfield, the Manager, worked on the pitch abandoned by the Bishops in 1856. They worked from 1909 for five years using an old shaft sunk to forty feet, sometimes coming on the remnants of Bishops' ironstone.

Another group, John W. Carr and William Hall & Co. of Kingsley Holt, worked near the Foxt Wood area. This was to the west of the Kingsley School woodland, just south of the Woodcutter Inn over in Gilbert's Wood which ran down to the stream entering Mosey Moor. From a couple of footrills in the bank side they reached the Sweet coal – two feet of coal split by two inches of dirt. They worked this for two years to 1916 when Williarn Lockett, the local Certificated Manager, signed their abandonment plans.

## Kingsley

The Bank Top Colliery at Kingsley Holt must be mentioned, not necessarily for its productivity, but for its two highlights. The first, its founder, Jonathon George Binns, who, for some unknown reason, left his home at Belmont Hall in 1862 to live at Froghall and start a new life. It seems he had broken with the Sneyds, his former landlord at Belmont Hall and estate, where for the past eight years he had mined for ironstone with a fair measure of success. Once at Froghall, Binns & Co., his new company, had a concession on Bank Top Farm in 1861 where he hoped to repeat his success in the Crabtree coal and ironstone. The second highlight was the majestic stone engine house built by the side of his two shafts down in the Bank Top wood below the farm where a track was already in use by the farm to get into Froghall. This was a failure as, according to A. H. Green's Geological Survey of that date, there was a distance of 62 yards under the coal to the very thin, useless ironstone and no one valued the Crabtree coal so near the Woodhead outcrops. He also had a shaft at Oakamoor in Star Wood, but again he found nothing worth continuing with. According to the Oakamoor Parish books, his shaft was filled in in 1915.

Binns died in 1866 and was buried at Kingsley on 12th January at the comparatively young age of 66 years. His tower, however, stood solidly for almost another century and gave we youngsters the pleasure of dangerously exploring it and watching the owls rear their chicks each year in a rectangular gap in the stone work near the top. Alas, all disappeared, shafts, engine house and owls in about 1960.

The Kingsley Mining Company began working the Shaw Colliery in 1893 with Charles Shaw as owner and the Certificated Manager. It employed on the average about eighteen men underground and eight or ten on the bank. His son, Charles Shaw, junior became Manager by 1896. One of the two shafts sunk was at the eastern end of Duke's Plantation and on the end of the Duke's Level. This, therefore, gives rise to some speculation as to the pit's origin since the 1836 Ordnance Survey 1 inch map marks a Colliery of some size at that spot. It was some five hundred yards south of the Kingsley – Kingsley Moor road and the line of the tramway to a wharf on a widened piece of that road can still be followed, as sections of the old embankment remain. Most of the coal was taken from the western side of the area towards Tomfields farm and the Cobble, Rider and Woodhead coals could be reached at eighteen, sixty and one hundred yards respectively over some ten or eleven years of the pit's twelve year life.

Interviewed by Dr. Auden, John Hood aged 83 of Kingsley, in 1939, quoted an older Mr. Gibson when he asserted that one of these shafts was working at least 130 years ago. The older Mr. Gibson, who was born in 1810 remembered the pit working when he was a boy and it was called 'Bottom of the Moor Pit'. It is marked on the 1836 O.S. inch map as 'Colliery'. The water from this pit was pumped into the Duke's Level. It was finally abandoned in 1907 leaving, as a memorial, its local title, 'Dog and Monkey'.

## Harplow

One of the most publicised of all Cheadle workings was started in 1899. It was run by a group with a Mr. Dickinson of the Potteries investing most of the money and Stephen Offer, a Certificated Manager. They had been at Cheadle Park and Draycott Colliery some twelve and fifteen years previously, but at different times. Both had been interested in coal projects of a doubtful nature and this sinking was by the west side of the Draycott road above the present New Haden complex. There had been worked many shafts within fifty and a hundred yards and without a specialist knowledge of the strata in that area many folk had shaken their heads. It was called the Wonder Pit and a second shaft was sunk further up the hill called the Surprise. In fact, the Wonder was an enlargement of one of the old Harplow pits of fifty years earlier and when a dog's skull was found at the bottom, one old man claimed it was his dog, Lion's, head. A sough was joined to the Harplow level to unwater the seams. The Wonder shaft was 12 feet in diameter and sank 102 yards to the Yard coal. The Surprise shaft was a tremendous 18 feet across and sank to 112 yards to find the Yard coal. They were joined by a level and the coal was taken up from the lower shaft. The coal was carried by raised railroad some three hundred and fifty yards down to the Deepmoor Wharf where it could join the Delphouse tramway and eventually the main line.

Unfortunately, one morning the pit was found flooded and the level bottom dry at Litley Brook. The men congregated around the dry sough end and the boss recited the consequences of prolonged flooding. The men looked at 'Owd Coddin' Summerfield, who was eventually persuaded to act the hero and creep up the sough to find the blockage and release the water. He crept into the sough, just shoulder width, and the others waited. Fifteen minutes, thirty minutes passed with anxious glances on the men's faces, forty-five minutes and a trickle of water appeared. Another minute passed and more water issued forth with 'Owd Coddin's' hat. Ten minutes later and a halfdrowned 'Coddin' appeared. Congratulations all round! The boss presented 'Coddin' with a gold Sovereign and a bottle of whisky!

The Wonder finished in 1901, but since Stephen Offer was in other workings, in addition to his engineering work for the last twelve months on the Cheadle Railway's tunnel, he did not appear unduly distressed. His other enterprises with the Draycott Colliery

Company were equally disappointing, especially to those investing and even the Draycott New Sinkings which, instead of passing to the Coal Board, passed to the Severn Trent Water Board!

## *The miners switch to iron ore*

The 1861 Census figures for the whole district illustrate the effects of the emergence of the Churnet Valley's iron ore mining in its earlier six or seven years. In the Cheadle district alone, that furthest from the Valley, the coal industry, had increased its working units, but lost some of the miners to ironstone mining. The switch began steadily from 1854 with only few organisations with any mining experience, having the legal contracts signed and sealed ready to start work. The fact was that in many cases, as at Ipstones, absentee landlords were involved and mining companies comprised iron masters from South Staffordshire and this delayed agreements. Although the legal men, Blagg of Cheadle and Challoner of Leek, may have enjoyed this rapidly increasing demand for their services, the valley could have become a legal battlefield without these guardians to overlook the working of all the transactions.

In Cheadle district the number of men in coal had fallen from 233 in 1851 to 160 in 1861 and among these we find William Bowers, junior Coalmaster of Parkfields with his two month old son, William Eli, and a certain twenty-one year old Robert Plant, who had himself registered as a Coal Prospector. William Swetnam was registered as a Sinker at thirty-seven years old. In the ironstone mines there were 120 Cheadle miners, most of whom had swapped black for red! At Ipstones those sixteen 1851 coal men had gone down the iron mines and were accompanied by 177 immigrants who swamped the village in the search for red gold. Across the valley at Kingsley, their 56 coal men were reduced to 40 including William James, a Colliery Manager, and Thomas Bishop, William's son, now fifty years old, as a Mine Agent. At Whiston there were 96 iron men and nearly half, 44, were immigrants, whilst only 19 natives had stayed with the coal mines.

The next ten years showed an equally dramatic change especially towards census year, 1871. There had been a rapid fall in ironstone output which was past its peak by 1869-70. Whereas the number of coal men in Cheadle had risen to 221 the ironstone industry had lost three quarters of its 1861 total and had retained but 30 men.

Both coal proprietors and local relief organisations must have felt the results of this degree of instability in their localities and Church and educational representatives tried to combat the effects, in the early days, of the surplus money earned which led to drunkeness and gambling. The Allens of Woodhead Hall and especially sister-in-law Miss Shepherd formed their Temperance Societies, Bands of Hope with the Temperance Halls such as that in Kingsley, but in the failing years an even greater burden was put on the relief bodies around the district.

### The Ipstones – Belmont Area

Little has been said about coal working in the Ipstones – Belmont area. This was because the earlier workings were in the Crabtree coal, which, though nearly 2ft 6in thick and of fairly good quality, was readily available on this side of the valley. Yet, west of the Churnet, it meant little or nothing being deep below the Woodhead seam.

George Barrow noted the number of shafts which were still recognisable in 1900 and he was able to mark some thirty-four of them between Belmont and Crowgutter Farm on the Foxt road. He says:

*"the coal has been extensively mined in the neighbourhood and one shaft is still being worked, the coal being 2' 10" thick and fairly good quality."*

He then goes on to say:

*"It was to unwater this coal that the old level was driven."*

He refers to:

*"an old level was accidentally found that must be at least 300 years old because it cannot be found in any Belmont papers."*

At the time he wrote this, Belmont was not two hundred years old being built in 1712. This does not detract from the meaning of his statement when he continues:

*"When we consider that every tub full of dirt was pushed along a wooden plank the labour and cost must have been great and the driving of it, a great engineering feat.*
*Starting by Belmont the name 'Coalpit Wood' gives a guide to the two shafts here with coal at 2' 6" thick. Other shafts could be confused with the 1860s ironstone shafts where this coal was often worked to supply the engines."*

At Pettyfields one of the three shafts was for coal and had a large spoil bank although much ironstone spoil was said to be tipped there. Nearer the canal the Bishop workings have been recorded. Barrow found, by the church, the Above Church workings with four shafts which had been started by a Mr. J. Golden in 1893 and found coal at eleven and twelve yards. After two or three years standing it worked under J. Davis with but four men employed. Mr. Harry Scragg's father carried coal from here as a boy. In the triangle below the Belmont road three faults brought up the first or Sweet Coal.

Five shafts had at some period worked this while the shaft at Oddo Hall had found the usual Crabtree at 41 yards deep. The Hay House shaft was recorded supplying the coal for the Ipstones Pottery in the eighteenth century. At Radfields what was probably a disused ironstone shaft started in the coal in 1893 with Harry Scragg's grandfather, E. Scragg, who was the acting manager at 6d. per day extra for managerial duties. It lasted but five years. Travellers along the main road beyond the former Red Lion at Ipstones Edge will have noticed a railed mound on the left. This shaft found the first coal at 18 yards and made bricks in the brick-kiln there. At Hopestones, northeast of the village, shafts on either side of the lane found first coal at about 20 yards deep. There were so many workings in that district that the thirty-four shaft remains that Barrow could record, for coal mining rather than ironstone, must have included many quite minor operations.

The only summary of the industry at around this date was given in Trueman's publication of 1954 when he stated:

*"In 1880 there were 14 Collieries (in the Cheadle Coalfield) now (1954) only Foxfield may be economic in 25 years time."*

Around 1930, I saw, for the first time, a copy of a book called a *History of Cheadle* by Robert Plant. I did not see another copy or have the opportunity of reading it for many years after I had come across an old copy of the *Cheadle Herald* of 1881 announcing the publication of this volume and its prices – ten and sixpence or fifteen shillings per copy. I was much impressed by this publication at this early date and set about identifying the writer. I found he came of a coal mining family and decided that I could not write a coal story without giving an account of this remarkable man.

Robert was the son of Thomas Plant, a collier living at the Back of the Town, who had married Hannah, a Kingsley girl and had five sons and a daughter, Hannah. By 1851 the eldest son, James aged 20 was already a joiner and George, was a fifteen year old book-keeper. Robert was ten and still at school as was Thomas, a year younger. The two youngest, Septimus was six years old and Hannah only four years old. *Hunt's Mining Records* of 1856 listed its collieries for the Cheadle district and contained two workings under the name of Plant & Co., one at Cheadle, the other at Ipstones. Just four years later a Directory names the partners in the above enterprises as Plant, James and Robert, coalmasters of Back Street. At this time Robert would be nineteen and James twenty-nine years old. The partnership appears to have finished by the 1861 Census. The Ipstones operation of Plant & Co. was adjacent to and just north of the Ipstones Park Iron Ore Company's mines by the Park Mill. This belonged to G. S. Herbert at that time, one of the most powerful organisations and working with the huge Consall Mineral concern in the mining of ironstone. The 1861 Census, when Robert was twenty registered him with his full qualifications *"Robert Plant, Coal Prospector employing 19 men and 7 boys"*. No ordinary coal man this! By 1863, *Blunt's Mineral Statistics* lists a total of sixteen pits on the coalfield, and finding Plant & Co. continuing at Ipstones also shows another branch of the company at Callow Hill, one of the first failures. At Callow Hill, Plant was hopeful of the Woodhead seam rising in the west, but after sinking for fifty yards found only the Dilhorne and the Alecs and so abandoned the area.

He was soon to move from Back Street to Ebenezer Cottage on Mill Road where, with his independence or perhaps a new wife, he could begin his dream of becoming the coal king of Cheadle living in some great hall. By 1865 he was the head of the Cheadle Colliery Company and by the following year had established his Cheadle New Colliery, nicknamed the 'Turf field', just off the first corner of Mill Road and opposite what is now the recreation ground:

*"In 1866 at a place called the New Mine*
*Three men did start a pair of Pits*
*The Woodhead coal to find*
*Some say its there, some say there's none*
*But we will try and the world will see*
*When we've got coal to draw away*
*There's a bunch of Plants set in this field*
*To see the business done*

*But it has been reported that one of them would run*
*There's Turdy a good old Cow Cabbage*
*And Tinclar a good old Brock*
*But Roberts red for winter time*
*And Rommer a runner among the lot.*
*And now my Lads do all you can*
*And you shall have some work at Home*
*And when the Bort hole's driven through*
*Old Ben will want some work to do*
*Then he will join old Turdy and Rommer*
*And fall the coals with wooden hommer.'*
*By Old Sod. (Noah Hurst)"*

A further lease was signed in 1868 in an agreement between Thomas Sillito and the Cheadle Colliery Company, i.e. Robert Plant, for:

*"Sale of a seam of coal under Wm. Allen's meadow for £200 known as the Woodhead Coal now being worked in neighbouring lands by the said company situate near the Ashbourne Road with garden adjoining 3 Acres 3 roods 22 perches."*

It was dated 27th March, 1868.

At Ipstones he found all around him feverishly mining the ironstone, although in his district, the ore had slowly changed to the brown coloured hydrate not so easily sold. I have found no record of his having any lease of the stone though his neighbouring operator, owning the Ipstones Park Iron Ore Company, was still mining, but finding the output somewhat disappointing, both in thickness and quality. Indeed, it had caused some trouble between himself and the landowner – lessor, the Slacks of Ipstones Manor.

On 8th November 1869, Plant had sent through Thacker, the solicitor, a letter to Mr. G. S. Herbert, the stockbroker and owner of the Ipstones Park Mines:

*"I am requested by Mr. Robert Plant to call attention to the fact, that H. Wilson (Herbert's Manager) is getting ironstone from under the engine house and new shafts lately belonging to the Ipstones Park Colliery Co. Ltd. and now belonging to Mr. R. Plant."*

G. S. Herbert replied *"These building were erected long after we became the lessees."* The parties offered to settle through an Arbitrator and Plant and Wilson agreed in early 1870 to accept the finding of Mr. Joseph Southall, who was also ore mining in that district.

There is no doubt that Plant was planning on coal mining in the Cheadle area to continue for many years. He had found small pieces of land purchased by some of his family from as far back as 1836. He set about leasing coal under properties from 1867, after he thought he had a success in the New Colliery, until by 1878 he had control of some further two hundred and thirty-four acres. Unfortunately, a large proportion of this coal turned out to be towards the east of Cheadle where the seams were near outcropping or deteriorating in both thickness and quality. Whether he worked the coals so leased or not he had to be prepared to pay the annual rents on this wide coal area and this added an increasing burden on his finances, reducing his returns to a minimum.

It appears that the agreement to purchase the coal in the Cheadle Mill area which Plant had contracted at the end of 1870 with Walters, through the solicitor, Benjamin

*Hales Hall (from Plant's **History of Cheadle**, 1881)*

Thacker, had been quickly put into operation. The two shafts were taken to sixty-five yards for the Woodhead coal, but this was not the usual quality, a large proportion of it being slack. It was, however, worked until 1876, an improvement on two other attempts at about the same time. He called one the Rakeway Colliery and the site of one shaft is shown just east of the footpath opposite Mill House farm and south of the Derwent Drive. At fifty-five yards deep the coal was said to be useless and engine and plant were up for sale by February, 1872.

A further attempt was made the following year at Lightwood, but this had even less success or no success at all since it is now known that the Woodhead had outcropped around Thorley Drive and in 1600 the iron people were delph mining the ironstone which was some twelve feet below the Woodhead. In July 1874, the materials were up for sale and there is not the slightest sign of where Robert Plant had made his attempt.

By the 1870s Robert Plant had other projects on his mind, two of which were connected with mining and a third to do with his own status. In the latter there had been something of a step up so far as the Directories were concerned.

The 1870 *Harrop Directory* chose to include him, though still in Ebenezer Cottage, Mill Road, among what it called the Private Residents, the Ladies and Gentlemen, with the Allens of Woodhead Hall, with residents of Harewood Hall, Hales Hall and members of the legal and medical professions. There is no doubt that, even though only thirty years old, he began to think in terms of finding a residence to match this category. He began to visualise what could be made of his conditions around Ebenezer Cottage. By this time there was no hope of seeing a branch railway being brought to the Cheadle area to encourage coal masters to further effort by providing transport to outside urban districts where coal was needed, such as Uttoxeter, Ashbourne, Derby and Burton. Railways, such as our nearest, the North Staffordshire Railway, took precious little note of Cheadle people and its coal masters until they formed themselves into an association of both coal men and others likely to become passengers and made much stronger representations showing that they would finance any short railway line from a main line to Cheadle. One of the very early schemes has left a map of the proposed line with a Cheadle gentleman. It was dated 1869 and left the main Stoke – Uttoxeter line near Normacot to pass through Caverswall with its station, on to Dilhorne also a station, to run by Brookhouses and under Majors Barn, circling to Charles Street for its terminal station. The idea faded and historians are fortunate in having the map preserved.

In the matter of coal transport, many people gave up hope of seeing a railway line into Cheadle and Robert Plant, with others, had been thinking of alternative forms of transport for the use of local coal masters. A Cheadle carrying company was formed in 1871 with Southall as secretary and Plant in the manager's position. The 1871 Census included a certain John Adlem, traction engine driver, who happened to be in Cheadle, having brought the first engine for the Cheadle company and spending a few days teaching David James, the Waterworks engineer, how to handle this monster when it towed its two wagons loaded with coal. A few days later, even A. S. Bolton was astounded to see it loaded, tackling Oakamoor bank:

"*May 6 1871 Saw traction Engine bring 2 trucks of coal into Oakamoor.*"

The traction engine service was of value in the rural areas but urban districts such as Leek found its cobbled streets so badly damaged by the heavy ironwheels that the machine was eventually banned there, so reducing its profitable service.

At about this time, with the introduction of the traction engine, more local folk began to take notice of the movements toward establishing a Cheadle line. The following verse describes the attitude of many local people on the question of a railway:

> "*Plant's traction engine goes ahead,*
> *It makes them fear that now instead*
> *An iron rail shall pierce the hill*
> *And join the town against their will*
> *With the Outer World.*"
> *Wakefield,*
> *Blythe Bridge.*"

By 1871 he had acquired the piece of land, behind Ebenezer Cottage, which stretched to the Tean turnpike and planned a much larger building in good Victorian style with decorative garden in front on the piece of land. Ebenezer Cottage was to remain only as the Mill Road back entrance, indeed the name was left carved over the lintel of this back door. Trees were planted all round the field and a very smart pair of gates erected to open onto a tree-lined drive from Tean road to the gardens, stables, coachhouse and later the grand dwelling called the Mansion. This was, from then on, Cheadle Park. The house itself, was slow in taking shape, indeed the stable buildings never were finished, but when complete, was the finest piece of Victorian domestic architecture in the town and should never have been demolished in 1980/1. We now have no other example remaining.

A quite remarkable event took place in February 1872, when Plant was entertained at a 'Testimonial and Dinner to Mr. Robert Plant at Cheadle'. The event took the form of a Dinner at the Royal Oak and was fully reported in the *Staffordshire Advertiser* on

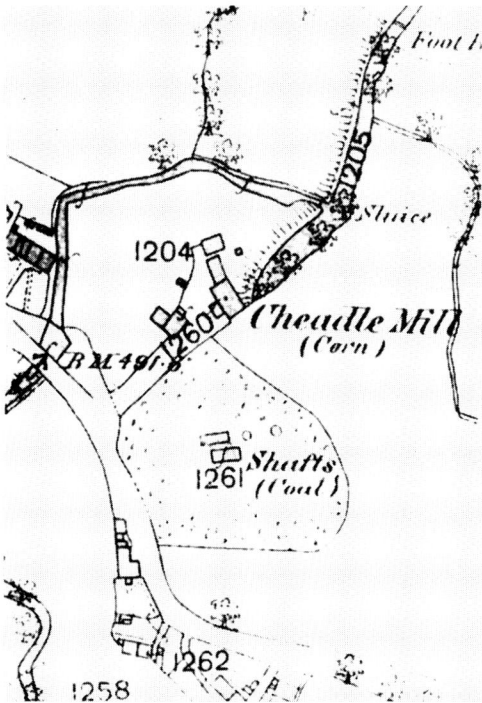

Cheadle Mill Colliery 1872

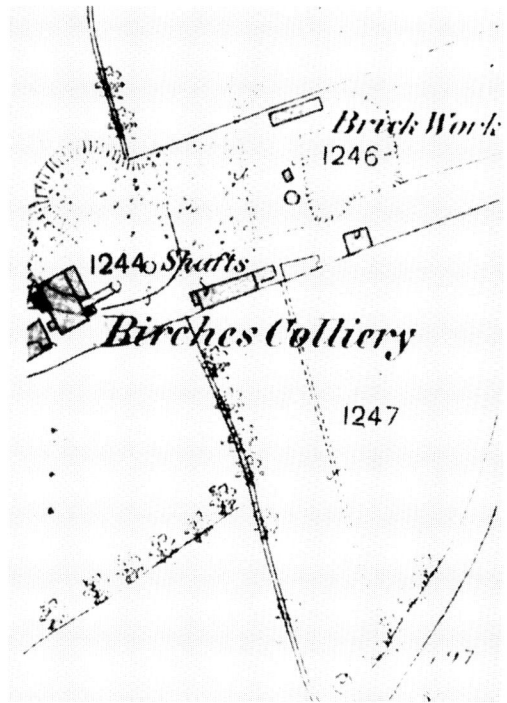

Birches Colliery and Brick Works 1874

February 17th. Forty guests came to pay their respects to the merits of this townsman. In giving the address, the Rev. J. Sneyd, J.P. said:

> *"This address and silver service.......are presented to you by 235 of your private friends and workmen in token of their admiration and appreciation of your unwearied energy, enterprise and abilityin giving at a time of depression increased prosperity to the labouring classe."*

The Reverend Chairman alluded to the traction engine, which he said:

> *"was introduced into the district by Mr. Plant for the purpose of supplying coal to the district at a cheaper rate than could otherwise be done."*

He defended Mr. Plant from the complaints which a few persons had made in reference to the traction engine and contended that Mr. Plant had as much right to take the engine along the turnpike road as any gentlemen had to ride along the roads in his carriage:

> *"It had been stated that the roads had been broken by the engine but he contended that if the roads had been in the condition which they ought to have been in, no injury would have been done to them by the engine."*

Mr. Plant thanked all present and referred to the effort to obtain a railway for Cheadle. Mr. Robinson proposed a toast to the Cheadle Colliery Company and Mr. Thacker responded. Truly a most remarkable occasion. When Robert Plant recalled these events in 1891 in a pamphlet he wrote for private distribution, he added the following:

> *"When I had a pig and a cow*
> *Everybody bid me 'Good morrow'.*
> *Richard's Proverb"*

On May 23rd, 1872, Lord Churston of the Dilhorne manorial family decided to sell his manorial rights in the Cheadle Manor which his ancester, John Holliday, had purchased in the Banks' sale of 1790. There were twenty-six lots with eight sizeable farms and woods. Robert Plant was there to join the town's gentry and actually bought Lot 13, Cheadle Park Wood at £1,575 (see also Chapter 12).

On the 17th September, 1872, Plant acquired more land around what was known as the Birches and eventually he decided that this must be worked for coal to raise the capital for his other activities. Before proceeding with the purchase of machinery, it was necessary for him to take a loan from the Blackburn and District Benefit Building Society to help with the building of his fine house and to install some very expensive machinery, for it appeared that he was setting out to make his Cheadle Colliery Company one of the most important in the field. William Bowers was already long established with his Woodhead Colliery as Cheadle's leading mining concern and Plant, having just had his failures at Lightwood and Rakeway, was intent on seeing his new venture at the Birches restore his fortunes. He was, however, feeling a certain financial squeeze for in the *Mining Journal* on January 3rd and 24th of 1874 there appeared the following advertisement:

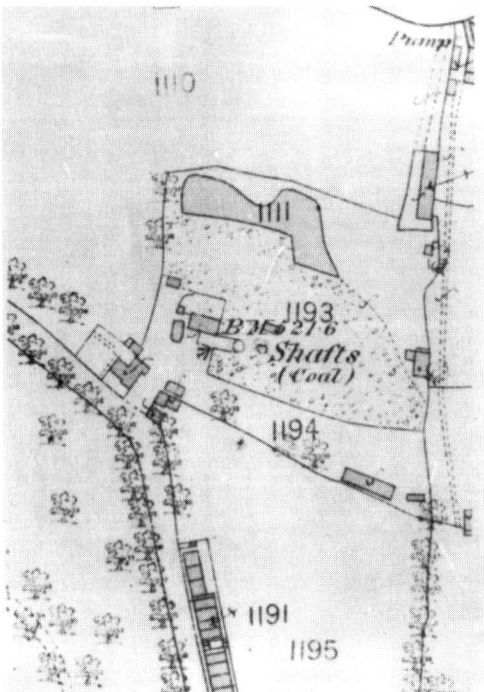

*Cheadle New Colliery "Turfield" 1866*            *Well Street Colliery, Hobbs Lane. 1870*

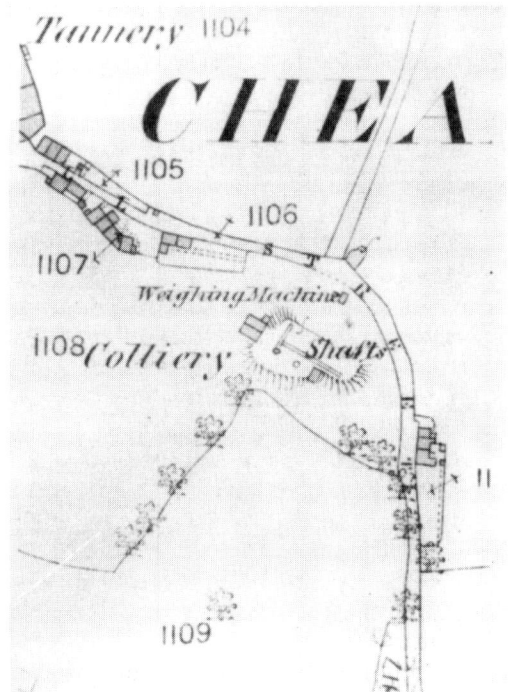

> *"To be sold about 14 acres of land or mines only adjoining Cheadle Colliery Company. Also excellent beds of clay or marl.*
> *Apply to: J. E. Keates, Burslem."*

By July 9th, 1874, Plant had met another industrialist who was becoming more interested in coal and mining in the previous two years. Alfred S. Bolton, who had been a partner in the highly successful brass and copper industry since his family had acquired the assets of Thomas Patten and Co. and their works at Oakamoor in 1852, had, by 1872, purchased the manorial rights of Cheadle from Lord Churston. By the time Plant was ready to sell up the Lightwood and Rakeway failures, Bolton was becoming familiar with colliery machinery and engines. He met Plant again during this time and by the 14th July had persuaded Plant to attend a sale of some ten lots of coalbearing land around Cheadle. The auction was held at the Royal Oak Hotel on the evening of that day and Plant was instructed that Bolton was interested in Lots 1 and 2, some fourteen acres of Sir Lionel Pilkington's land called Foden's Field lying near Bolton's Litley Colliery land. The sale was advertised in a Birmingham newspaper, the only local contact being Messrs. Blagg & Son, Solicitors, Cheadle.

Plant managed to oblige Bolton by buying at £1,300, a large sum at that time. This contact was to lead to further connections with Robert Plant and other partners which terminated twelve years later, in a most unhappy atmosphere, even in the law courts.

In the meantime Plant pressed on with his Birches project so that by October, 1874, his latest colliery was all but ready for working. He was given every encouragement by both mining engineerers and geologists and so confident was he of the success of this venture that he decided that the opening day should be the greatest day of celebration even surpassing that of a coronation day. The Head of the National Boys' School entered in his Log Book:

> *"6th October 1874. Holiday all day on account of the festivities of the opening of the Birches Colliery."*

On October 10th, 1874, the *Staffordshire Sentinel* gave a full report of events in Cheadle under the heading:

> *"Opening of the Birches Colliery, Cheadle.*
> *Monday was a day of high festivity at Cheadle, the occasion thereof being the opening of the Birches Colliery by the spirited proprietor, Mr. R. Plant. With a view to signalise, Mr. Plant entertained the whole of his workpeople and a large number of the poorer inhabitants of the town, in all about 850 besides something like 450 guests invited from the town and neighbourhood, including the whole of the members of the North Staffordshire Institute of Mining and Mechanical Engineers. The day was observed as a general holiday in Cheadle; nearly every shop was closed, flags floated from many of the houses, there were festoons of evergreens crossing the streets in several places and everything betokened a great fete day."*

So wrote the *Sentinel* reporter. He then went on with another four thousand words describing the events of the day, but readers will, I hope, be satisfied with my shorter account.

The important visitors came out of the Potteries by special train and in saloon carriages thence by seven open carriages from Blythe Bridge, the leading wagonette drawn by four grey horses with scarlet outriders. The church bells rang and Tean brass band played at the head of the line to Cheadle Park. They were taken to the Birches Colliery where visitors saw the pumping engine of 50 horse power with 36 inch cylinder and two winding engines of 40 horse power with 18 inch cylinders. Mr. Homer, President of the Engineers, started the great engines. There were many cheers for Mr. Plant. The party proceeded to view the Roman Catholic Church after refreshments in Mr. Plant's office. They then returned to assemble in two spacious marquees in the grounds of the Park for an excellent spread including game, venison and wines by Munro & Co. of Hanley. Some nineteen guests gave toasts and speeches. The top table included Messrs. Homer, W. Bowers, Stirrup, Haines, all in mining, with Messrs. Adamson (Ship Canal) Goddard, J.P., Messrs. Blagg, Thacker (the legal profession) and Sutton. The whole was arranged by a committee with Mr. Webb as Chairman and Mr. F. Cox as Secretary. Mr. Webb, in proposing one of the numerous toasts – there were some twenty of them – recalled that forty or fifty years earlier there had been a colliery at the Birches but *"it was somewhat mismanaged"*. This was the colliery which had left the old shaft to collapse around 1970, leaving a gaping hole on the Grammar School playing field site of the High School, just off the school drive and opposite the caretaker's house. Notice of the sale of all its engines and machinery in 1817 was mentioned previously.

The feat finished with toasts to the Ladies and the Press who reported that the great tent was overcrowded with listeners. The whole day was wet, but many stayed on to watch the fireworks *"which were on a large scale, not often witnessed in the town"*.

The Colliery was not ready to start for some time after the opening, but the shafts eventually were at one hundred and forty-five yards deep at the Woodhead coal. Very shortly, however, the reason for its predecessor's failure was found in a fault within a few yards of the new shaft which dropped the coals by some ninety feet.

*Cheadle Haulage Traction Engine at Cheadle Mill Colliery, 1872. Robert Plant is in the centre by the wheel. The Driver was David James and the Red Flag was James Critlow, who had to walk in front of the vehicle with his flag.*

The Birches, therefore, had bad luck from the beginning, either tackling the fault or the old workings of its predecessor . It was reported in the *Staffordshire Advertiser* of 12th June 1879, that the machinery and shaft sinking had cost the best part of £20,000 which had again to be borrowed. It was likely that the only overall profitable section of this enterprise was the brickworks which continued to operate after mining had finished for many years under Robert Plant's brother.

At about this time the carrying company ran into trouble and was dissolved. The traction engine which had been rented was taken over by Plant, but shortly returned to the owners at Leeds. just another disappointing failure.

By 1876 the local railway question once more raised its head. Its leaders could now claim that the needs of the coal industry were even more urgent in that within the last two or three years two more collieries, the Park Hall and the Birches, with new finds of coal, made it necessary to promote another scheme to join with the North Staffordshire line. A letter from the Bullers to possible Subscribers to the Cheadle Railway, said to be $5^1/_2$ miles long, was published on 27th November 1877:

> *"The Railway will traverse a good Mineral district, with four collieries now in work close at hand. Two of these are already in a position to raise 1,000 tons weekly and others only waiting for this line to open."*

## Cheadle Colliery Company

A new Company was formed at a meeting at the Royal Oak Hotel in January and the Cheadle Railway Company had Parliamentary sanction for the line by 1878. The Direc-

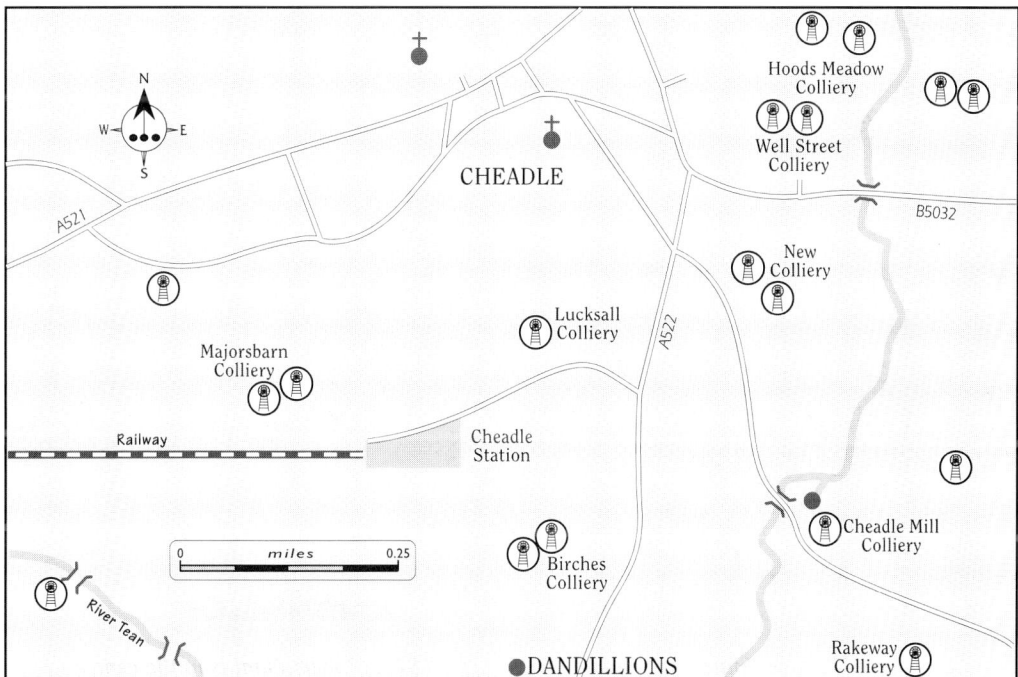

*Plant's Collieries, 1874-5*

tors were Mr. Craig, M.P., W. S. Allen, M.P. and three coal men, A. S. Bolton, J. Mann and R. Plant. A pamphlet was despatched from Blaggs, the Company Solicitors, calling for the purchase of £10 shares with the deposit of £1 10s. to be paid before the end of that month into the Company's accounts with either the Midland or the District banks in Cheadle. Some £23,000 was raised, but £50,000 was necessary to lay the line and build stations. *The*

*Plan of Plant's Mansion, 1870*

*Staffordshire Advertiser* reported on 24th April 1880 that the new Cheadle Colliery Company was incorporated with a capital of £100,000 and it had taken £5,000 worth of railway shares. This colliery company was now working the Major's Barn pit which had opened in 1875 under Robert Plant and his new partner, Stuart Miller of Delphouse. Although they did not reach the Woodhead which at Major's Barn, would have required a further five hundred feet of shaft sinking, they were, to some extent, fortunate in finding the upper seams readily to hand. These were the Dilhorne at 27 feet, two thin seams at 60 feet and 120 feet and the Alecs at 225 feet deep which Plant claimed at 6 feet 3 inches thick, but this was some two feet better than the Alecs at its best.

In addition to his mining and railway work Plant ventured at this period into an entirely new field. He set out to become something of a literary gentleman and historian. He was collecting material for his *History of Cheadle* and neighbouring places. This could only be done in the 1870s by finding the writings of other collectors of local historical material. Research, at a period before local Record Offices or university libraries, was out of the question for a man with so much in the way of industrial and railway problems. In addition, he had his domestic concerns in finishing his grand house and park at Cheadle Park. He does, however, mention Pitt's *History of Staffordshire* of 1817 and the William Salt Library at Stafford as though he was well acquainted with both.

In June 1880, the three-year old *Cheadle Herald* announced the publication of the History of Cheadle by Robert Plant, F.G.S. It was an excellent account of what the author had set out to achieve in this piece of writing and thanked Charles Lynam, the Archaeologist, and William Molyneux, the Geologist, for their contributions on Croxden Abbey and the Cheadle Coalfield. The work was dedicated to the memory of the late John Michael Blagg. It was to be bound in cloth at 10s. 6d. or in half calf with gilt edges at 15s., prices which, in 1880, must have put this excellent piece of work out of the reach of the great majority of the Cheadle people. When the book appeared in 1881 that ten to fifteen shillings was a week's wage. Dare we compare it with today's wage, a century later, and contemplate the purchase of a book at that price? In 1885 the *Herald* was, advertising it at five shillings.

By 1877 Plant was anxious to extend the mining area since the Birches was not coming up to expectations and Major's Barn, could not last for many years working the Alecs as its main source. He knew that Bolton had taken more interest in the Litley quarter of his estate over the previous four or five years and he was persuaded by Plant and partner, Stuart Miller, to allow a trial. Within a few days Plant had found only old workings and began filling in the shaft. By early in 1880 Bolton was prepared to lease part of Litley to Plant. He met him in May with his partners, a new one being Saul Isaac, ex-M.P. for Nottingham, at a lunch. They proceeded to Litley where Plant explained that he could reach a six foot seam below the Alecs which would crop out on the Cheadle side of the brook. By October, Plant reported to Bolton that he had found a five foot coal near the brook opposite Litley farmhouse. This working must have continued until June of 1882 when Plant was accused of having 'Forgerently' (Bolton's term) obtained a truck of coal from the Cheadle Colliery Company. The case went to court but no report was made on the result.

At the same time as the publication of his *History of Cheadle* in 1881, perhaps because he found that it was not going to make a fortune for him to clear his debts, he filed a petition of bankruptcy in August. He had borrowed very large sums from the Blackburn Building Society and it was claimed he had debts of £70,000. In February 1883, the Building Society foreclosed on him by selling a large share of his assets. All colliery machinery, including the monstrous engines at the Birches colliery and the New Mine were auctioned at the North Stafford Hotel. His confidence must have been shaken to the roots. Incidentally, the Building Society was wrecked!

By 1886 the coal spirit had returned to Plant and now, with his old partner, Miller of the Major's Barn Company, had again taken a lease from Bolton for Litley coals. At the interview and lunch on 28th April only Miller was present. They agreed on a 25 year lease at £100 rent per acre of Woodhead coal and £25 for another thin seam. There was some pretence of searching for coal, but Plant does not seem to have met the lessor although Bolton often visited another more successful venture at the other end of the town.

In 1887, with the Major's Barn Pit still working, Plant needed still more financial support. Another company, with Plant in the chair, was formed. Its title indicated its interests and ambitions. The Cheadle Railway, Minerals and Land Co. Ltd. decided that if the railway could not be completed as quickly as they wished, they could make a start on minerals, for coal was known to be available. By 1891 the *History of Cheadle* was still not selling well enough and before his trip to London he was handing out complimentary copies, one of which went to Marshall, the chemist, at that time next to the Police Station. A much happier occasion came in March of 1888 for, on the 22nd, the first direct step to getting the railway into Cheadle was taken. On that day the Cheadle company held a ceremony of cutting the first sod. A very large number of railway enthusiasts had gathered to see young Edward J. R. Plant cut the first sod followed by Robert Plant, his father, and Mr. C. J. Blagg, the Solicitor. It was announced that the Company had a capital of a quarter of a million pounds. After the ceremony at Totmanslow, the procession of vehicles entered the town to the sound of church bells. This was followed by a cold meal washed down with a number of toasts. Mr. Blagg proposed *"Success to the Cheadle Railway"* and the final reply by Robert Plant assured all that the railway would be open in fifteen months!

The coal men did, however, meet in April 1888 at Blagg's office, along with William Bowers, Sir M. Buller of Dilhorne, Mr. E. E. Almond when some of the geologists had nearly convinced them that the Froghall ironstone could be found under Cheadle and turn the town into a Shelton or Black Country within two or three years. The Cheadle coalmen agreed to call in the Aqueous Boring Company whilst Mr. Almond agreed that they should be allowed to bore from the bottom of one of his shafts at the Woodhead coal. After a bore of 570 feet the effort was discontinued and Plant saw one of his last chances to retrieve his fortunes disappear.

The Litley lease from Bolton to Plant turned out to be a miserable failure. It continued with little or no effort until 1893. But for the comparative success at Cheadle Park Colliery, Bolton would have had the Litley business terminated much earlier, but on 24th May 1893, he gave notice to Plant, through Blaggs' office, that he must quit the Litley estate. That same afternoon they met at Blaggs to patch up some agreement on the various problems and clear Plant's rent debts by paying £500 within two months and a further £700 within seven months. It was also agreed that Plant should show some intention of using the lease by sinking for coal within the next two months. Nothing, however, happened through 1894 and by February 1895, Bolton had completely lost patience with this unusual character. He called in Mr. Blagg's office to ask him to write and terminate the agreement over Litley coal:

> *"I must have Litley Minerals free of the deal with him as he had not carried out his payments."*

From this time on, Plant seemed to have forsaken his early enthusiasm, Little is heard of him, either in railway or coal except that in 1891 he had compiled a list of his brightest moments. There was mention of his Cheadle Carrying Company and the traction engine which kept his name on everyone's tongue for widely differing reasons; the glorious day of the Birches Colliery opening and the proud moment of the first sod cutting of the railway by his son in 1888.

By now he was fifty years old, not much in the way of age, but few of his generation had used so much effort and energy with so little to show for it and such a great burden of debt near the end.

Signs of bitterness crept in with his last few writings. Even those who had followed him through thirty years of scheming and planning now appeared to have left him to face the leaner years:

> *"If Mr. Blagg, who has taken much interest in Cheadle Railway, had carried out one tithe of his promises as set forth in this little memoir, it would have proved that a rich prophet as well as a poor prophet could be honoured in his own country."*

His last line also shows a change of outlook:

> *"Hardened to sustain the load of life."*

The railway he had dreamed of for more than thirty years opened on the first day of the twentieth century and Robert Plant missed the opening. He died in London on 19th January 1902. He probably managed a first when his coffin was brought to Cheadle on his railway for his funeral just six days later.

This most remarkable of Cheadle's characters at least retained his name in style for with Prince George Street and Queen Street, we still keep a Plant Street!

# THE BOWERS' EMPIRE 11

By 1853 William Bowers, junior, sometimes called Eli, had enough coal under lease to last him for his working days. He had taken his tramway further north-east knowing full well that a considerable amount of coal had been taken on the Shawe fields, though not exactly how much. He had been informed of the activities of Beech some fifty or sixty years earlier. He was preparing to open another shaft for the Longhouse Colliery when he was involved in the early ironstone rush. As early as June 1854, he had been fortunate enough to sign a lease for all the stone under the Shawe estate, either in Kingsley, Foxt or Ipstones and this included, along with the Kingsley Banks and Hazelwood area, the Ruelow Wood, Hermitage and the Mosey Moor district, probably the most important section of the ironstone field. In addition to mining ironstone, he had agreed with Beech on the erection of two blast furnaces to smelt the output when the volume of stone mined justified this.

Where conditions for mining the stone were favourable the profit was much greater than that earned by coal mining. The census returns show that it was becoming more difficult to retain men in the coal working unless they were assured that they could maintain earnings to match the ironstone men. There was, therefore, in the case of the Bowers' and other coal enterprises, a slowing down of new work and this effected the speed with which the tramway extension and new shafts could be put into operation. When Bowers rented the Consall Mills from the Leigh trustees he held the flint grinding mills that he had helped Leigh bring back into commission. In the 1840s this was reckoned to be a profitable enterprise so that Bowers had a third business to attend to. He had the ability to organise this working and especially when he found the mill adding to his profits.

A further extension of the tramway took place by 1863 when, leaving a large rail wharf and passing place outside the Booth's Farm, it took the line a further two furlongs up the lane to sink a shaft nicknamed 'Coopers'. This was followed by a further extension of 200 yards in sight of Shawe Hall, sinking a pair of shafts which became the Longhouse Colliery. There was, no great area to be mined on this piece of the Shawe land as Beech's father had mined with five shafts back in the 1790-1800 period and this cleared most of the Shawe Hall land south of the Hall. The Cobble coal was, however, available at a mere twenty yards deep at Lady's Well and there was only little Woodhead left. At the Coopers shaft the Cobble was at thirty yards and there was considerable evidence of old workings around both pits. The Woodhead seam, which was said to be eighty yards deep in those upper Shawe mines, was proved at one hundred and twenty yards, a variation this, as at the Dog and Monkey half a mile north, it was said to be only one hundred yards.

A gruesome accident is recorded on a gravestone in the Bethel churchyard:

> "To the memory of William Machin, aged eleven years, who was killed at the Woodhead Colliery on March 30th 1863."

Knowledgeable older colliers recall the accounts of this accident from their grandparents and the circumstances of the boy's death at the Cooper's shaft belonging to the Woodhead company. One version tells that boys at the shaft bottom coupled the loaded little trucks to be hauled to the shaft top. As a bit of a thrill they would swing on the rising axle for a short lift before letting go to land back on the bottom. In this case the truck rose rapidly before William let go and fell to his death.

Mr. S. Atkins, a descendant of the family, living in Machin House, Charles Street, related a remarkable sequence to this dreadful accident. William's mutilated body was recovered and carried away from the shaft. It was, however, seen by his younger brother, nine year old Joseph, who decided, there and then, never to have any work to do with pits. He persuaded his parents to get him apprenticed to a printer in the Potteries and having completed his time, he returned to Cheadle. He set up his own printing works in Cross Street and by August 1878, published the first *Cheadle Herald*, the first local paper, whilst he took up residence in Charles Street.

The coal under the Booth Hall estate was not under contract to Bowers. The mining plans for these last three pits show only working from the tramway to the Beech's old shafts. It is not surprising to find Ladyswell closing by 1863 and Coopers and Longhouse by 1870. In fact, there is no evidence of spoil around these two pits, though Ladyswell has some ten feet of spoil around its two shafts, all now covered by good turf. East-west faults ran through both Claypits site and Longhouse site probably accounting for their shortened lives.

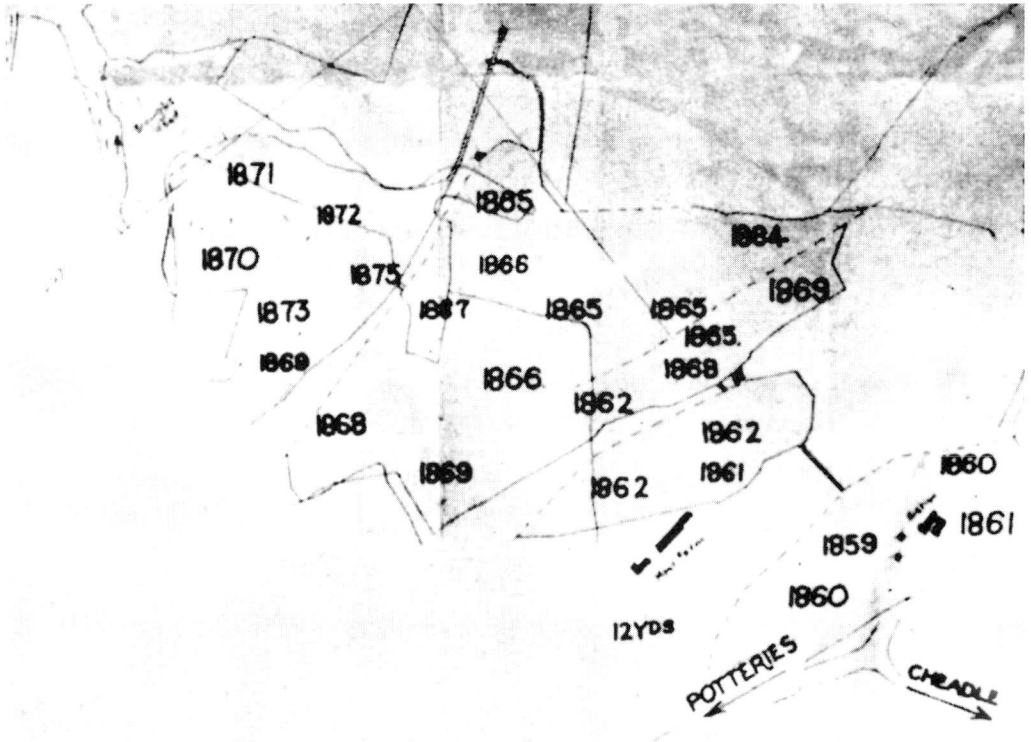

*Kingsley Moor New Sinkings Plan, 1880.*

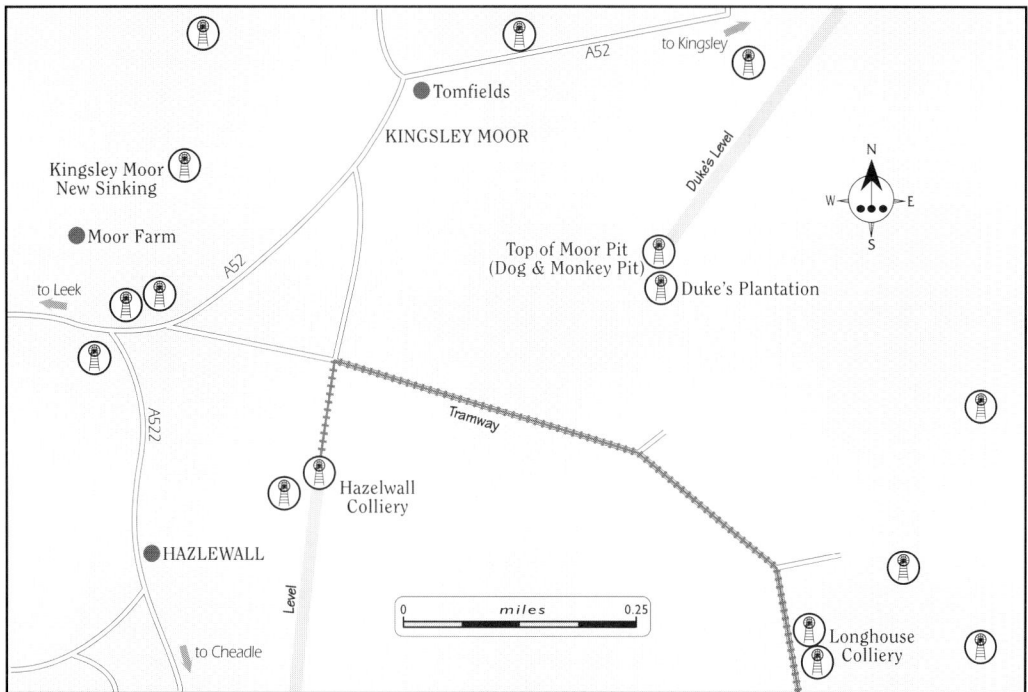

*Hazelwall Colliery and Kingsley Moor Area.*

At that time Bowers was in a position to continue the most northerly part of the Beech estate, the Moor Farm. The Mission Church at Kingsley Moor was later to be built on the site first mined, and was but thirty yards east of the two shafts sunk in 1859. This was a promising site, for the Woodhead was only sixty yards deep and was nearly half a mile by three hundred yards in area. Bowers could only call it '*The Kingsley Moor New Sinkings*' and, having finished the patch near the road junction within three years, 1859-61, crossed under the road, contacting a north-south fault before turning to work just north of the Moor Farm.

He continued to use the first shafts for the next five years until, driving north-west, he sank two further shafts nearer the remainder of the working, but both being in land he owned toward Church Gorse Farm.

Again he found an inconvenient fault as his workings approached the northern put of the Moor Farm land. This was east-west, cutting through the lower part of Brough's Wood and just south of the Woodhead seam northern outcrop.

It was fortunate that the tramway had been extended beyond Longhouse towards Kingsley Moor for these workings continued to 1875, a total of sixteen years working for a comparatively shallow Woodhead. The seam, however, was dipping here quite steeply for in a later shaft just fifty yards south of the road junction this same Woodhead was one hundred yards deep. Just a quarter of a mile further to the south-east of the road junction it had sunk to one hundred and fifty-six yards deep, but this was not measured until thirty years later.

William Bowers had by now been fairing well in his industrial enterprises so that by the time his mining was succeeding at Kingsley Moor he decided to build himself a sizeable mansion as befits the prosperous gentleman. He set about building along Harwoods Lane, now Leek Road, and to improve the sound of the name an 'e' was inserted so that his house became Harewood Park. It was completed by 1860 and his son, young Williarn Eli, was born in 1861. At the age of nine young William E. Bowers was mentioned in *Harrod's Directory* as a limeburner at Froghall Wharf, but living at Park Fields off Oakamoor Road.

By 1856 William Bowers had acquired the Holly Bush Colliery in Longton and the Berry Hill Colliery between Bucknall and Victoria Road. He had built property as soon as he became established after acquiring the Woodhead complex and starting the tramway. A pair of cottages he built by the Leek Road had the inscription 'E.B. 1841' but his son, Williarn E. Bowers, was to exhibit his initials in many places before the century was out.

At the Churston sale the Hazelwall Farm was bought for £9,400 by a Mr. F. Hordern who had been in the town but a few years. He lived at Butler's Hill opposite the Osborne building and had a wine and spirits store on High Street. He also had a Brewery at Macclesfield.

## *Hazelwall Colliery*

Within two years Bowers had made arrangements to mine the coal and by 1874 John Carr had sunk the shafts of what was to be Hazelwall Colliery. It was to work for more than thirty-six years.

The first Manager was David Bettany who had been in ironstone at the Consall Chase Fields pits and returned a few years later to work Cherry Eye ironstone near the top of Ruelow Wood until the end of the century.

Many Kingsley men and their families worked here for it was regarded as a Kingsley pit with its annual holiday at Kingsley Wakes when the ponies and a donkey were brought to the surface to take their holiday. Bettany was followed by Abraham Edwards also an ironstone man under Bowers on Kingsley Banks when he closed the Hazelwood mine in 1885. G. Forrester became under-manager and Thomas Mellor the engineer. By the time the 1890s arrived there were almost eighty men on the books with some sixty underground. By far the greater part of the output was trammed the two mile journey to Woodhead, though many carted north and west from the wharf at Hazelwall. The Kingsley men, the Woods, Booths, Moretons, Copes, Carrs, Halls, Hoods, Weavers and Carnwells looked upon Hazelwall, at this time, and for the next twenty years, as the main source of employment.

This management was followed by one of the earliest Certificated Managers. Benia Parker came out of the Potteries and knew the workings of the much larger and deeper pits. Owners like the Bowers gave these men much more responsibility, so that he could visit his Potteries' units regularly.

Old Mr Bowers reckoned to collect Tom Mellor, who lived in the Victoria Cottages, Kingsley Moor, before the larger pair were built, at the road junction. He came from Harewood Park in his trap, drawn by his high stepping horse, to pick up Tom at 6.00am on the way to Berry Hill. *"We're late this morning, Tom"* was the usual greeting. A couple of years later an accident with a beam in the shaft caused Parker to sack Mellor without Bowers' knowledge. Bowers called later and demanded to know why Mellor was not tackling the job only to be told that Parker had sacked him. Bowers then retired Mellor with a pension.

Benia Parker demonstrated his progressive outlook by starting a tramway underground worked by endless rope which reached north-west for more than half a mile under the

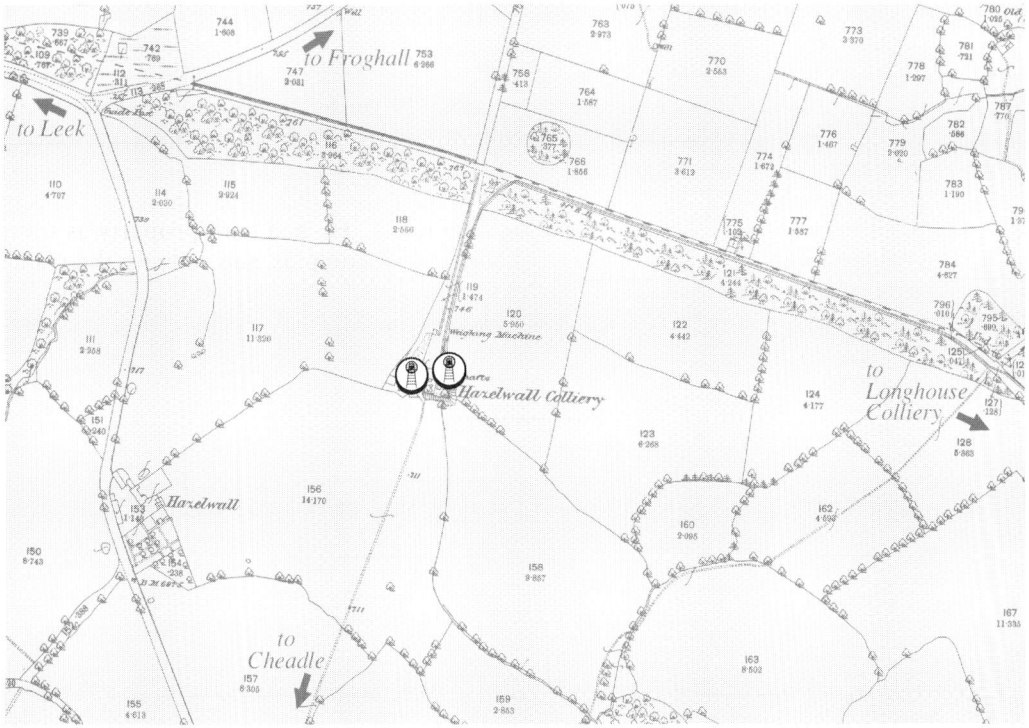

*Hazelwall Colliery.*

Wagon and Horses by 1904. Shortly after he left to be manager at the new Shafferlong Colliery near Wetley Rocks. There were nearly a hundred men employed by this time and the seven ponies and the donkey were brought out by Thomas Barker, the ostler, when the men had their annual holiday at Kingsley Wakes.

William Bowers died in January 1880, and for the next three years his affairs were in control of Trustees until William Eli came of age, at 21 years in 1882. There is no doubt that William, the second Bowers, had been a hardworking and astute business man. A few years earlier he had gone into the Alabaster and Plaster of Paris business near Tutbury around the village of Fauld where the mines became long tunnels. These were used during the second World War for the storage of ammunition and became notorious in 1944 when the largest non-nuclear man-made explosion in the world occurred there killing many people. The Bowers' tonnage sheets were forwarded from Fauld to his solicitors, Blaggs' office over many years. His elder brother, Eli of Parkfields, died in 1883, but was 76 years old. He had continued with his farming.

William Eli continued at Harewood Park with his widowed mother and took charge of the general workings. He was prepared to put his stamp on what was now his own property. He decided to fence the Park property and the iron rails along both Harewood Road and Bate Lane still stand though wellover a century old. The iron gate at the farm entrance carried a plate with the now familiar 'W.E.B.' in the middle, but the plate disappeared; only the space is easily visible. His manager must have had a dwelling near his work and two larger houses were added to the Victoria Cottages with the date, '1897' and 'W.E.B.' on a stone above the doors. Later when he purchases a piece of woodland adjacent to Hawksmoor, the boundary stones carried the initials as did the house on the road side, 'W.E.B. 1906'.

In 1885, at the age of twenty-four years he married Miss Blagg and this event brought a full day of celebration with High Street, decorated with garlands stretched across, for the whole length to the Church.

The Hazelwall colliery was still promising plenty of profit. All his other enterprises had helped to make him a wealthy man. The railway shares he and his late father had accumulated were still healthy stock and having stayed with his mother at Harewood Park for five years, he decided to show that he was Cheadle's most successful coalmaster.

In 1890 he took over Caverswall Castle and within a short time a new gate house was built and W.E.B.' was carved over the lodge door.

The wharf at Woodhead was kept very busy since the Uttoxeter area had now to be served by horse and cart. [It had been the case since the canal closed in 1846]. In fact, one of the older carters there, Tom Stephenson, told how he was expected to load, cross the road to the new weighbridge and complete two return journeys to destinations as far as Rocester or Ellastone in one day. He tended his horse and stabled for the night before finishing. It is doubtful whether he would see Mr. Hammond, the wharf manager, at that time.

New steam ventilation was installed and there was not no sign of candles, as the new safety lamps were well established.

On 26th March 1905, William Eli's wife died quite unexpectedly. She was only forty-two years old and he was deeply affected by this turn in events and threw himself more energetically into his work.

Shortly after this period there was talk of another attempt on that narrow strip of coal just off the north of the Cheadle coalfield called Shafferlong. It had been attempted much earlier and in those days the water problem had defeated all attempts, but by 1905 the experts, Marshall Fox and J. Haines, the top surveyors, had reported confidently to the Westwood Manor Coal and Iron Company. When Benia Parker moved from Hazelwall to take charge there it appeared to be one of the strongest organisations in the district.

This left a vacancy for William Eli to fill and he chose J. H. Lister from the Leeds district who was housed in one of the larger houses, the one with the plaque, 'W.E.B. 1897', in Victoria Cottages. He was a man obviously prepared for his job and shortly gained the respect of those working under him.

There had been some water trouble which necessitated the use of pumping and a level. The shaft was sunk well below the Woodhead seam and water pumped was taken by the level in a southerly direction.

There was no shaft strata diagram for Barrow to use and publish in his survey. Lister set about correcting this and in 1906 his copy showed the following:

| "At | 10ft coal | Foxfield | 21ins thick | |
|---|---|---|---|---|
| | 62ft | Mann's | 24ins " | |
| | 94ft | | 2ins " | |
| | 193ft | coal cobble | 21ins " | |
| | 245ft | | 2ins " | |
| | 325ft | | 6ins " | |
| | 345ft | coal Rider | 18ins " | |
| | 468ft | coal Woodhead | 36ins " | |
| | 471ft | Buster Coal | 3ins " | " |

Lister signed his diagram in October 1906, and I am fortunate enough to have found his copy among the old Bowers' papers. The abandonment plans, however, of 1913 give the shafts at 610 feet and 613 feet to account for the drainage.

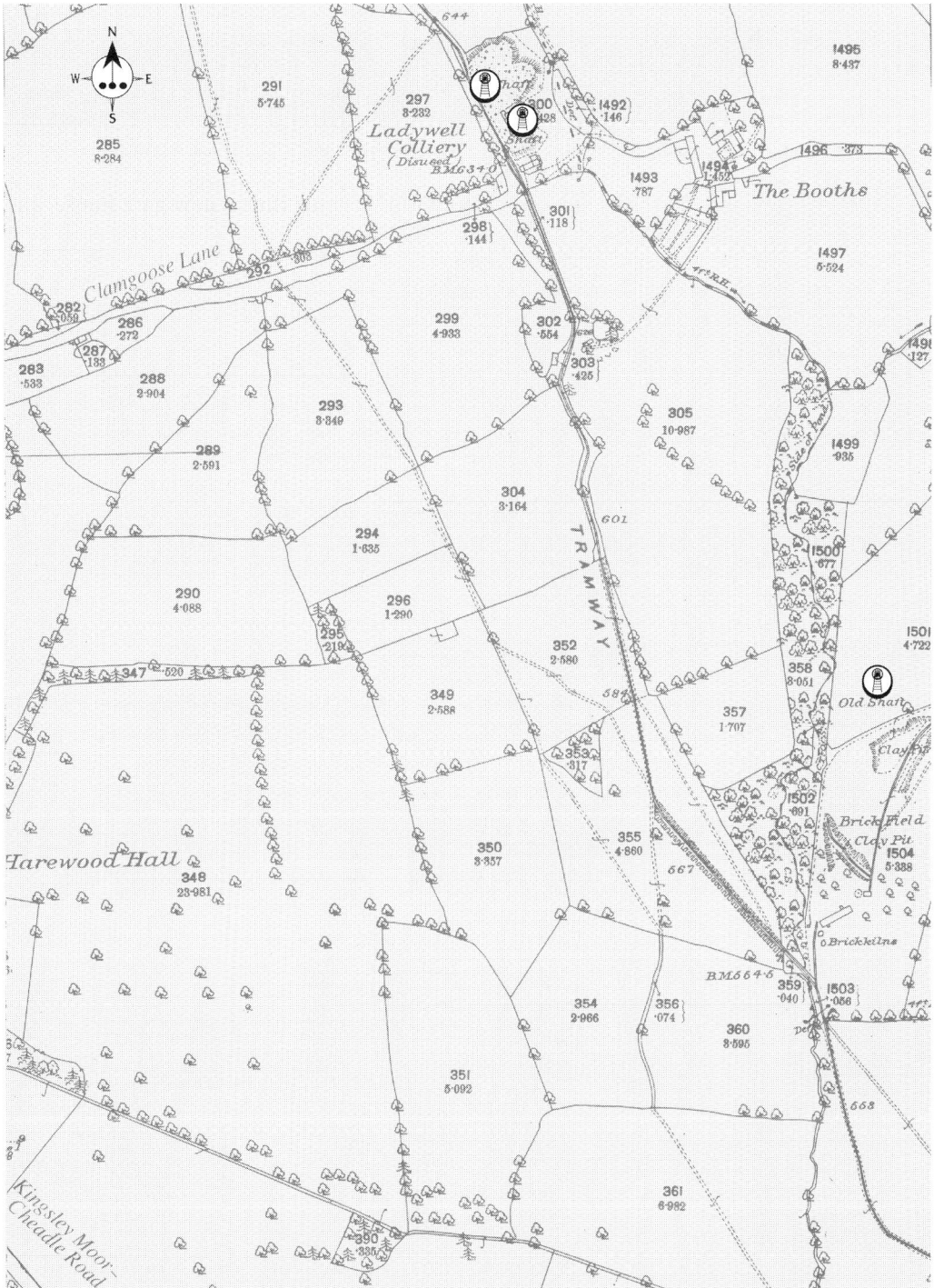

*Ladywell Colliery and tramway. The extension northwards is on page 137*

In January 1907, W.E.B. entertained his workmen and about sixty sat for the meal at the 'Unicorn' in High Street. The Chairman was a Mr. Hoyland and both Lister and Hammond were present, the latter being recognised especially for his long service as Manager of the Woodhead Wharf.

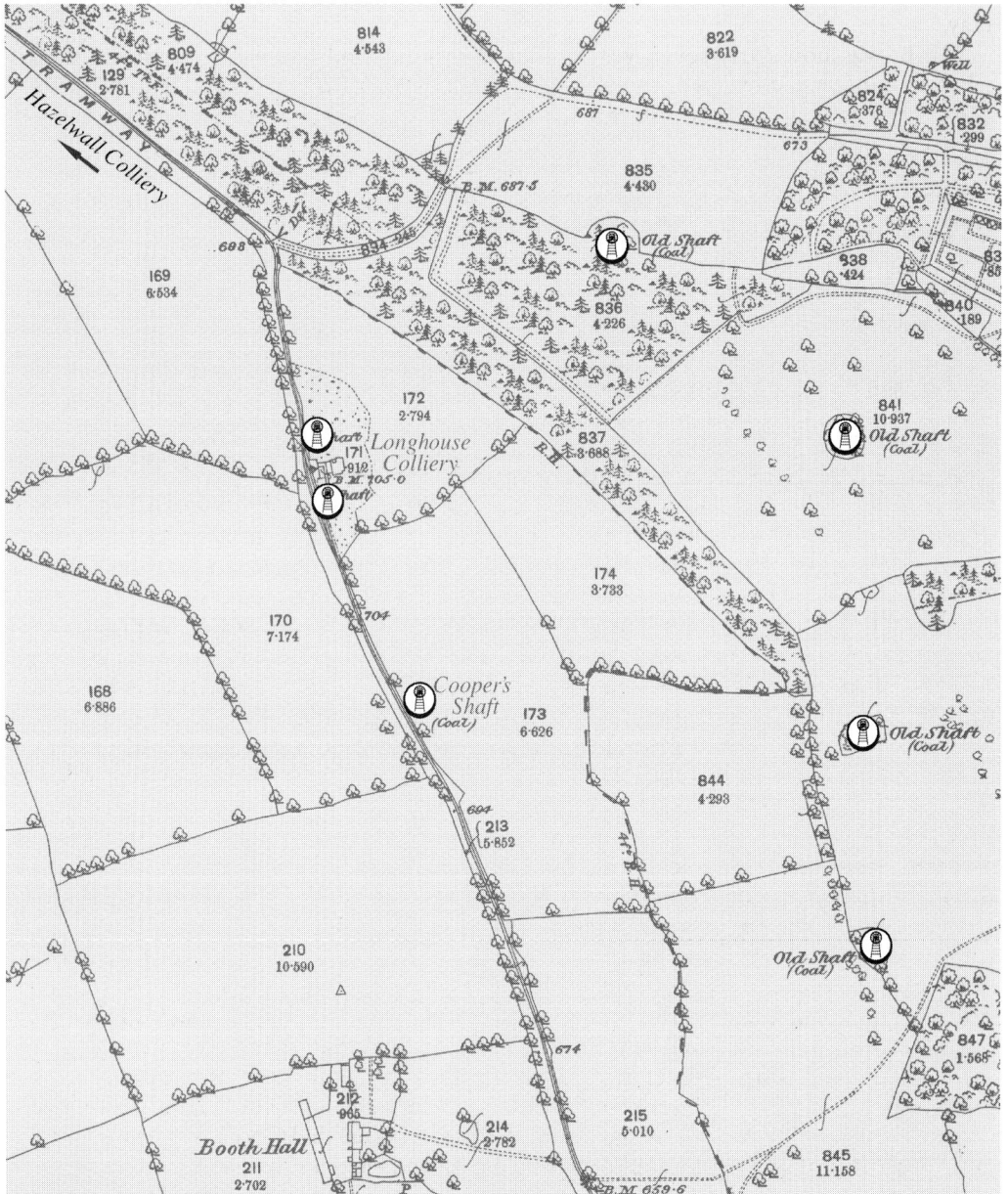

*Longhouse Colliery with the grounds of Shawe Hall top right*

In 1908 there were more celebrations at Caverswall at the coming of age of Mr. Aubrey Bowers, who, had been educated at public school and was then at Oxford University. In August of that year there was the usual Rent Audit, a social rather than financial gathering, for all the Bowers' tenants and officials, at the Royal Oak with toasts to W.E.B., Mr. Aubrey and both of his two younger sisters.

In the same month W.E.B. attended the Kingsley Holt Horticultural Society's show as its President and he welcomed Mr. & Mrs. Almond of Park Hall Colliery and Abbot's Hay.

W.E.B. was now forty-seven years old and thriving and had a rare sense of humour when in contact with his workmen. On a certain pay day at Hazelwall, he approached a banksman, shaking his head and muttering about his inability to pay his wages that week:

*"Why, Mester Bowers, ar yer shoort er brass? Ha cun let thi hev er quid er tow." When asked how much he had saved up he replied "Twenty quid." "How much do you earn? "*
*"Foertine an six er wick."*
*"Then if you've saved all that money, I'll have to drop your pay to twelve and six-pence!"*

This came from the man everybody expected to be a millionaire!

In January 1909, W.E.B married his second wife, a Miss Owsley from the south, and this meant great celebrations at Caverswall.

In early March 1911, news quickly spread that W.E.B. had purchased Park Hall Colliery from the Almonds. This was a break from the normal Bowers' strategy of digging their own pits where they thought best. Consultations with manager, J. H. Lister, must have shown that the coal land leased from Beech was, by 1911, nearly worked out, for nearer Kingsley, Mr. Shaw had closed the Dog and Monkey and it appeared that Hazelwall must prepare to close. The local papers took the view that *"while Bowers meant progress, Almond was always a good boss."* Lister was now nominated as Manager of the Woodhead and Park Hall Collieries. The closure of Hazelwall was shortly completed although the Abandonment Plan was dated 1913.

Before five months had passed the local coal industry was shocked to hear of the death of W.E.B. on 28th July 1911. He, like other gentry, had acquired his own car and died at the wheel while returning with his wife from Stone to Caverswall. He was fifty years old.

Lister was appointed executor in charge of the Bowers' coal business, as young Mr. Aubrey Bowers had only recently completed at Oxford, so that the whole burden of the change-over fell on Lister's shoulders. Only a few of those seventy workmen could be transferred to Park Hall and this meant that many moved to either New Haden or Foxfield, but there was still a measure of unemployment and, inevitably, the blame fell on Lister. The coal had been taken on the south-east side as far as the old Longhouse pit and in the north-westerly direction well beyond the Wagon and Horses Inn.

Just before this change-over in 1911 a mining man from Lister's old country, near Leeds, arrived at Kingsley Moor to join his old colleague. This was Charles Hullah, who stayed until nearly 1920, leaving his son, Fred, to work a lifetime in coal and leave grandsons also to follow, though only one has stayed the course.

W.E.B's will was published late in 1911 and surprised many in that it only amounted to £105,987. It appears that his railway shares had suffered since the boom had turned to slump. Aubrey took the major part of the estate whilst his sisters received £15,000 each. The services of his solicitors, the Blaggs, was recognised as they received, the one £500, the other £200 per year for life which was not long in either case. At the same time some of his servants were named as benefactors – John Stevenson, a Manager; John Wm. Salt, carpenter; Herbert Sedgewick, screen foreman; Isaac Hammond, engine driver; and a friend, F. H. Wynne, Inspector of Mines.

Legislation to do with mining mens' pay was published in 1912 under the title *"North Staffordshire Schedule of Minimum Rates Fixed for Cheadle District"*. The word *'minimum'* is obviously the operative word:

| " |  | s. | d. |
|---|---|---|---|
| 1. | Contract Colliers | - | - |
| 2. | Other Colliers | 6 | 0 |
| 3. | Loaders | 5 | 6 |
| 4. | Datallers | 5 | 3 |
| 5. | Assistant Detallers | 4 | 6 |
| 6. | Coal Cutter Attendants | 5 | 6 |
| 7. | Ass. Coal Cutter Attendants | 4 | 6 |
| 8. | Onsetters | 4 | 6 |
| 9. | Motor engine men | 4 | 6 |
| 10. | Road men | 5 | 0 |
| 11. | Boys 2/- to 4s. 6d. at 21 years" | | |

On the 16th May 1913, to mark the change-over, a presentation was made to Mr. Aubrey Bowers, now married, by the workmen of the Woodhead and Park Hall Collieries. There were speeches and songs, even one from J. H. Lister. Charles Hullah was present.

By the following year, Aubrey Bowers was in the Army and another tragedy occurred when he died of wounds in 1916. A memorial service was held at Caverswall at which Lister, as Manager, attended, accompanied by H. Molyneux the under manager and many other workmen. Also a Mr. H. B. Land, schoolmaster at Caverswall, who was soon to be the Headmaster of the new Council School in the Avenue, Cheadle, was at the organ.

By 1913 Hazelwall Colliery closed and its Abandonment Plans were forwarded to the Ministry.

## The Park Hall Colliery

In 1872, Lord Churston, Head of the Buller family of Dilhorne, decided to sell those sections of the Cheadle manorial estate, purchased by his ancestor John Holliday, at the Bank's sale of 1790. The sale was once again conducted, at the Royal Oak on May the 23rd, but this time under a local auctioneer, Henry Walters. Once more the Manorial Rights of Cheadle were coupled with Cheadle Park Farm.

Again the sale attracted the coal men including William Bowers of Harewood Park, Robert Plant of Cheadle Park and one of the Southalls of Ipstones, whose main interest had been in ironstone mining as a contractor, but since that had now passed its peak, he was returning to coal.

*Parkhall Colliery, south-west of Kingsley Moor*

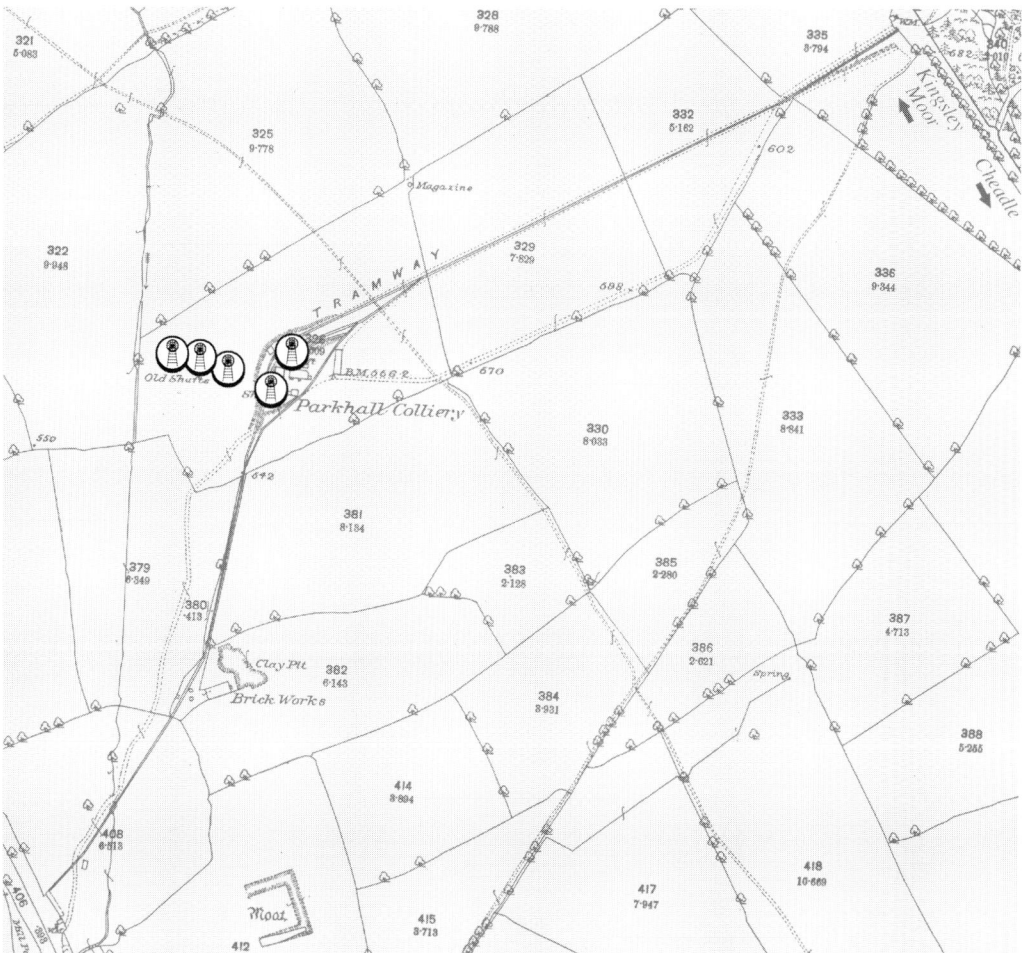

The twenty six Lots contained near a thousand acres of land containing sewn farms of up to two hundred acres, including Litley Farm and Park Farm of some two hundred acres each. Hazlewall Farm contained one hundred and fifty acres and Park Hall one hundred and forty acres.

Bowers bought Lawns Farm of sixty two acres and three smaller pieces in the Gawbutts area down the Green. Plant bought Cheadle Park Wood for £1,575, while Southall satisfied himself with the mineral rights of Draycott Common for £250.

There were, however, some surprising bids. Cheadle Park Farm with Manorial Rights and Litley Farm with Sweet Hills, its near neighbour, were purchased by a Alfred S. Bolton. His bidding for Lot 10 (Litley) caused some consternation as it reached £13,400 with a mere £2,000 for Sweet Hills. He then bid up to £20,000 for Park Farm and Manorial Rights and, having spent £35,400, he returned to 'Sunny Side' Oakamoor as Cheadle's Lord of the Manor. One other stranger on the bid was a Mr. Ferguson who paid £7,850 for Park Hall Farm and within the next year agreements had been made to start Ernest Almond working the Park Hall Colliery, which was to last another half century.

It will be remembered that Holliday paid £4,400 for the farm and rights in 1790 which cost Bolton nearly five times as much just eighty years later. It was not realised until ten years later that this sale was instrumental in starting four medium-sized collieries, i.e. Litley 1873, Park Hall 1873, Hazlewall 1874 and Cheadle Park 1884.

Edward Ernest Almond was joined by his brother. Both had come from Walsall where they had been in the town's leather industry. Ernest took up residence at Abbot's Hay, pleasantly out in the country, within sight of Woodhead Hall. in taking his walks he must have noticed the remnants of the Leigh tramway, Woodhead to the old canal in the valley.

Within four years, by 1877, his Park Hall colliery output had risen to 10,000 tons per year and its sale must have become something of a problem. He had two tramways, which are described later, but these did not supply nearby Cheadle very conveniently. He heard of the five or six wharves along the old canal and thought of having these sale depots by the railway stations. In that year, 1877, he approached Allens at Woodhead with a proposal. Although no plans are available, Almond may well have thought of continuing his Leek road wharf line for a further half mile to join the Woodhead tramway. Early in 1877 Almond approached the Allens about taking a lease on the old line through their Park and land. They appeared helpful at first and steps were taken to repair a section of the line which had not been used for nearly thirty years. On the 21st May, A. S. Bolton noticed some work being done and entered in his diary *"Noticed that the tramway by Woodhead was being put in order."*

However, when the agreement was to be signed Almond found certain clauses which made the scheme impossible. The most awkward laid down that locomotives should not use coal. The old embankments erected by Leigh could hide ponies and trucks from the Hall, but could not prevent the smoke from drifting to the Hall. Almond considered the use of coke too expensive. Another clause forbade the use of the line from 6.00pm until 9.00am. Almond found both clauses too restricting and the scheme was abandoned.

There is available, however, a report on the progress of the colliery at ten years old written in 1883 by a Sebastian Smith. It reads, however, as though the colliery might be for sale as so little of the report is of a critical nature.

*"Report on the Park Hall Colliery 16 Ocr 1883. The only profitable coal is the Woodhead which is 190 yards deep. This coal is got under 26 acres and there are 171 acres left – ( Park Hall Farm itself had only 141 acres) – of this 103 acres will have to*

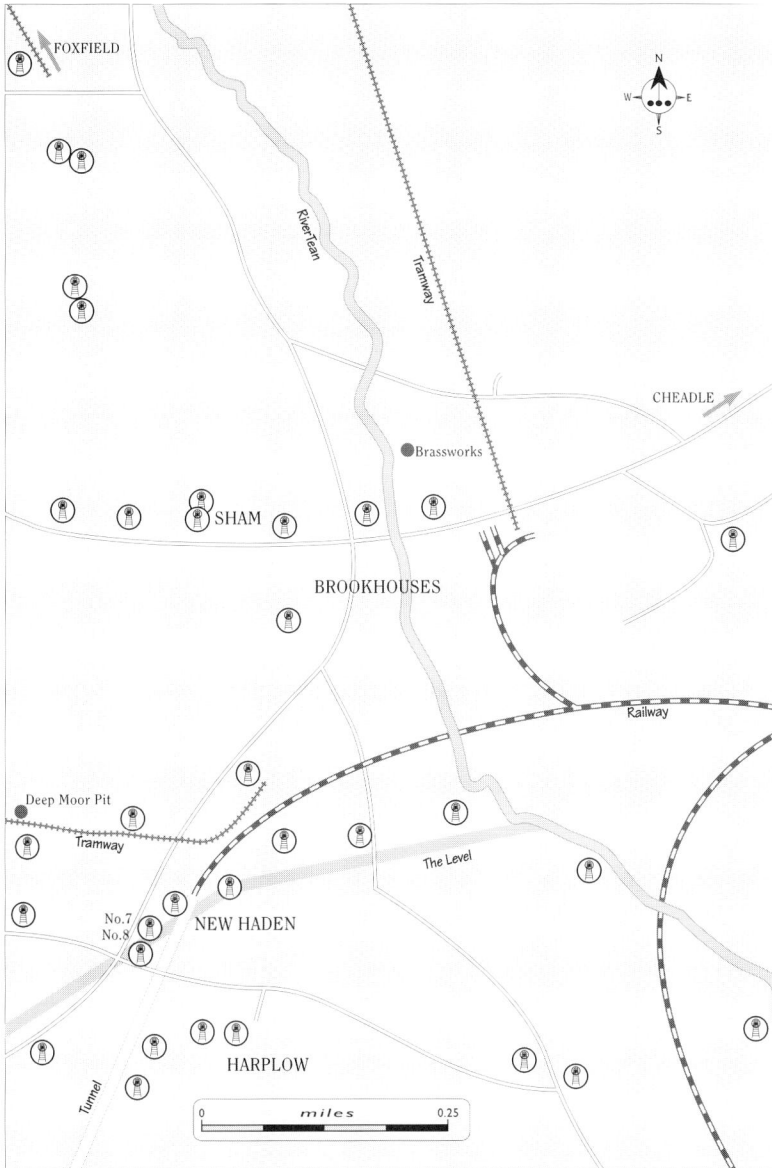

New Haden
Colliery,
Brookhouses, west
of Cheadle

be pulled up to the pit bottom.  Little timber is needed,  There is a inclination of $1^{1}/_{2}$
inches to 1 yd. After the coal is undercut it comes down without powder.  There is
practically no gas, but locked lamps are used for safety.  There are 20" tramways and
ventilation is by steam jet, halfway down the  Upcast shaft with 8,000 ft if air in the
North workings and 7,000 ft in the south workings.  About 100 men and boys are
employed underground.  The Upcast winding shaft is 12 ft in diameter with wire rope
conductors with cage of two trams side by side.  The Downcast shaft of 9 ft in diameter is used to wind water out of the sump.  There is a pair of winding engines 20"
horizontals with a 3ft stroke and drum of steel, $2^{3}/_{4}$ winding ropes, head stockes good.
There are four boilers 6" pumps only to a wet seam 40 yds from the top, worked by a
12" engine.

*There are two horses underground and seven above for carting. There are two tram-ways worked by one stationary engine and ropes and one horse. The Buildings consist of engine houses, chimney shaft, sawmill storeshed, stabling for 12 horses, Blacksmith's shop, lamp room offices with a weighbridge and offices at the main wharf.*

*The accounting is poor and there are no books. It is reckoned that there is raised 21450 tons per year or $6^1/_2$ acres per year. Profits are said to be about £3000. There is no royalty as the coal belongs to Mr Almond who manages the pit. There is one contractor who is paid 3s/10d per ton and 3s/1d for Cobbles and 1s/6d for slack. The colliers and workmen have no coals given them.*

*Cheadle's 4000 inhabitants are supplied from here and one other small colliery. Prices at the wharf: Coal 10/- per ton, Cobbles 9/2d per ton, Slack 5/- per ton. The colliery is getting at the rate of 50% coal, 10% cobbles and 40% slack. It seems that at the present rate 171 acres will last for 26 years. I am informed that a large area on the south side of Park Hall estate could be rented at a low royalty. The surface rental here is £400 p.a."*

The report gives a good description of the colliery and workings but if the report was designed to sell the colliery, it did not succeed. It did, however, make a good assessment of the colliery's length of life before it took further coal land to rent.

The second tramway and wharf mentioned in the report was a simple selling wharf opposite to Adderley Mill on the Dilhorne Road. Unlike that on the Leek Road there are no buildings remaining or record of the weighbridge which was used there. The remains of the track prove that it was laid on pit spoil and this wharf would be quite useful until Foxfield decided to have a wharf just two hundred yards nearer Brookhouses at New Closefields corner.

*The No. 1 Brigade Rescue team at Park Hall c. 1914/15*

In 1875 Tildesley had recorded seven collieries on the Cheadle coalfield and although most were not to last long it must have meant a measure of competition to Almond.

In 1878 the *Cheadle Herald* reported on what it called Cheadle's first football match. In this context it is the membership of the team, which beat the Leek team, we find of interest. It included to two Almond brothers as backs, seventeen year old William Eli Bowers as a forward, along with Mr. Judge the Midland Bank Manager as captain who scored and David Hancox, the Grammar School master as a forward. There were three Briddens belonging to the blacksmith's shop at the Watt Place end of Bank Street, and of course two umpires. No wonder Cheadle won!

PARK HALL COLLIERY.

REDUCTION IN COAL.

5/10.

Coal delivered in the Town, 7/6 per ton.

Always a good supply ready.

E. E. ALMOND.

CHEADLE PARK COLLIERY.

BEST COALS delivered in the town of Cheadle at **7/6** per Ton.

S. OFFER.

*Prices of Park Hall and Cheadle Park Coal, 1900.*

The trial for ironstone in 1888, noted in the last chapter, was of great importance to Almond as he was the one participant without the experience of this acticity. He had heard of the fortunes to be made in that period just prior to his sinking Park Hall and was just as disappointed as his partners when the boring team reported *"no ironstone"*.

Shortly after the 1883 report W. Southall, the Ipstones contractor took over the managerial duties at Park Hall and at about that time Mr. Wardle was followed by Mr. H. Molyneux and Mr. Seabridge as Under managers. Engineers Riley and, later in the early twentieth century, Charles Steel were on the books as specialists in their field, for time had brought changes, and additional mechanisation demanded engineers to maintain the machines. After an explosion in which three men were burned while using candles, a change was made and Davey lamps, the early type with complete gauze chimney and no glass, were introduced at Park Hall. These lamps were but a half candle power. At about the same time, the steam jet ventilation and, later, the Hopkinson compressed air coal cutter were introduced. When previous to this, the coal cutter was first introduced to the district at Foxfield, it was deemed to be robbing the miners of their work. Some talked of strikes, but the machine was called *"the Iron Mon* [sic]*"* for many years. Almond was, however, more humane than most coalmen of the.day for both he and his wife insisted that their ponies should be brought out of the pit at the end of each day.

The shafts had gone down to 583 feet to get the Woodhead coal, the deepest at the time the mining heads met in 1888. This probably accounted for Almond agreeing to the bore for ironstone being made from the bottom of his shaft. This bore took the known strata depth to 1,151 feet, piercing the Crabtree 'Stinking' coal at two feet thick and continuing to the Grit without finding the ironstone.

Barrow, on his 1898-1900 Geological Survey, had rooms with Marshall, the Chemist, trading where the Co-op furniture store now stands next to the Police Station. He was taken down the major workings by John Carr, the expert sinker. He wrote of the trial, but concluded:

*"this corroborated the evidence already given that the seam does not extend south of the line described."*

Lister was, along with most other Certificated Managers, both interested and knowledgeable in the Geology of the workings. The Ministry demand evidence of such qualities of all men taking charge of collieries and it was shortly to be the case with under-managers and again deputies and shot-firers.

Lister, by 1917, had collected 'eratics' from the Woodhead seam while at Park Hall. These were pieces of a 'foreign' stone which had no place in the seam except by some unaccountable accident when the seam was laid down. He despatched these to the Geological Section of the North Staffordshire Field Club, where, after examination, they were entered in the Report for 1921. They were of white quartzite, quite smooth, weighing some ten pounds each. In October 1918, a new company was formed which brought Arthur Leighton as a Director, from Lancashire and later, his brother Jeffrey joined the board.

At about this time production increase at Park Hall made it necessary to get some connection with the railway so that, as soon as the war was over, plans were made for the line. It ran from the Colliery south towards the railway just over the main road to Brookhouses, over the roads at the Gas Works and then the Green. Here screening and tipping dropped the coal on to the N.S.R. trucks for shunting to the main line and joined New Haden wagons on the main line to Cresswell. Of course, a deal of embanking was necessary and part can still be seen at the old Gas Works site. It was completed by 1920 just at the time Lister left both the W.E.B. service and the cottage at Kingsley Moor. He probably resented the loss of authority under new Directors.

There were accidents at the Park Hall – some fatal – for in 1920 two men lost their lives. "Rifter" Coxon of Cheadle was killed by runaway tubs and in the same year, William Oliver, also of Cheadle, was the victim of gas.

There were other changes around the Park Hall colliery at about this time. There seems to have been a change in the board of directors, members quite unknown to both workmen and management. Lister's place was taken by Thomas Dobson, who had already been in the district for some time. The new company of Mrs. V. A. Bowers and the two Leightons were later joined by a third Leighton and these three lived at Ash Hall when in the district. They were joined in 1920 by Messrs. E. Adams and O. W. Hesketh. Mr. Mason was later introduced as an agent and Mr. Griffiths became under-manager.

*Parkhall Colliery*

*The Park Hall Colliery manager's in 1928. From left to right: Messrs. Griffiths, Under Manager; Mason, Agent; Dobson, Manager; the two Leighton brothers, Directors; Steel Engineer.*

By 1925 definite efforts were made to increase production with three hundred and eighty men working towards the clearing of Park Hall coal land. Within the next eighteen months the board were making plans to use the capital under their direction. They decided that efforts must be made to take over the big neighbour, Foxfield, and with the consent of Mr. Fielden of Dilhorne Hall, the change came in 1927. The new colliery could use that direct line to the railway and also have connecting haulage roads underground between the two pits.

Park Hall completed its history by 1930 and the illustration shows the men in charge at its end.

## The Foxfield Colliery

About 1874 an attempt at mining the Woodhead coal was made on the west bank of the Dairy House brook. This brook rose near the top of Richmoor Hill and made its way to Godley Brook and once provided the Mill leet to work the Adderley Mill.

It seems that prospects were good for the promoters, who erected sheds and constructed a tramway from near the ford across the brook by Dairy House Lane up to the Bank Top road. Here a wharf was made from which the coal was sold. The site of the old tramway can easily be found today after a spell of dry weather.

The Whitehursts had probably explored this area for coal and ironstone some three centuries earlier. In fact, the area had been called Above Park Pits. Some coal had been mined in the vicinity as long ago as 1850 when Alexander Bowers had worked both Rider and Woodhead near to their outcropping. As early as 1817 a sale notice for the fifty acre farm emphasised that *"The coal is of superior nature, may be got at trivial expense"*.

No mining had been done near the Foxfield. Mrs. Holliday at the manorial hall at Dilhorne had refused her business colleague, Samual Bamford, the right to look for coal there and even threatened, through Blagg, her lawyer, to have her gamekeeper and his assistants remove him and his friends if they were found on the Foxfield trespassing for game! However, around 1881 some one by the name of Twigg was sinking a shaft either for himself or perhaps the Mann brothers, who had found the Above Park working unprofitable.

As yet there do not appear to be any lease documents available, at least on the Mann's side. A grandson, Peter Mann, of Derby informed me that there are no documents, but he does have a barometer stamped '*Foxfield Colliery*'. This void is most unfortunate for the venture was to develop into the coalfield's most important feature, mining over a wider field and lasting longer than any others, continuing to nationalisation in 1947 and exhaustion in 1965, a total of eighty-four years production.

At that time a new colliery would normally take the place name if that was a worthwhile feature such as Park Hall, Cheadle Park and the Birches, but this time, the name of the owners was preferable to that of a field. It, therefore, became Mann's Pit with E. Jones as Manager and stayed so until ten years had passed when it reverted to the field name in its new limited liability company status. The Mann brothers were Directors and Mr. Sims as Manager, to be followed shortly by Mr. A. Fisher, Mr. H. Pointon and shortly by Cheadle's first Certificated Manager, Benia Parker.

The first of the twenty-six underground plans made during the whole working period shows the area worked in 1882 in what the men were calling the Wallsend seam; a local nickname this, whilst another group used an even more unlikely name, 'the Daffodil'.

The Dilhorne coal was but twenty-five feet deep here and it was said that the first pithead gear was using the Dilhorne seam as a foundation. These workings went northerly to approach Whitehurst, but did not extend beyond in that year. A similar block was mined south of the shaft some fifty yards beyond the school. In 1885 a working plan was made by H. Goodwin, another Manager, and by 1887 the shaft was down to nearly 750 feet. In September the following year, the first Woodhead coal was lifted from 751 feet. The Foxfield seam at 1ft 8 ins. thick was being worked at 278 feet deep.

As usual this first Woodhead coal demanded a celebration, not the usual procession around Dilhorne, but a grand supper for all staff at the Wagon and Horses; a first for the Milwards.

It was necessary to provide transport and a wharf for the sale of this Woodhead coal to compete with Park Hall and Cheadle Park for Cheadle custom. The Old Engine tramway of fifty years earlier was to be re-opened, but worked in the reverse direction. The line was built to cross the road at the Rose and Crown to reach the pit where wagons were loaded, trammed along the line past the Old Engine to a new wharf somehere much nearer Cheadle at the Newclosefields Lane end. Small locos were used for this transport while the system was in operation for the next five years.

As the output of Woodhead increased Foxfield found it necessary, as had other pits, to find means for wider distribution. The Cheadle railway, at this time, appeared after the sod cutting of 1888, set to reach Cheadle without offering any help in the Foxfield direction and the management decided to 'go it alone'. Along with the Newclosefields line they had already constructed the track and wharf for another line to serve any customers to the north, i.e. Cellarhead, Wetley Rocks and on towards Cheddleton. The wharf was on the Bank Top roadside just to the south of the Little Above Park Lane and this site also can still be found with the track running down to join the pit area.

There became a real need to solve the distribution problem. By 1892 Foxfield's own railway line was started and completed in less than eight months and coal was being put on the main North Staffordshire Railway at Blythe Bridge to serve a much larger area. In this respect Foxfield had an eight-year advantage over all other Cheadle collieries. Times must have been good for another Wagon and Horses Supper, with owners and Manager; Benia Parker, took charge of the celebrations. Within a couple of years steam jet ventilation was working well and there were 107 men down underground and 30 about the Bank.

Allan Baker gives an excellent account of the Foxfield line construction in his book *The Cheadle Collieries and their Railway*, 1986.

From 1897 with the working of the Woodhead coal, it became most urgent to get those trucks full and onto the main line. The most important working extended up to 1904 towards Dilhorne village until 1904 and shortly after another group worked on to 1925. With another working toward the Newclosefield area in the south from 1912-23 the colliery was thriving. Its total manpower had risen to over 200 with an output of 50,000 tons per annum.

Of course, Foxfield had its accidents and these were reported in the *Cheadle and Tean Times*. In July, 1907, John Whitehurst of Cellarhead was killed by a roof fall. It was four years later in October 1911, that Luke Harvey of Godley Lane was killed at the age of 72 years. Just one year later Thomas James aged 45 years, a banksman, badly injured his foot and died shortly after.

A fourth heading into the Woodhead had been started in 1916, working towards the Hazelwall and Park Hall boundaries whilst in 1923 the Dilhorne seam was tackled towards the old Delphouse site. The former was followed for thirty-six years, the latter for only sixteen.

At about this period, 1924-5, the successful Foxfield enterprise, having lost its original founders, the Manns brothers, and also the son, Abel, appeared also to lose some of its drive from the Board Room. Although its production was maintained by the increasing manpower, now totalling nearly four hundred persons, it came as a shock when rumours spread about the relations between Foxfield and little brother, Park Hall. The latter had been working for fifty years and must have been approaching its boundaries, but in 1918 it had become a different organisation. There were now no male Bowers partners, only Bowers capital under Mrs. Aubrey Bowers, to push it along, but by 1918 it was a company led by Arthur Leighton, and Cheadle miners were, within five or six years, to witness something of a miracle. The dying old Park Hall was, revived by a new Board. J. J. Leighton, E. Adams and O. W. Hesketh were the new Directors by 1920 and in the next four years they were working Woodhead to the east of the Leek Road. There was a deal of negotiation before the Fieldens, who had taken over the Dilhorne estate from the Bullers, agreed to the change. Some heard that it cost the companies £10,000 and the revived Park Hall organisation had taken over Foxfield in its prime. By 1928 we began to see the newly named Park Hall and Foxfield Colliery railway trucks.

Thomas Dobson was once again on the scene, holding by now the most important mining position, Certificated Manager, to this new coal empire which was working with nearly four hundred operatives. By 1930 the Park Hall company had gone into liquidation. It had been in existence for fifty-seven years and up to that time was the longest lasting pit on the Cheadle coalfield. Indeed, it had come up to the expectations of that 1883 report.

The Foxfield Colliery now took over all operations and although there were underground connections, it was more logical to use the direct railway facilities from the Dilhorne side. The other wharves had been closed for many years and all output was railed.

Every effort was made to bring the Foxfield equipment up to date, in fact, more than

£30,000, an enormous sum in the depression days of the 1930s, was paid for it including electric air compressors, screens and slack washers and now a real innovation on the Cheadle coalfield, new concrete headgears for the shaft.

From this date onwards every possible means to increase production to pay for the capital expended was used. The Woodhead, Dilhorne and Four Foot seams were worked in one section or another continuously. Two major stables were constructed underground, one housing nine ponies, the other four, attended by two ostlers.

A succession of managers and under-managers, men like Messrs. Bowden, Cutts, Brown and Venn had the growing responsibility for the mine. Cutts joined the Workers' Educational Association's branch in Cheadle and others showed that the examinations had broadened their outlook on life.

By 1935 one of the earliest workings in the Foxfield or Wallsend seam had been re-opened and worked on and off until 1939 when it was abandoned. J. R. Ball, the Certificated Manager, extended Goodwin's 1885 plan and again marked down the section as unprofitable.

In the early years of the 1930s the government, faced with a most severe depression and, therefore, reduced use of coal, cut down the output of coal from each mine, so that the quota at Foxfield came down to 150,000 tons for the year. This was considerably less than it was capable of, especially since some hundred men had been transferred from the old Park Hall workings to start in new workings at Foxfield. There were new workings in the Woodhead toward the New Haden boundary from 1932 to 1934 but output was cut to a half of capacity. This was continued for another three years after restrictions ceased from 1939 to 1942, with Woodhead working in a westerly direction, under Kelson Well. A further set of workings in the Woodhead started in 1935 working southeast until 1952.

Every effort was made to use the Dilhorne coal so that by 1946 the Woodhead, Dilhorne and Fourfoot were producing quite heavily. During the war years production was encouraged although many men volunteered for the Forces. New Haden reckoned some two hundred and fifty volunteers had joined through the six years 1939-45. With the introduction of the Bevin Boys scheme (when Ernest Bevin, the trade union man, was asked by Churchill in May 1940 to organise man power for industry) the working force was partially returned to strength. By the time the forces returned in 1946, although a number of the Bevin Boys left for other employment, the work force had risen to 540 men, both underground and on the bank.

The next year, 1947, the coal industry was nationalised and Foxfield worked for eighteen years as a National Coal Board unit. During the first year the Alecs seam was started in the direction south toward Cheadle Gas Works which was approached by 1959. This joined another heading which had worked the same seam in 1946. It was a great block south and west, stretching from Dilhorne to Newclose Fields and further south to Adderley Mill and on to the Blake Hall boundary. Another working in the Alecs was started in 1947 – a large block taken out by 1959 around old shafts. Three of these had previously been down to the half yard coal at 2.2 yards and another 60 yards to the Yard coal while a third had sunk 75 yards to the Litley coal.

The work force in 1947 had been 545 men and the total output had risen to 167,410 tons when the manager, R. F. Lovatt, had signed Abandonment Plans for a large section of Woodhead mining in 1952. This was the beginning of prolonged increase of both manpower and output tonnage until 1954 when the figures had reached 551 men and 210,813 tons. At this period of expansion management had been in the hands of Mr. Bowden and Mr. Brown, but by 1959 Mr. D. Alcock was the manager to sign another Abandonment in that year.

After 1954 both tonnage and manpower decreased, the former quite evenly until the year before closure. It had finished at 115,478 tons whilst manpower began a more even fall from the 1958 high down to its finishing figure of 361. For the previous years many men had moved into the Potteries coalfield while in 1965 the Board had distributed the remainder among the most convenient units.

Foxfield had mined nearly all there was from the three seams mentioned earlier and had worked for eighty-three years. This was certainly a record for Cheadle pits, but in the last thirty years its boundaries stretched much further than any other had.

Total production over the whole period is not available, but the figures from 1947 to 1965 show a production of more than three million tons in the eighteen years. There is no doubt that this total will appear small in the Potteries Coalfield, but from a sixty year old unit at Cheadle it proved a worthy swansong!

## The Delphouse Colliery

The earlier years of the Delphouse were dealt with in Chapter Nine where it was shown that Offer had followed a number of operators who had worked the site for almost a century. Readers will recall the Old Sawney Pit in the Scriven Reports of 1842. Its attraction was that a number of seams had been found in the vicinity, but at Delphouse the main obstacle, the Bunter Sandstone, could be discounted. Offer brought his Draycott Colliery Company in 1885 to this site when there were at least a dozen other workings on the coalfield. Unfortunately this did not last for long, a matter of three years, but offer was not particularly concerned as the money lost was that of the investors. He merely drew his salary as manager until the next job appeared, in this case Cheadle Park.

When the Cheadle Park changed hands in 1887 before A. S. Bolton's death, (in 1901) Offer brought a new Draycott Coal Company to make a more determined effort at Delphouse. The occasion is best described by the Reverend Carlos in his magazine for February 1895:

> *"Good news for Cheadle Everyone has noticed that the winding machinery at the Delf-house Pit, and at the Pit on the opposite side of the road is being put in order. It is found that the pumping at the Draycott shaft is draining these Pits, and it is intended therefore to open these Pits again and get out the lower coal. This means, we hope, plenty of work for Cheadle colliers."*

There must have been every confidence in the success of the operation at this attempt for the number of men employed increased from forty in that first year to over fifty in the second and up to eighty by the end of the century. It was also necessary after two years to employ G. Wright as under-manager.

The Reverend Carlos appeared to reflect the satisfaction of the Cheadle mining community when he included another item on Delphouse in his magazine for August 1896:

> *"It will interest some of our readers to know that in the course of opening the Delf-house Pits, various relics of old workings of 50 years ago have been found. A pit wagon, some miners tools, and even some candles which were quite hard and burnt as well as any bought in Cheadle today."*

The management seemed to be concentrating on the four feet coal and, with the exception of a short break in 1898, things went very well. The fact that Offer was holding the colliery managerial positions was not conducive to good all round relations. This was even more forcefully indicated when, by the end of 1898 Offer accepted a position of Engineer to the struggling Cheadle railway company. He continued with the Delphouse works though there was no doubt that he was more concerned with completing the railway tunnel and line to Cheadle station.

Unfortunately his railway work had many unforseen difficulties and, although at its completion all cheered him, the faults began to show within two years. Offer discharged himself from both colliery and railway positions, being quite disillusioned and prepared to leave the country.

The Log Book of the Wesleyan School of Charles Street for January 14, 1903, carries the following entry:

*"Charlotte Offer ceases duty today as she and her parents are going to South Africa."*

The date and style of the entry indicate a more than usual haste.

Over the centuries the Delphouse area had been an easy site to mine. Before the nineteenth century, coal men had found the upper seams had been mined during the period when no one worried about planning the workings or even filling disused shafts. The Yard coal, generally reckoned the best quality, had been mined in the early nineteenth century. The four feet seam had been found first under the lower reaches of the district, especially approaching the Tean brook. It was found at the Sham at a mere one hundred and thirty-five feet. Nearer the Boundary all seams were slightly deeper, but at the Delphouse there was no Bunter to cut through with the result that by the end of the nineteenth century it was possible to find a total of nineteen shafts. Many of these were left unfilled into the early twentieth century. A good sough or level was taken from one of the lower shafts for a distance of just over half a mile to the Tean brook where it emptied its water just one hundred and fifty yards from the bridge. This doubtless helped to unwater many of the pits. These shafts gathered some quite unusual nicknames. The Bull Engine pits were the two shafts by the main road on the bend leading up to the Elms entrance. Many will remember that after the war they were used for dumping superfluous material and have been used quite recently. The Bull Engine nickname was derived from the fact that the engines were of Bull type and manufacture. Coal was brought out from these shafts at only forty yards deep.

No. 1 and No. 2 pits, one hundred and fifty yards from the road were called the Garden Pits because they were sunk in the gardens of the original Delphouse. This old house, home of the generations of Colcloughs, stood near the old pre-turnpike road, the lower end is marked today by two tall yew trees near the field gate. The Four Foot coal depth here was some eighty yards.

The Wood shaft was sunk in the little piece of woodland which thrived there in the early nineteenth century and some sixty yards to the west was the Willow shaft, again in the woodland. Both shafts had been used in the early days to mine the two yard coal as had three or four other shafts.

The No. 3 shaft, one of the latest, stood by the side of its engine house. The tramway ran by the side of this when it was built later to take its coal to join the New Haden sidings.

About 1902 Stephen Offer's son, who now reckoned himself a surveyor, was allowed to take a level from No. 1 shaft, through the fault marked on the Barrow map, to contact the Bull Engine shaft. The intention was to go through to get some of the remaining Blake Hall coal. Unfortunately, the Bull shaft was completely waterlogged with Blake Hall water which followed the men so quickly that they barely escaped up No. 1.

Since that time the New Haden company, under Slater, employed most expensive pumps in these shafts to keep New Haden workings below quite dry.

By 1903 with the departure of its manager, the enterprise collapsed, but by the following year there were strong rumours hinting that it was likely to reopen with a definite attempt on the Woodhead coal.

In the Parish magazine for January 1905, the Reverend B. S. Carlos wrote:

> "We were most thankful and most hopeful when the new coal was found at Delphouse (1904) but the town has not felt any benefit from it."

Although, in that previous century the Delphouse area could offer prospectors a variety of coals – the section of the beds under Delphouse Hollow shows that all five upper coals were available – the Woodhead had not been tackled. At the same time, it was one of the three workings connected with the railway and not dependent on local demand.

When, however, Delphouse did reopen it concentrated on the Dilhorne seam at 2ft 8in thick. This was continued until Slater took over for New Haden.

## The Litley and Cheadle Park Colliery

Over the last quarter of the nineteenth century, the student of the history of the Cheadle coalfield detects a slightly different atmosphere to do with the setting up of workings, the style of working and the people who came to take part, in one way or another, in the winning of the coal. As has been previously stated, this field was quite small, indeed compared to coalfields such as the North and South Staffordshire, the Cheadle was looked upon as insignificant. Usually, the folk mining the coal belonged to the district or had estates, even small estates, or some rights in the soil. Even the Duke of Devonshire had his own estate here in the eighteenth century. Those who busied themselves in coal getting were people the locals knew, who had been in mining before . In the late 1800s, however, mining men took employment from owners and managers they had not met before and it appeared that they were intent on introducing methods and tools from the larger coalfields.

*Cheadle Park Colliery before the headframe was built.*

One of the earliest was the Birmingham Brass and Copper manufacturers of the family of Bolton who came in 1852 to make real success of the Oakamoor company, previously the Patten's Cheadle Brass and Copper Company.

Alfred Sohier Bolton has been mentioned in an earlier chapter, more particularly in his dealings with

Robert Plant, but his activities had a much wider scope than those portrayed. He moved when Moor Court was completed and, knowing that the works was progressing satisfactorily, tried to discover if the coal industry had anything to offer him. From 1870 he began to show a greater interest in mining. He went to Ipstones to look at an engine which was to be auctioned at the Newhouse Colliery, the disused *'Skin and Grief'* pit closed for more than three years. He looked over the Ipstones Park ironstone mines. He went to watch men sinking the exploratory shafts when Charles Bill, who owned the Gibridding woods off the Woodhouse property, hoped to strike the stone. In 1872 he visited one of Plant's failures, Rakeway Colliery, to look at an engine up for sale.

A previous chapter dealt with the Churston sale of the Cheadle properties in 1872 and here A. S. Bolton took the first definite steps to becoming a coal master. He paid out some £35,000 for property having seams of coal and, one step further, acquired the manorial rights, becoming Lord of the Manor of Cheadle, a title he held until he died in 1901. His diary reads *"1872, May 23. A.S.B. bought Litley Farm, Sweet Hills Plantation and Cheadle Park Farm (+ Manorial rights) from Lord Churston."*

By the following November the, first positive steps were taken:

> *"Went to Litley to meet Jos. Hurst of Majors Barn* [the lane, the Colliery not opened] *about getting coal under Litley."*

His diary entries throw light not only on his own activities, but also of others in the industry, from small-time men to officials. He enjoyed learning from such men and shortly began to show the capitalist attitude in his dealings. He had descended from a

*A group of men and boys at Cheadle Park Colliery who worked half day for the South African War Fund on Saturday December 16th 1899.*

*An early view of the Colliery*

strong non-conformist family. His grandparents had been buried in a Quaker Meeting House graveyard in Birmingham which had been cleared when in 1837 the London Birmingham Railway had required the use of the site to erect its station. In 1877 he had borrowed the rails from the Litley coal workings to carry stone from the quarry in Moss's Wood to build his Free Church in Oakamoor.

His connection with Joseph Hurst at Litley lasted until 1880 and appeared to be a useful and worthwhile partnership. No reason was given after 1880 as to why the diary does not mention his name. After the first meeting things moved quickly. Hurst informed Bolton on November 11th 1873, at the Brassworks (Oakamoor) *"that he could get 4'coal at Litley at5/-"*. Within a few days they had agreed where the shafts should be sunk and they were to be lined with bricks taken from some old shafts. Whilst removing the bricks they also came across a few cwts of slack. In the first few days of January 1874, a serious effort was made by Hurst on a shaft near the Huntley Lane, just off the Litley drive and paddock. Just across the line and in the corner with the Harplow Lane, Taylor Bagshaw, from the Elms, was also sinking. After just twelve yards sinking, they found the four foot coal, but the following day found old men workings. These were worked through after a short distance and Hurst with his assistant, Booth, continued by digging a second shaft. This Litley working continued apace though there is no mention of the quantities of coal mined. There were some few altercations when Bagshaw was warned that his workings must not cross under the lane and Blagg was called to instruct him about trespass.

Bolton had a full three months buying second-hand cage timber for pit head gear and a portable engine. He also had his share of frustration: *"Went to fix engine at the colliery but driving wheels too small."* The engineer in Bolton delighted in this period.

Within another three months Bagshaw had failed and Bolton had bought him out. He also continued to spend money as in the case quoted in the Plant chapter. He bought coal under fifteen acres of Pilkington land not far from his Litley estate and in 1875 Edward Blythe went to a London auction to buy land at Harplow next to Litley at a cost of £1,790. In August a new pit was being sunk to find the coal in that Harplow piece not so far from Bagshaw's working. It proved successful and they were now searching for the Litley and the yard coal.

Bolton was, without doubt, one of the most interested coal master capitalists in the district, despite the experience in coal that W. E. Bowers had with his family's long connections. The Litley enterprise must have continued for there are no further mentions of Hurst, Booth and Litley until early 1880 when Robert Plant made a request for a lease of the Litley coal and this was agreed in April. The story, a sorry one for Bolton, was told above.

At the end of 1883 F. Southall, who had been, for twenty-five years, contracting in the ironstone field around Ipstones and Foxt, approached Bolton for a lease of any ironstone that could be found under his small piece of land in Foxt. Bolton agreed, but by January, 1884, the two men met again in rather different circumstances. He was invited to Blagg's office where he found Alfred Barclay, a mining engineer he had met some ten years earlier over the Bagshaw transactions. He was accompanied by Fred Southall. and Samuel Pointon, who had spent twenty years, and had already been bankrupt, in the ironstone industry. He was, however, now living at Butler's Hill while Southall was in Watt Place. They asked for a lease of the coal under Cheadle Park, a request which probably surprised Bolton, as, for the last ten years, his interest had been in Litley. It appears that some form of verbal agreement was made at Blaggs for a week later the three met at the Park to find a likely spot for the pit. A site was chosen at the southern end of the flat stretch, long known as the Racecourse and used as such for local competition on Fair days and holidays. When the pit was sunk, known officially as Cheadle Park Colliery, it retained its old nickname as Racecourse Pit.

*The first load of Woodhead Coal was raised at Cheadle Park on 17th June 1887 and was taken to Alfred S. Bolton at Moor Court, Oakamoor. The mine closed in 1915.*

There is no doubt that in the first three months there were signs of feverish activity for Pointon and Southall, the leasees, paid an initial fee of £50 to enable them to begin on the layout without fear of interruption.

Southall, who, apparently, had also become manager, set about arranging for a wharf at the bottom of Park Lane to serve the nearby Leek Road and running a tramway from the pit to this wharf which would be 600 yards long. The pit itself was 350 yards from the Leek Road and west of Harwood Park.

The following twelve months were very disappointing for Bolton for there was little progress. Southall had only half finished the tramway which meant that Bolton had to pay a trespass fee to the farming tenant, Mrs. Whitehurst.

By the middle of 1885 little seemed to be moving although Bolton visited monthly and had given it a suitable name, the Manor Colliery, because of its strong connection with the manorial rights, but this never took precedence over the Racecourse in local favour. There was, however, a new name mentioned. *"Drove in trap to Cheadle Park to see the new Colliery there which Stubble is working (or rather proposes to work)."* The name was not mentioned again and Southall had finished.

By the middle of 1886 the two shafts, both the 10ft and the 8ft were completed while Plant and his partner, Miller, were asking for a lease on Litley. By this time Bolton could not understand the reason for this delay and when he was approached by partners from the Draycott Colliery Company, Mr. Dickinson and Manager, Mr. J. Lockett, with a view to taking a lease on the colliery, he agreed, although Pointon was to remain a partner. Indeed, hoping for the best, Bolton had offered to make the new company a loan by December 1886.

Within a few months in the new year Pointon had fallen out with his partners, although they were not far from the Woodhead at 522ft deep, and had left, whilst Stephen Offer had been appointed manager. On Queen Victoria's Golden Jubilee, June 17th 1887, two very large pieces of the Woodhead were mounted on a waggon to be decorated and photographed, with Offer leaning on the waggon. The whole workforce surrounded the load, many armed with picks and shovels and the under-manager, bowler-hatted Mr. Hollinshead, showing the safety lamp. It paraded the town and then took the journey to Moor Court, a

Cheadle Park Colliery in 1890

very welcome present to the Boss after three years of waiting! He entered in his diary on that June day *"They sent me from Cheadle Park Colliery a load of Woodhead coal, the first that had been raised"*. It was April 1888, before the endless rope tramway was quite completed and in working order down to the wharf by Park Lane. During the next month things must have improved to such an extent that Bolton discussed with Offer the question of building him a new house although, strictly speaking, Offer was put of the company, rather than servant to Bolton. This did not materialise for in a short time Offer was in Monkhouse Villa, a big house, until 1894 and by 1896 he had promoted himself to the 'Elms'.

By 1900 Offer was appointed engineer to the new Cheadle Railway, specifically to complete the last section of the railway to Cheadle which included the scourge of the scheme, the tunnel. James Lockett, now assumed the managerial position at Cheadle Park Colliery.

It is possible that A. P. Dickinson stayed for as long as he could. He was initially an investor unfortunate in the choice of partners. He had been with Offer on a number of drastic failures and hoped the Cheadle Park would recoup some of his losses. In that year, when Dickinson became Company Secretary it was decided to mine the Cobble coal at some 270 ft deep and this branch continued until the Cobble was worked out by 1913.

In 1904 there was a great celebration at the *"Finding of the Dilhorne Coal at the Draycott Colliery"*. This was Cheadle Park's other partner, although no Cheadle Park people are mentioned in the notice in the local paper. There may, however, have been something to crow about as in June 1905, a quite positive account appears:

> *"Another Recovery of Coal at Cheadle Park.*
> *On the 8th inst. the Dilhorne Seam was won at Cheadle Park. After a long and expensive search by James Lockett at Draycott Colliery a year ago, Mr. Lockett has been busily engaged in laying down modern screening plant and electric coal cutting machinery. In addition, Mr. Lockett, one of three Directors of Cheadle Park Colliery Company Ltd. has, for some years, been working a neighbouring property to Draycott, under the management of Mr. Lockett's son, Mr. William Lockett, F.G.S., Agent at Draycott Colliery.*
> *An impression has for some time been prevalent that Cheadle Park was getting rapidly worked out. Between the Cobble workings and the borehole midway between Cheadle Park and Draycott, which proved the Dilhorne last year, discovered at Draycott a great fault. Mr. Wm. Lockett had a tunnel driven upwards through the fault for 71 yards, met a rich seam 60 yards from the surface 5ft thick. This was the Dilhorne seam. Under this lay the Cobble and the Woodhead. It is calculated that these could yield 3,093,550 tons of saleable coal!"*

This must have been wishful thinking!

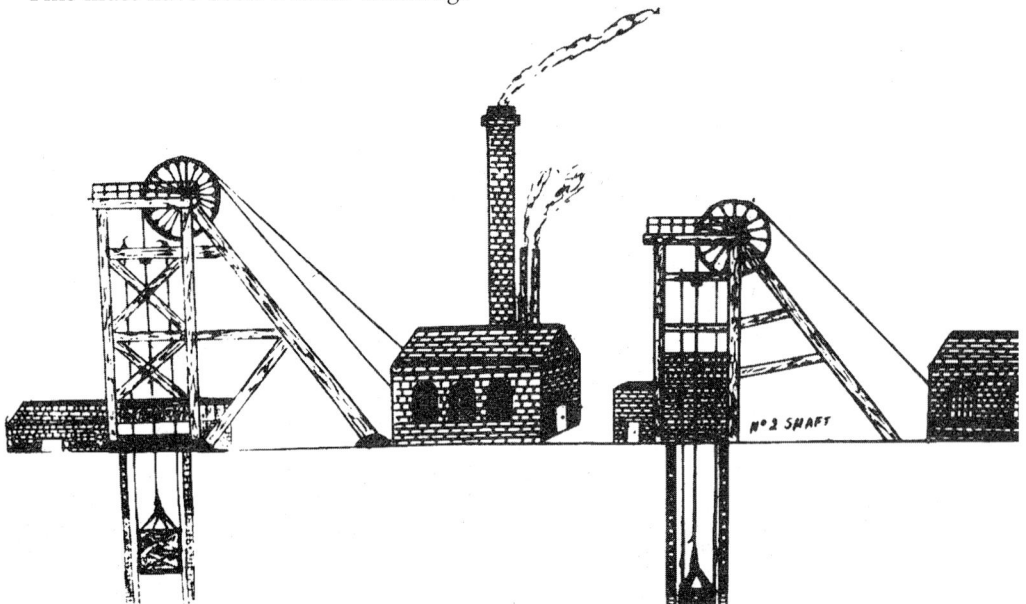

*Parkhall Colliery in 1929*

A. S. Bolton had died in 1901, no doubt a shock for many of both Oakamoor and the new Froghall Mill men but the coal men had mostly forgotton him. Stephen Offer had left the country in 1903, but many coalmen continued to remember him for many a year! The work at the Racecourse continued without making fortunes for anyone. Some men remembered when Dickinson, in a moment of depression confided in some of them, with tears in his eyes, recalling how he had come to invest in the 1880s under Offer's management in the Draycott projects with £60,000 to make a fortune, but left Cheadle Park with nothing.

By 1908 there were but forty-nine men underground and slowly reaching the boundaries of their lease.

The Cobble seam working was completed in 1913 having worked well under the Harewood Park ground to the north and well beyond Park Farm and the pool to the

*Foxfieid Colliery in 1929 (above)*
*Delphhouse in 1920 (below) These*
*were drawn locally for the author*

south-west where Lockett's crut to that Dilhorne 5 ft is shown on the plans. The Woodhead was not mined to beyond 1914. When J. H. Lister asked to see the plans in 1920 he said he was concerned with the accumulation of water.

At closure William Lockett took a few men to work a level at Lockwood but this only lasted two years.

On July 30th 1915, the following advertisement appeared:

*"CHEADLE PARK COLLIERY. Tenders are wanted for willing up two coal shafts at the above colliery. For particulars and to view: Apply Geo Pyatt, Majors Barn, Cheadle."*

## The New Haden Colliery

We have seen that toward the end of the nineteenth Century there was increased activity in the Draycott Cross and Harplow area. Since 1845 when Vavasour wrote of his 'Infant Colliery' to the end of that century there were failures. There were, however, no high hopes when another sinking was tried near the Cheadle end of the new railway tunnel, although it was known that coal had been despatched by rail over a short period from the Draycott end of the tunnel. As the construction of the tunnel was completed at the end of 1900, a subsidiary of that company with the grandiose title, The Cheadle Railway, Mineral and Land Co. began a shaft near the east end planning for sidings to operate with the main railway line to Cheadle. At last the coal men had their ideal transport system but, apart from Foxfield and this new enterprise, the others had to find ways of connecting.

The earliest efforts found a Mr. Dickinson, who, it was thought, had capital to invest as a senior director and in this small concern he was expected to take, on occasion,

*A procession with the first New Haden coal raised. Taken outside the old Roebuck Inn, 1904.*

## PARISH OF CHEADLE.

At a largely attended Meeting held in the Assembly Room at the Royal Oak Hotel, on Thursday evening (Mr. T. B. Cull, Chairman of the Parish Council presiding), it was unanimously decided to hold

# A DEMONSTRATION

**And Decorate the Town with Flags and Bunting on**

## Saturday Afternoon, May 21,

### TO CELEBRATE THE FINDING OF THE

# DILHORNE COAL

### At the DRAYCOTT COLLIERY.

The Celebration to take the following form—

# PROCESSION

To start from the Colliery Office at 3 p.m. The Public are invited to join in Procession at Brookhouses and proceed to the Church, at which a short Service will be held, after which the Procession will be re-formed and proceed through High Street, Tape Street, New Street, Charles Street and Watt Place, there dispersing.

### Order of Procession—

Mounted Police.
Cheadle Town Band.
District and Parish Councillors.
The Draycott Colliery Directorate.
Clerical Staff.
A Piece of the Newly-Found Coal.
Draycott Colliery Workmen.
Fire Brigade.
General Public.
Church Lads' Brigade.
Carriages, Horsemen, Cyclists, &c.

Cheadle, May 19th, 1904.

J. CUMBERBATCH,
Sec. to the Meeting.

J. LOWNDES, PRINTER, CHEADLE.

*A notice issued in 1904*

secretarial and probably other supervisory duties. A photograph of the sinking of the shaft shows, among others, Jack Carr, the well known shaft sinker and Bert Plant, 'old Uncle Bert Ninety' who had spent his working life with the Delphouse and Draycott company and was not to stay on until this venture became the New Haden. From 1901 we heard of Klondyke with S. Offer and J. Lockett in charge.

That shaft was to become the No. 7 much later and by 1902 the four feet coal at 3ft 8 ins. thick was being worked at some sixty yards deep, but when No. 8 shaft was completed, it was sixty-four yards deep. It worked to both north and south of the shafts to find old men workings on all sides. At one time the men took out the Litley coal, a 2ft 8 ins. seam, some thirty feet above the 4 ft at this point. It was abandoned in August 1904 after the celebrations shown in the illustrations, leading to one more bad period in the coal story.

The two new shafts, however, could not be left unused. Mr. John Lockett had joined Mr. Dickinson for a second attempt to use the shafts to good purpose, for all felt that they knew more about the business after the publication of Barrow's Survey in 1903.

On March 1st 1905, Lockett set out to let Cheadle and its engineers know of his qualities. He gave an address in the Town Hall, advertised as for miners, weavers and copper workers on the subject, George Stephenson, the engineer.

The following week the *Cheadle and Tean Times* carried a most optimistic article describing progress. Such was the enthusiasm that the locals adopted the name of the gold working in the extreme north of America. The paper described the impatience at the delay in getting this "Klondyke" to work:

*"There is a large amount of work, both above and below. There are about 200 people at present employed, these include those who send up 100 tons per day."*

After mentioning that it was but a short time since the second shaft had been fully working, it continues:

*"Mr. Smith* (this was J. Smith, the manager) *hopes for a thousand tons per day in a few years. The screens are well advanced and the sidings setting ready to load five trucks at a time. Electricity was being used to drive the machinery, for lighting, engines dynamos to get good quality coal. The wharf will open next Monday for the sale*

*of coal at Cheadle Station."*

However, despite the enthusiasm the enterprise was not paying. It appears that this over-manning of the new colliery, led by the end of that year to another closed period.

The February 1906 number of the Parish Magazine carried Rev. Carlos' impressions of the situation:

*"KLONDYKE*
*It is with the greatest regret that we see the Klondyke Colliery once more stop work-*
*ing. In former days the work there was always irregular, but we hoped that the new*
*coal would provide constant employment for its colliers for many years. It is a great*
*disappointment to find the work there already stopped, – and the most serious part is*
*that no one knows how long the stoppage may last. If the 200 men working at Klondyke*
*have to scatter to other collieries in the district, it will be as great a blow to our little*
*town as when the Silk Mill stopped, and the mill girls had to go to Rocester, or any-*
*where, for work. We hope such a disaster may be averted."*

Shortly after an appeal was made for the Klondyke men and the Rev. Carlos wrote as follows:

*"KLONDYKE*
*The appeal for the Klondyke miners and their families has met with a fair response,*
*but we urge all Klondyke men to face the painful necessity of seeking work elsewhere.*
*They have our full sympathy, but the number of men is so large that it is beyond the*
*resource, of a place like Cheadle to do more than help them for a few weeks. We hope*
*each week will find fewer and fewer dependent on the fund. It is unreasonable to*
*think that so valuable a colliery will. not be able to find a purchaser at last, and then*
*the present Klondyke miners ought to have the first offer of work, so as to return, if*
*they please, to their home-place."*

On August 10th, 1906, *The Cheadle Herald* announced that Klondyke had closed.

John Smith's confidence was not well placed and both he and his under-manager, George Wright, had to make a change. Wright was a local man, born in 1848, working in coal from the age of nine and later at the face. By 1888 he was certificated and was under-manager for the Draycott company for eight years.

John Smith's son, Joseph, moved to the Minnie Pit in the Potteries just in time to be near the great disaster there in 1918. The Potteries newspaper *The Evening Sentinel* published a photograph showing him as a member of the rescue team.

There must have been a measure of publicity around the closing of Klondyke, for by the autumn, there were signs of activity around the shafts and a new name, Higginbottom, was mentioned, after he had been seen inspecting the preparations for work. It was not long before two other gentlemen, the Bassano brothers, were seen and the strange name, quite unknown around this little town, was said to belong to the new purchasers with that Mr. Higginbottom as the Managing Director. It had happened in October 1906, but the Lease document was signed on the 16th March 1907:

*"made between the said Thomas Edward Milborne Swinnerton Pilkington of the one*
*part and Bassano Bros. Ltd. of the other part being a lease of mines as the same*
*stand."*

The following April the men were called to work by a new Blower, as the coal face was ready to produce. By October, of 250 men, many were connecting with Delphouse.

A further Indenture varied the above. It was dated 15th September 1910, and made between the Bassano Bros., Thomas Pilkington, Henry Sharrock Higginbottom and Richard Taylor of the third part and New Haden Collieries of the fourth part. These established the framework of the new Colliery and the *Cheadle and Tean Times* proclaimed the new name, New Haden Collieries.

Although Cheadle was loathe to forget the Klondyke it only stayed for four or five years. This new name, Haden, had been brought by the new owners from Old Hill in South Staffordshire where they lived at Haden Cross. This name was destined to stay, even though new owners have come and gone, indeed the coal industry has gone, but that name lives on, having been adopted by new industry and the district.

The colliery must have become a stable unit sufficient for the colliery to have its first football match on the first anniversary of the re-opening and A. H. Bassano kicked off. The Players were not to know what a tradition they were starting in October 1907.

The week before the *Cheadle and Tean Times* had written:

> *"It is now twelve months since New Haden was acquired by the present proprietors. It has been a wonderful year's work. It was a fortunate day for this place when the attention of Messrs. Bassano Bros. was drawn to it."*

This note of praise was often found in the local press. We also heard of our old friend, Benia Parker, who had left Hazlewall for Shafferlong with his contractor, Hollinshead, and now, in 1908, they celebrated by carting a 30 cwt lump of coal around Leek before presenting it to the local Cottage Hospital. A succession of managers took over duty in this period. W. Lockett, H. James and Thomas Dobson did service while the pit worked in the four foot, the Little Dilhorne and the Big Dilhorne, although there are no plans to give definite information.

In December 1910, Mr. Pearce, the successful Liberal candidate in the previous election now claimed to his Cheadle audience that he had instituted the negotiations which had brought the Bassanos to buy the Klondyke and re-open the pit. Within a few days H. S. Higginbottorn, the new Chairman of Directors, and both Bassanos had denied that Pearce had started anything. The working went on apace under a new manager, Harold James, who had taken over by 1912. It was said at this time that there was plenty of work at 27s 0d per week. There was, however, a bit of trouble between a butty and his

*Pit props stacked at New Haden.*

men, which came to the court. Mr. Robinson was a butty on No. 46 Drift who had some disagreement with some of his men, and decided to leave his employ to move to No. 17 Drift. The men then noticed that the No. 17 tallies on the loaded trucks were being changed for No. 46 tallies. One of the No. 17 men named Bentley saw this and the checkweighman agreed with him. The result was that Robinson was fined 10s 0d with £2.2s. costs.

The increased output from New Haden demanded more publicity and from June 1914, there appeared a half page advertisement in the *Cheadle & Tean Times* offering Best large coal, Best Cobbles, Rough Slack and this continued through the year.

By the Christmas of 1914 the War was the most important subject of conversation and prompted many unusual events. A new notice read:

*"The New Haden Collieries Ltd.*
*GRAND PATRIOTIC FOOTBALL MATCH*
*on the*
*GAWBUTTS GROUND CHEADLE*
*on XMAS DAY AT 11 O'CLOCK*
*Grand Medals will be presented to*
*The Winners*
*SURFACE VERSUS UNDERGROUND"*

Among the players were many good old Cheadle names – Brunts, Crook, Hawley, Shaw, Whitehursts, Thorley, Mellor, James, Rowe, Hammonds, Summerfield, Beardmores and Shenton.

The notice continued:

*"Admission 3d. All Pay.*
*Entire Proceeds Given to the Cheadle Belgian Refugees."*

As the industry progressed there were also a number of accidents, some fatal. In April 1915, James Chandler, who lived at Woodhead Lodge, now demolished, was killed by a fall of roof and electrocuted. By the following October, Higginbottom had decided to buy a colliery for himself and purchased one near Manchester.

There appears to have been a greater incidence of absenteeism. A miner's letter in a local paper reads:

*"I recently got coal at 9$^1/_2$d per ton 65% per ton including the loading of it. There is no class of workman who habitually distresses himself as does a miner."*

Work continued through the war although New Haden had a large number, some reported two hundred and fifty, who had joined the forces with the promise that their jobs would be waiting for them on return.

By 1917 either through New Haden workings or other 'old men' workings there was trouble with the railway tunnel construction and, with the need for large scale repair work, certain colliery work was discontinued. By 1918 a larger fall of tunnel roof completely closed the railway siding work and a large amount of other colliery workings.

Miners began to recall all the old stories of tunnel delays and the tales spread around so that the commotion with the Peace celebrations completely over-shadowed the most important news for New Haden.

There had been rumours spreading for quite sometime as neither Higginbottom or

The opening of New Haden Colliery in 1902

Bassano, Bros. appeared as interested in the New Haden affairs. At last the men learned that a new man, John Slater, had taken over from the beginning of 1917. He was only twenty-eight years old, but from later accounts had had an extraordinarily successful business career since he married the daughter of a coal factor, shared in the business, but soon moved on to bigger enterprises.

At first the press concentrated on his early footballing career with Bolton, but later in 1917 when he brought his family to the Elms, the locals began to hear, a little at a time, of his prowess. In just over a year he had bought the local Gas Works and gradually we heard more of the other twenty concerns he governed, through his acquisition in 1919 of Amalgamated Industrials Ltd. as a holding company. That same year the press gave him a further build-up entitled *"Footballer to Millionaire"* – A romantic story of a £5,000,000 Deal! and went on to tell how he employed 20,000 people and had said *"I believe in putting money back into business rather than making a splash"*.

But there was a splash. Having acquired major interests in three other local coal units, New Haden became part of Berry Hill and progressed to a manpower unit of nearly a thousand. At this time a brick works was established to use the very good material found above the Little Dilhorne coal. This was dumped on a special spoil bank to be retrieved as required. The earliest bricks made were stamped 'Jayess' before they reverted later to the New Haden Bricks. Both Mr. and Mrs. Slater, the latter also a Director, were present at the opening alongside the new manager, Mr. Cowgill, who resided in the Avenue. Everything seemed to be going remarkably well. The two new dynamos fitted were named after his wife and daughter, Elizabeth and Irene, whilst a new disc coalcutter was installed to cut three feet under the coal along a hundred feet face before being dropped by firing.

*The procession to celebrate the finding of the New Haden coal, January 1905.*

He began to play a special part in the social life of Cheadle. He presented the new Recreation Ground to the town and was accompanied by Dr. Ernest Mackenzie at its opening. The Football team was restarted with its headquarters in Bank Street, where the New Haden band practised. It had new uniforms, but more important, when each man was presented with a new silver instrument, Ernest Mackenzie was there to hear the band and its conductor, Peter Starkey, put the new instruments to the test. Not surprising, therefore, that he was voted onto the County Council with a good majority.

While New Haden itself appeared to thrive, by 1922, the holding Company, Amalgamated Industrials, was in difficulties so that it was in the hands of the Receivers and shortly after the Liquidator, Mr. W. A. Hayward, was a major shareholder and Managing Director. Slater had a tragedy at the Elms when he ran his car and family through the fence of the steep corner, resulting in the death of his young twins. He left Cheadle though there was always a car and chauffeur waiting for him when he wished to visit this district. Hayward now occupied the Elms and a manager followed by the name of W. Plant, while Nixon became a Managing Director.

*Two further views of the New Haden procession.*

By 1924 Slater found a mansion at Eastbourne where he created much the same impression as he had done at Cheadle. It is not surprising, therefore, to find that this gentleman, with car and chauffeur also at Eastbourne should show some interest in politics to the extent that by 1932 he was put forward by the Conservatives in a parliamentary election where he was unopposed. He had nearly reached the top when, after three

*Mr Slater & Dr. MacKenzie with New Haden Silver Band, 1921*

*New Haden Colliery with the railway cutting and tunnel portal in foreground*

years as an M.P. he collapsed at a dinner party and died. He was only forty-five years old and was buried with his three children at Dilhorne in a large grave covered with granite slabs next to the Buller tomb.

By this time New Haden itself had expanded enormously. Following the very early days before Klondyke and the Four foot coal, there were no Abandonment plans for the Bassano workings through the Great War. It was vastly different through the Slater regime, for the plans show the workings in the Little Dilhorne at 2ft 4in thick up to the 1920s. Once the times were more settled, Slater continued his industrial pursuits and took over Berry Hill Colliery in 1922 whereupon New Haden became a part of the

No.8 (Woodhead) shaft, No.7 (Dilhorne) shaft behind it, New Haden

combine. There was, therefore, an incentive for production. Its workings in the Big Dilhorne coal, which were almost six feet thick and of good quality, were greatly extended and lasted until the 1930s. It was extensively worked from 1920 to 1931 on the north and west side as far as the Boundary and well beyond Draycott Cross, whilst the workings to the south-east extended in the Litley direction until 1940 and in the south prior to closing in 1943. The Cobble was mined for a mere three years from 1938 to 1941.

The Woodhead also had been mined in a similar area, but on the north-west side under the old Delphouse all through the 1930s to early 1940s, whilst to the south-east it was mined towards Litley into the 1940s, closing in 1943. It seemed that it was destined to follow the ambitions of Slater when he arrived and claimed that New Haden was going not only for the Woodhead, but for the Crabtree and that elusive haematite.

In 1925 it appeared that he had found the manager likely to help achieve his ambitions. G. H. Dixon came and was promoted to managing director. He resided at the Elms and had a manager, H. McGowan, to work under him. Dixon was recognised as a well-qualified man, but he could also express himself in language specifically designed for use underground.

Below: Old Loco shed, New Haden, with the brickworks kiln to the right

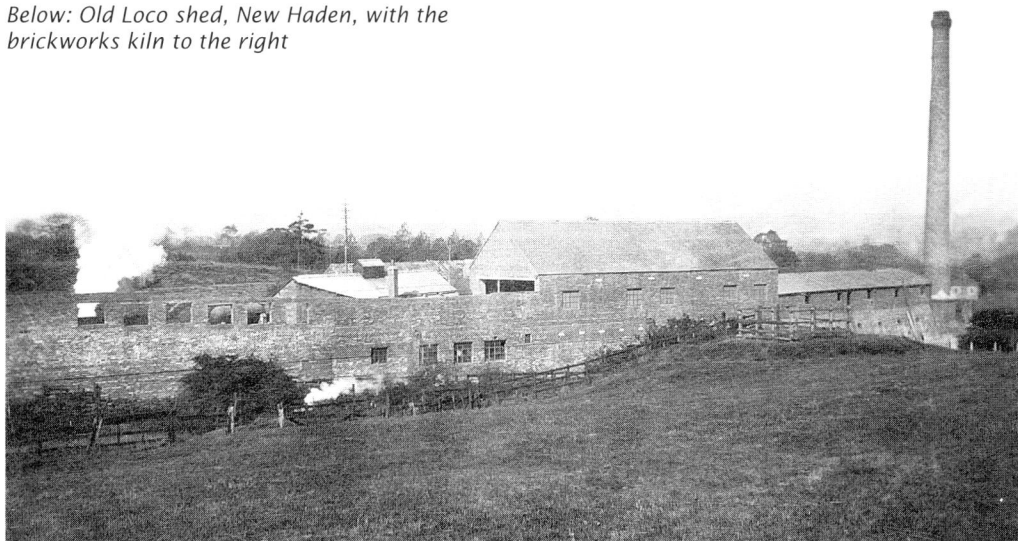

After the tragedy of 1935, Mrs. Slater was joined on the Board by Messrs. Redmayne and Maitland. The combination of New Haden and Berry Hill Collieries seemed to be flourishing. Not until the outbreak of the 1939 war did the miners begin to consider how much coal remained to be mined. Many thought that government regulations, with the need for energy, would keep the old pit going. The shock was quite unexpected when, in 1943, those same regulations, asserting that New Haden was costing £10,000 per year, demanded immediate closure.

## Deaths at New Haden

Collieries had their disasters and through the nineteenth century, mining records covering all the coalfields quoted those with a hundred to three hundred deaths. The Cheadle coalfield, as Dr. Plot pointed out in 1680, would not be subject to such catastrophes.

Local collieries, however, often lost men, sometimes as many as three or four a year from a variety of causes. My list of twenty-five fatalities at New Haden is by no means complete and probably omits those of the very early days. There were in the 1908-1910 period cases of two men losing eyes in a shot firing accident. One man from Tean named James lost his life when he fell down No. 8 shaft. Another in the early period was when Ernest Hughes was so severely injured when a haulage rope snapped and damaged his neck and head. A more dramatic account says the rope cut off his head.

The more modern underground transport systems had their mishaps and often resulted in very serious accident or fatal injury. From the 1930 period, Jim Steele, a fitter was killed and Messrs. Rushton, C. Bloor and W. Dale were also killed. A most unusual accident occurred in March 1939, on the bank. Tubs just out of the cage broke lose, ran down to a lower level and injured Peter Starkey, the store man and bandmaster while he was at the door of his stores. The severe leg injury deteriorated so that he died within a week.

Most deaths came, as expected in those early days, from roof falls. In 1908 Joseph Warrington was killed as were Joseph Fowell and Joseph James in 1910, whilst Thomas James, having suffered a foot injury, died shortly after. In the late 1920s and 1930s Messrs. W. Northwood, Hammon, Len Cashmore, Clarence Weston and Norris Ellis were killed followed by Jack Cammell.

The installation of electricity brought additional dangers. Jabez Hurst was one of the earliest victims in New Haden. Jim Barnes in the 1930s was another victim, while my neighbour Arthur Whitehurst, W. E. Brunt and a Mr. Morris were severely injured by electric sparking and explosion. The first two died within a couple of days of the accident whilst the third recovered from his burns.

Black Damp killed a few. In the 1930s W. James was killed and in the early 1940s a Polish worker, who had intended hiding his tools in a disused roadway, crept into the dark, but was not found until the following day.

Even the ponies had their accidents. Indeed, two were killed in the Big Dilhorne seam, but the usual quota of nine could be seen skipping about after a day or so when their eyes became acclimatised to the surroundings when they were brought up for the annual holiday. Messrs. Bartlam and Alcock were their ostlers for a long period.

By July 1943, the New Haden property was to be auctioned. Not only the colliery buildings, but many cottages in which the workers lived. There was some consternation when it was announced that all the band's new silver instruments were to be collected for the sale.

The deeds of this sale contained information on the financial standing of Slater's New Haden holdings which amazed Cheadle mining folk. We had heard of some irregularities in the working of the Amalgamated Industrials Ltd., Slater's holding Company which had been liquidated before 1930, but by this date, Slater had borrowed some £125,000 from an important Assurance company at 7% interest, a high figure at that time. Within a short period, a further £35,000 brought his debt to £160,000 and again in 1934 an-

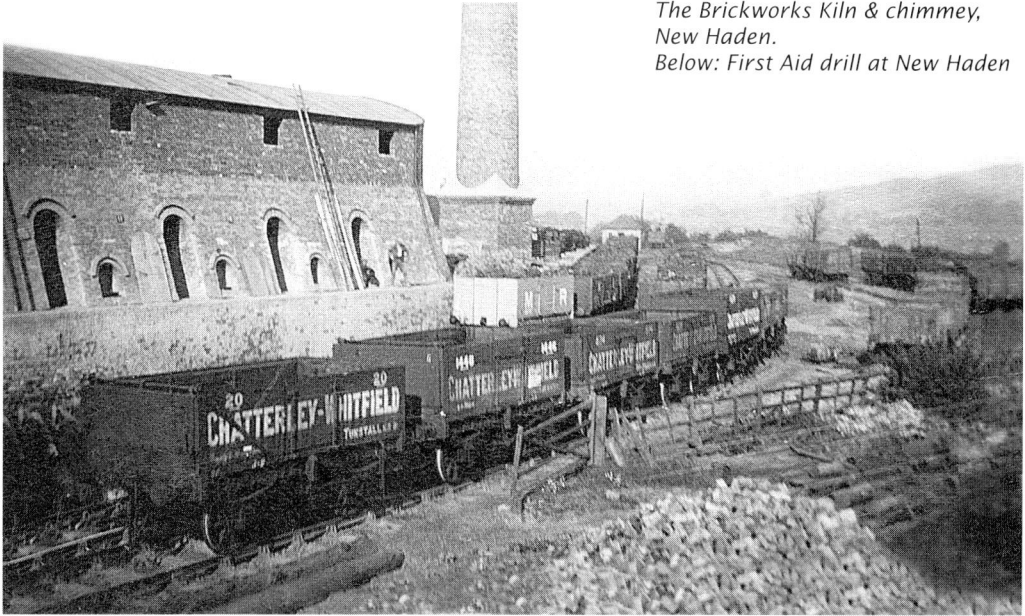

*The Brickworks Kiln & chimmey, New Haden.*
*Below: First Aid drill at New Haden*

other £40,000 was added to his debt. At his death his wife and daughter were left with the burden of this £200,000 debt to balance against whatever assets came from the sale.

The days had gone when redundant miners could move to one of the four or five pits a mile or so away. There was but one, Foxfield and few were taken on there. Many moved to Florence or Stirrup and Pyes, whilst some travelled into Derbyshire or even Yorkshire. The name still remains. The Colliery gave its name to the whole district and a new engineering concern has assured its future use.

## The Mosey Moor Colliery

James H. Lister left the Park Hall Colliery in 1920. He had served the Bowers business for fifteen years, but this business had suffered losses in personnel so that it seemed that Lister spoke only for the past and the new Directors probably felt that he could not look to the future. He chose to join Thomas Bolton & Sons at Froghall Works just as it seemed there might be problems if the miners acted as they threatened in 1921, when the government spoke of reducing the war-time coal subsidies which would mean a reduction in miners' wages.

Lister began to explore a coal supply less than half a mile from their boiler house beside the canal. The Crabtree coal was 2ft 4in thick in the valley side between the Ipstones and the Foxt roads and, indeed, the tramway built for the ironstone trade in the 1862-3 period had left its mark here and could easily be relaid to its wharf on the canal side where the notice board today announces that this spot is part of the Froghall Way.

He set a level into the hillside to the west in the direction of the Hermitage, but when only forty yards from the tramway he found old workings which went more than a hundred yards ahead and more than two hundred and fifty yards to either side. But Lister and the old men's workings were halted by a fault which was obviously too much for the 'old men' who had worked here long before the ironstone fever of the preceding seventy years. Lister, however, with his dozen or so men, did find some coal at that depth to tram to the canal wharf and boat down to the works to keep the metal men at work.

This was a change in coal supply for, prior to this time from 1890 when the first mill started, its fuel was carted from the Cheadle collieries. Horses and carts faced either the Stakes or Kingsley Banks; both uncomfortable stretches for the horses and their drivers. The carts, however, were supplied with brakes which screwed tightly onto the wheel's inner axle and slowed the wheel and the loaded coal cart. It did, however, make a dreadful screaming sound all the way down the hill until the bottom was reached with the brakes smoking. The number of loads going into Froghall could be easily counted, but the system did not last throughout 1921.

Within a few months Lister had set a crut at 6 feet deep, a good sixty yards to the north-west and found an untouched block of coal one hundred and fifty yards by two hundred and fifty yards eventually lost through a fault only fifty yards from the Ipstones road. This block was worked until December 1925. It seemed the Gilmoor Colliery was at an end.

There was threat of further strikes when the government announced that this time it was definitely stopping the subsidy and miners would have to take a cut in wages. This resulted in the General Strike which lasted but a week whilst the coal men remained on strike through the summer. Few mills in the Cheadle area suffered any inconvenience as the miners with their outcropping work satisfied the needs of local factories, whilst domestic use fell through the summer months.

The Gilmoor workings were hardly closed when Lister found a chance of the Sweet coal only two hundred and fifty yards to the north, but this was only 1ft 9in thick. In fact, the area had been explored as early as 1924-6 but it was found that old ironstone mines were waterlogged at the lower end of Massey's woods. Further work in the direction of the Ipstones road continued into early 1927 but it was unprofitable once the the strike was over. Lister completed his abandonment plans in 1928 and also showed by a strata chart how the coals lay around Mosey Moor. He had found coal at eighty-five feet some 11 inches thick followed by the Crabtree 2ft 4in thick at two hundred and twenty feet and the Sweet coal 1ft 9in thick at two hundred and eighty feet.

Lister had been in the district for twenty-three years and could only find work acting in an advisory capacity in workings in the Lockwood ground. Primrose Thorley, the lime burner at Froghall Wharf, living in a large house at Windy Arbour recently demolished (i.e. as at 1980), had invested where the Woodhead outcropped previously but in neither case did he repay his expenses. Both Liner and Hullah returned to Leeds. In Lister's twenty-three years he had made a name for himself in the district, but as time went on the Cheadle coal industry had too many managers for all to keep their positions. Lister was last heard of as Manager of Denby Colliery in Derbyshire in 1938.

## On Strike

The Great War finished in November 1918, and the government's main business was to get industry on a peace time programme. This meant that many factories had a slowing-down in production and inevitably a measure of unemployment. Boltons at Froghall, instead of making copper shell cases, were looking for the old line of electrical goods orders. These were slow to arrive with the result that men were working part-time by 1920. The government found a measure of over-production from the pits and decided that the war-time subsidy must be cut, resulting in a fall in wages for the miners. Hence the 1921 strike.

This did not last for more than three weeks, but it gave a few groups of miners time to look around where shallow seams came to the surface or outcropped as it came to be called. They were just learning the practice of shallow mining, what tackle was necessary, how many men could group into a unit with a job for everyone without overcrowding.

The government withdrew its threat on subsidies and work continued until 1926 when the problem once again arose in the spring and this time quickly became the first General Strike. This, however, lasted but a week and since we are dealing specifically with the Cheadle coalfield we must see how the striking miners coped with this more serious position.

*The Liberal Club. from left to right: Charlie Beardmore, H. Wetwood, E. Turner, Arthur Beardmore, Arthur Woodward, Harold Harris, Leslie Beardmore*

They soon proved that they had benefited from that short 1921 practice and since all the signs indicated that this was going to be a very long dispute, preparation was made on a much larger scale. Local miners had among them a number of practical amateur geologists, knowing where any of half a dozen seams cropped out and they also knew that when coal stopped production from Cheadle's three collieries, a large local demand was waiting for them to satisfy without the necessity of using the railway, although if they achieved a surplus, that facility would attend to its despatch.

*Keelings Hole. from left to right: Arthur Wilshaw, Bob Kirkland, ? , Aubrey Waugh, ? , Arthur Mace, Charlie Kirkland, Jack Boon, ? , Jack Keeling, Will Bentley*

Before the first week finished the areas known to be near outcropping seams were invaded by mining groups in fives and sixes. They had staked claims to sink their holes once the landowner or occupant had been persuaded to accept the small royalty, maybe sixpence or a shilling per ton lifted. There were some occupants who, perhaps for political or maybe agricultural reasons, would not allow any sinking on their ground while a few even brought out a gun to drive enthusiasts away. Generally, most saw good coming from evil especially on pay day!

The Racecourse site we had considered some forty years earlier, for the Cheadle Park Colliery, was now nicknamed the Racecourse pit. Now miners with their brothers, fathers, sons and in-laws came to take their luck where they knew that the old colliery did not take out the Alecs coal when they intended to sink for the Woodhead. The Alecs surfaced on the Harewood Park side of the road and was plenty good enough for emergency use. What was more, Lawyer Foster, in charge of this piece of land, was pleased to encourage groups to stake a claim here, for every sixpence royalty on the coal sold from this field was a contribution to the fund for the erection of the Guild Hall. Within a few weeks the whole length was nearly occupied, at least the number of 'holes' was counted in scores and those nearest the road need only sink some six to eight yards to reach the coal – those further west needed nearly double the depth. The family atmosphere was very strong. The four Shakeshaft brothers, the Rushton father, uncles and grandfather, and many similar groups led to good 'labour relations' and on this site alone many estimated that over one hundred small pits operated. It was worth the time of the photographer to visit and take pictures of each group. The members all obliged with a smile. The half dozen workers in one illustration had given their little pit a well known name, '*The Dog and Monkey*' copied from the Kingsley Moor pit which closed in 1907, whilst they may have intended to give a clue to the group by advertising '*Salts Pale Ale*' on the primitive headgear. The venture was quite lucrative. Thirty shillings and two pounds a week colliers were transformed to twenty and thirty pounds a week coal masters. They had never worked under these conditions before, but by the end of three months they did not know how to spend the money. A number of stories were circulated about the refurnishing of cottages. One told how, after setting up with piano, new suite, beds, etc., Dad had money left so he bought another piano!

This coal, along with the product of other sites, providing fuel for mill boilers far and wide, meant a large increase in the number of carters. They either took loads to the station or delivered anywhere within the ten mile radius and were gratified with the prospect of having this employment for the duration of the Strike.

Not all, however, were as content as the Cheadle men. Pottery men came to join in this Cheadle second 'Klondyke' and once started, employed buses to carry them night and morning. The Union men in the Potteries, however, saw this as defeating the general principle of the action and formed a large group to march to the sites. They demanded that this work was to stop. The Cheadle men argued that their struggle was with the three Cheadle Collieries which were not working. What they did with their time did not constitute a breach with the unions. The outcropping continued and was extended.

There must have been some sympathy for the colliers' cause, as managers and other officials were seen on sites. It was said that Thomas Dobson looked to the safety precautions of some sites, while one of his son's helped with smithy work such as pick sharpening and chain repairs.

No other site was quite as busy as the Racecourse, although groups found plenty of outcropping seams from the Dilhorne area. The Cobble and Woodhead seams outcropped to the east and north. East of the Churnet, the Crabtree was well worth mining too. Around the Adderley Mill a few shafts were sunk and a complex of seams were found and lost. Little Dilhorne, the Four Foot and the Alecs were found, but an unusual trial

*Leek Road, Hole 90*

was made down the well in Pegg's Farm yard, near the Trimpos road, where some of the Fourfoot was also won.

Just west was Blake Hall where men had initially been refused. Within a few days work was started after negotiations and before the end of the strike this proved to be second in size to the Racecourse. There were around twenty shafts in five different fields around the farmhouse where some were lucky enough to find the two yard or Old

*Leek Road, Hole 106. from left to right: Stan Prime, Tom Prime (father), Harry Prime, Ernest James*

Delph coal, while a further half dozen shafts in what was called 'the meadow' found a two feet six inch seam they nicknamed the 'Billy' coal.

Across the main Boundary road a group tackled the old Delphouse colliery area and in the meadow three shafts found the Old Delph coal, while in the nearby Lower Delphouse Wood three other shafts found the Yard coal. Further down towards the Brookhouses other shafts again found the Yard coal.

At Kingsley Moor around the Above Park Farm outcroppers found the old workings of 1850, but they continued to mine the Rider coal they found outcropping only eighty yards to the west. Further west at Little Above Park three other shafts went into production.

To the south the Big Dilhorne was found between Whimpney Wood and Godley Lane and several shafts worked between these points.

Further to the north men were working the outcropping Woodhead seam at Broad Oak Farm not far from the woodland where there was a water pump worked by the stream. Four shafts had been sunk and men were surprised to find much older workings.

Men from Kingsley came around the Kingsley Holt area starting in the north western end of the Broad Hay land where it reaches the road between Top Shawe and Bottom Shawe gates. Woodhead coal outcrops on the Broad Hay land where shafts were sunk and when worked out the men were allowed to crut under the road on to the Shawe Park land, but were instructed that no mining would be allowed within sight of the Hall. Some five or six shafts were sunk where the Woodhead was quite shallow. Indeed, the site of these sinkings can easily be seen today.

Nearer Cheadle this Woodhead outcropping zig-zagged under the road on Booth Farm land but here was misfortune. Miners dug their shaft from the Booths Lane to the north to meet the main road some two hundred yards away. Unfortunately, they also found the old men workings. They brought up an old pit haulage sledge which crumpled to pieces when at the surface. These colliers allowed their disappointment to overrule their experience and took out the coal pillars, left by the predecessors, as some form of recompense. Each pillar brought them two tons of coal and they moved to another site.

Within a few weeks the strike ended and they disappeared into the Potteries. However, as I rode to work some ten months later over that Shawe road on my cycle, I did notice an unusual depression in the middle of the road and turned to examine it. By the time I returned in the afternoon the depression had become a gaping hole and the county workmen were trying to fill it with many tons of large limestone. A glance down showed that this was the 'old men' workings without any support.

Other Kingsley partners traced the Woodhead seam down the brook between Kingsley and the Holt where many shafts were sunk whilst others came into contact with the three older shafts on the west side of the brook. Also at Kingsley Holt and in three or four places in the Lockwood Hall ground miners, once more, found the Woodhead seam outcropping where it overlooked the valley just as those early men had used this seam to mine that *'Brode Delphe'*. Some of those later men continued long after the Strike had finished.

The Dandillions Farm site was a favourite for Cheadle miners for here the Dilhorne seam, which further south become the Huntley coal, cropped out just behind the farm. There were as many as a dozen shafts here which did very well. Not far away, the Litley site also had a dozen shafts working the Litley coal and these also came across many *'old men'* workings.

Near Majors Barn on Pyatt's site shafts were sunk to the Little Dilhorne coal. The quality was good and satisfied the sinkers of the half dozen shafts. On a nearby site behind Lawns Farm shafts were sunk close by the tramway belonging to the Park Hall

*Another view of Hole 106*
*From left to right: Ken Carr, ? , Dickie Brunt, ? , Sam Harvey, standing is Tom Brunt, ? .*

Colliery. Both the Litley and the Yard were mined and I am informed that the railway was used to transport the output to the main line on the Green.

Many workings were started in the Lightwood area and the shaft remains could still be seen until the 1970s. These men found the Woodhead and, although Robert Plant had one of his failures here, these men had a very rewarding four or five months despite the discovery of old workings.

The Eaves and Mobberley had been worked a century earlier, but men still found that their shafts contacted the Cobble coal. This again was worth the working for its quality and the eight or ten shafts were quite successful. At Brookhouses a unit worked just west of the brook with half a dozen shafts at six or eight yards deep. This was a very wet area and here, as in a few other attempts, a water pump was necessary to keep the shafts working. Here they used a Merryweather pump, making it possible to continue mining the Four Foot until the Strike was over.

There were, no doubt, many other workings on the east of the valley where it would not be difficult to find the Crabtree which would be most useful to the farming community in that wide area.

The Strike finished after some six months but so far as the Cheadle coalfield and its workers were concerned, it had been a most unusual period or even adventure. It had

*Leek Road, Alcock's Hole*

not only brought together most grades of workmen and management to different degrees, but in many cases, brought out the best of mens' characters. It had also taught those who moved from one set of shafts to another, more of the geology of their coalfield than they could have learned had they stayed at the old face for six months.

## *Licensed Mining*

With the coming of nationalisation in 1947 all coal under the surface belonged to and was under the control of the National Coal Board. Licenses were, however, granted to certain applicants to mine coal in certain areas under quite strict supervision by the Board's mining surveyors. Very often these men, of the highest qualifications and with practical experience, were of great assistance to operators venturing underground on a comparatively small scale.

There were a number of such applicants working to the west of the Potteries in the Betley-Madeley district by the early 1950s. It was, however, some five years later before any attention was paid to the Cheadle area. Harry Scragg had been interested in coal and mining for many years and had been working in both Australia and Canada but on his return he went back to farming.

When opportunity arose he had joined with a group beyond the Potteries but continued to study old maps and plans dealing with earlier Cheadle mining and the results of Barrow's survey. After the 1926 working most would have thought that there was little or no easily-mined coal left even for the least expensive of trials. They would have judged that the most sought after, the Woodhead, would be only in the depths of the field, bedevilled by faults, and too costly to attempt. Harry Scragg, however, had read his plans, listened to the 1926 outcroppers and with a first class mining engineer, Butler,

*Leek Road, Hole 126 (Mick Campbell's Hole). from left to right: Fred Plant, Ted Bolton, Wm. Campbell, ? , ? , Keeling, Brunt, Fred Bough, Harry Slack.*

began, in 1955, to dig into the outcrop of the Woodhead at Blakeley Lane some fifty yards before the old Methodist Chapel (turned farm building) on the south side of the road. This became the Moorland Colliery.

As expected they immediately found the 1926 workings which proved to be of little nuisance except in the wet season when the water had to be cleared. From the outcrop the seam dipped fairly steeply through the first ten yards of working at a one in two ratio, but levelled out gradually to one in four at thirty to forty yards deep.

The Abandonment plan shows that the working continued in this south side of the road to a distance of some two hundred and fifty yards and covered about an acre while across the road, after two year's working, approximately a half of that area was taken. Indeed, they were probably within sight of some of the strike workings which continued to 1928 and according to that plan had been taken over from Mrs. Brassington by the Park Hall Colliery for 'Protective Purposes'.

Indeed, this same district, according to the Directory of 1850 was being worked much earlier – "*Here is a Colliery worked by Mr. Alexander Bowers.*"

With the help of electric pumping an average of ten men managed to win some one hundred tons weekly and worked for nearly ten years. The Abandonment plans were submitted to the Board by March 1965, by which time the area had been cleared and the Moorland Colliery had finished working.

It took some eight years before Mr. Scragg could make further application and in 1976 had followed that same Woodhead outcrop about six hundred yards down the Dairy House brook to a spot where an old colliery had worked with the help of a small tramway to carry its coal up to a wharf near the top of Dairy House Lane adjoining Bank Top road. This was where the Mann Brothers had first ventured on the Cheadle coalfield nearly a century before that date. Scragg's activities became the Above Park Colliery with the farm of that name by the side of the A52 between Greenhead and Blakeley Farm. There was also Little Above Park Farm where the Dairy House Lane joins the Bank Top road.

The Mann's old workings were something of a nuisance, for at times, after a rain period, they carried water that had to be cleared, but before the fifteen operatives could approach two hundred tons weekly further investigations were necessary. It appeared that this colliery was likely to continue working for a much longer time than did the Moorland.

However, this chapter cannot close with an ending. Harry Scragg and his surveyors knew that there were other areas similar to the last two, though perhaps in different seams, to be tackled when the need arose.

## Opencast Workings

By 1946 men were returning from the forces and looking to get back into civilian work as quickly as they could return to a peace-time economy. However, Cheadle was never to be the coal town of the earlier part of the century. Only one unit now remained and half the miners and their sons had to change their employment or follow the coal mining in the Potteries with its much larger pits with workings and seams such as we had never seen on our coalfield.

There were, however, small areas of Coal Measures near the surface, but these were in districts where, in the twentieth Century, coal men thought only of the Woodhead, something almost three feet thick and worth sinking shafts for.

There were others also who had paid more attention to what the increasing number of geologists had been saying about the Cheadle coalfield and, indeed, since the 1903 survey and publication by Barrow, there was much less guess work about where the coal had been taken and where shallow coal remained.

For a century or more iron ore had been mined in and around Northamptonshire by employing machinery to lift the top soils, two or three layers, pile them on one side and lay bare, at a depth of twenty to forty feet or more, the ore required for smelting. Unfortunately, when the ore was collected the land was left and can in many cases still be found, rendered completely derelict. Not so today. When machine men considered the use of such methods for coal getting the government had legislated to compel complete replacement of soil, but the machinery men found no difficulty here, requiring just a little care and extra expense.

*Hole 170, the Racecourse*

The firm experimenting on the earliest site, Bilton's, had begun in late 1944 on the Harewood Racecourse area. Here we first saw the huge machine which moved slowly on its wide rotary feet, the great arm above fitted with its line to lift the bucket and its drag lines to pull and fill the bucket. It then lifted and laid the sod in its proper order at the side of the working. Next we saw it getting to the coal, swinging forward the bucket, dragging it back to get it full, perhaps with three cubic yards of coal and lowering it into waiting lorries.

The machines were American built by Monaghans and we saw the 3W which was designed to lift that three cubic yards. Biltons only lifted nine hundred tons, a very small total compared with later operators. It did, however, demonstrate that the produce could quickly be transported by Cheadle station to the big coal users, the power stations, who were not, at this time, critical of quality. The Stinking coal was most useful for this purpose.

By the time Biltons had finished, another operation had started in very late 1944 which was to last for two and a half years. Paulings were working the Leafields site where the Alecs coal actually outcropped and could be lifted at an average of only thirty feet deep. The site stretched on the east of the B522 road, Cheadle – Kingsley Moor, from behind Leafields Farm for a quarter of a mile towards Hazlewall Farm with a width of some 150-200 yards.

The Alecs was split by a six inch layer of Pricking or rubbish with approximately one foot three inches of coal above and two feet of coal below. At well over three feet of coal, this was well worth the getting and Paulings managed a total of over fifty thousand tons here and they erected screens which were operated privately.

The next operators working were caught up with the nationalisation legislation of 1947. The All Counties Engineering Company began digging in late 1946. They intended working from Bate Lane toward Dairy House Brook some two hundred yards to the north of Hatchley Farm. The site became known as the Hatchley site. Here All Counties found a useful area of some six hundred yards long and three hundred wide and the Alecs coal outcropping two hundred yards to the north and about thirty feet deep in their area. The National Coal Board took over within a few months and the

*Hole 9. from left to right: ?, Bertram Shenton, Heathcote. In hole: Wm. Shenton (son of Betram), to his left Godfrey Heathcote*

screens along Leek Road at Perkins Lane corner were thereafter under the National Coal Board supervision. All screened coal was transported by lorry to be put on rail at Cheadle station. The All Counties were now under stricter supervision with regard to replacement. By the end of the operation they had lifted nearly sixty-eight thousand tons.

Even as these had started, another contractor, Holloway, had started on two sites, neither of which was far from the earlier sites, for they also worked the Alecs. One was called the Booth Hall site because it was on that farm's land, although, being by the side of the Leek road it was a third of a mile from the site of that once reputable old Hall. It stretched for a quarter of a mile up the road side, though only some two hundred yards wide. It was, however, in a good position to get the Alecs coal. This was also the case on the Harewood site where again the Alecs was within twenty yards of outcropping so that the old Racecourse had its first opencast treatment, although it had seen plenty of activity in the 1920s. This site stretched along the left side of the Leek Road beyond Harewood Park for a quarter of a mile and was more than two hundred yards to the west. Both were handy for the screens at Perkins Lane and since both sites were operated in both coal getting and restoration until early 1949, a useful 120,000 tons were despatched by the Cheadle station.

Many folk can recount, with some excitement, the stories of how the monster transferred from one site to the next with that stately rotary mechanical movement of their outsize feet along the roads, a motion very sedate and equally sure.

From 1950 for the next decade this form of mining was completely under the Douglas concern. The responsibility for all transport and screening was taken from the National Coal Board by Douglas and Reg Gamble was in a managerial position over the mining and Perkins Lane Screen site. Its first operation was between the Old Engine farm and the Godley-Dilhorne road. It had a rather thick, wide horseshoe shape, a quarter of a mile from toe to heel and some three hundred yards across the heel. This found the 20-inch Little Dilhorne seam which outcropped just a quarter of a mile to the north and was thirty feet deep at this site. Although it was nearer Godley Brook, the operators called this the Old Engine site, quite ignorant of the fact that the name came from the fact that here was installed, in 1778, the first 'fire engine' on the coalfield.

*On the Racecourse, Leek Road. from left to right: ?, ? , George Shaw, Whitehurst, Fred Robinson, Jack Yovatt, seated: Ernest Wood and Fred Croft*

The site operators here were quite successful as they won some twenty-two thousand ton in a matter of seven months, completing in August 1951.

At this time Douglas found other necessary operations in Derbyshire so that all machines and equipment were away from the Cheadle area for some two and a half years, when in April 1954, they returned to tackle a most unlikely spot. The official title of the site was New Haden, but it actually covered a large area of the old Delphouse Colliery site and readers will recall that this had been mined to quite shallow depths from around 1800 until 1910. The site was only some eighty yards from the main road and stretched some two hundred and fifty yards south at a width of one hundred and fifty yards. In fact, it appears that the great machine must have disturbed the upper section of at least five of the old Delphouse shafts.

The surprising thing is that the operators managed to win some ten thousand tons of the most valuable, tonnage-wise, Dilhorne Two Yard coal at somewhere around forty feet deep within a four month period ending August 1954.

From 1954 to the end of 1959 Douglas worked continuously on the Cheadle coalfield. They then tackled, in February 1954, a rather more intricate piece of work behind the Waggon and Horses pub in a number of sections stretching toward the brook. The site had seven sections, three quite small which stretched over a length of half a mile and width to the Dairy House brook of five hundred yards. The most unusual feature of this operation was that it was possible to lift three seams in some way or other as the Foxfield 1ft 8in seam outcropped near by, the Mann's at 1ft 5in thick was only some 40 feet or less below and the Cobble was also available, but much deeper, probably sixty yards and one foot three inches thick, but very good quality.

Means were found for working from one level to a lower one, so that after nearly two and a half years in July 1956, 87,342 tons had been recovered and the land restored.

*Plant's Hole, Lightwood.*
*From left to right: Arthur Plant, Jack Alcock, Albert Plant, Mrs Albert Plant, Mrs Boon, Plant, George Rushton, Levie Johnson (kneeling), Ned Plant, Bob Plant*

*The Dog and Monkey Pit, Alton Castle shaft, Racecourse. from left to right: 'Young' Barnes, Arthur Chandler, Bill Heath, Alf Barnes, Ernest Hammond, Arthur Beardmore, Bill Collier, Joe Day*

By August 1956, Douglas had started in an area we do not usually reckon as being in the Cheadle coalfield. They also gave it a most strange title in the N.C.B. records. They called this area Overmoon (wherever did they find this name?) and it lay by Consall village stretching down to Consall New Hall. Barrow had shown that the Crabtree coal outcropped in a line running through Consall towards the old Chase mines where previously miners went through the Crabtree to mine the red haematite.

The site was almost a mile in length and was in three sections with the largest to the south-east of the village. The Crabtree, although not the best of coal was called 'Stinking' in some areas. At 2 feet 6 inches thick and around this site about twenty-five feet deep, the area was well worth the operating. After six months in February 1956, Douglas had won more than thirty-five thousand tons, but it was the only site to tackle this coal, as across the valley much of it had long been outcrop worked. The site was restored before 1957.

By the middle of October 1956, Douglas had turned their attention to an area which was being heavily mined only forty-five years earlier. The area was in two strips about one third of a mile long, but only one hundred and fifty yards wide. Both strips ran east to west, the northerly ran under the long stretch of woodland where the Hazlewall tramway was set. Hence the name, Waste Wood. The southern strip ran over the old shafts and spoil bank, but whilst Douglas were anxious to fill the shafts and level the spoil bank, such arrangements were not made with the N.C.B. with the result that the spoil bank is still plainly seen.

When Lister made his section diagram of the Hazelwall shaft strata in 1906 he marked his first coal at 10 feet deep as the Foxfield coal at 21 inches thick, followed by the two feet thick Mann's at 62 feet. There was nothing more worth considering, as the Cobble was at 193 feet down and still only twenty inches thick. The operators worked the two upper seams for nearly a year, restoring all the land except the old shaft area, and the operation won more than fifty-six thousand tons.

By November 1957, Douglas then moved further down Clamgoose Lane around the bend near Shawe Hall but concentrated on a large area near the Leek road just east of the ten year old Booth Hall site. The main section was nearly half a mile long and a quarter of a mile wide but in irregular shape. There were, in addition, one piece north and south of Booth Hall and four other pieces inside the Longhouse pit bend in the old tramway.

This was an awkward section split into eight pieces. It had the name Leafields East although most of it was near Booth Hall. It was worked for some twenty-one months and was the only Cheadle operation to be lucky enough to find signs of four different seams.

They were attempting in various places to find seams that had not completely outcropped and disappeared. It will be remembered that the Booth Hall operation near the Leek road worked the Alecs and it would be in the large block next to this that the Alecs would be coming to the surface. In the next five sections, the smaller ones nearest the lane at Longhouse, there would be the last of the Foxfield and more of the Mann's coal while the diggings on either side of the Booth Hall would be likely to produce both Mann's and the Cobble, for the Ladyswell adjoining found the latter at around sixty feet, while it was only forty feet at the Remington just a quarter of a mile away. By the time the operation had finished in August 1959, around one hundred thousand tons of this four seam mixture had passed through the Leek road screens to Cheadle station, and this was the most productive opencast working, Douglas were to have on the Cheadle coalfield.

In 1959 Douglas had their last operation, a very small site at Kingsley Moor in the Blakeley area near the lane running down to the Scout camp. It was on the opposite side of the main road from Mr. Scragg's Moorland Colliery, so Douglas, in deference to the existing colliery, named the site Moorland. It worked from July to October, two and a half months on this two acre site to win nearly five thousand tons, but since this Woodhead seam was near the outcrop, Douglas must have considered this small 'take' worth while.

After this 1959 operation Douglas moved on. They had, however, managed to win more than three hundred thousand tons of coal from the seven ventures some thirty years after the striking miners had been outcropping often in the same districts.

Two other firms came in the sixties. The first by the name of Currall, Lewis & Martin began in June 1964 to work land west of Majors Barn towards Litley Brook in three

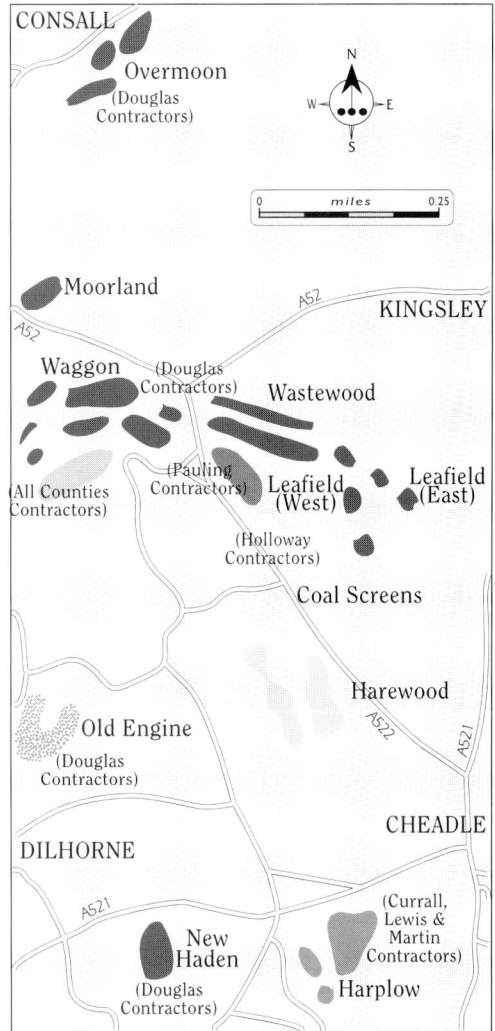

CONSALL
Overmoon (Douglas Contractors)
N W E S
miles 0 0.25
Moorland
A52 A52
KINGSLEY
Waggon (Douglas Contractors)
Wastewood
(Pauling Contractors)
(All Counties Contractors)
Leafield (West)
Leafield (East)
(Holloway Contractors)
Coal Screens
Harewood
A522 A521
Old Engine (Douglas Contractors)
DILHORNE
CHEADLE
A521
(Currall, Lewis & Martin Contractors)
New Haden (Douglas Contractors)
Harplow

sections. The largest section nearer Majors Barn approached the railway on the south some quarter of a mile by two hudred yards on or near the Old Gawbutts enclosures. Two smaller sections approached Litley Brook in the west, much smaller in area, and local mining men were right when they talked of 'old men's' workings hereabouts.

The official name of this site was Harplow, but locals still called it Litley. They uncovered two seams which the Coal Board called Upper and Lower Litley probably at twenty to thirty-five feet.

Of course being closer in to Cheadle this operation had interested visitors especially among retired miners. My old friend, George, could report the opening of 'old men' workings in the Litley and finding a collection of clay pipe heads in one chamber. Obviously, the Smoke Room! His interest took him much too close to the working monster, so that the driver threatened to drop a load of soil on his head instead of its collecting area. The driver did, however, call for his opinion when he broke through a small brick tunnel. It was an old sough and may well have been that Fowell – Mylles sough from 1668.

The Dog and Monkey Pit, Alton Castle shaft, Racecourse. from left to right: 'Young' Barnes, Arthur Chandler, Bill Heath, Alf Barnes, Ernest Hammond, Arthur Beardmore, Bill Collier, Joe Day

The work then went to the Four Foot coal at more than fifty feet deep, but since it was nearly four feet thick it is not surprising that in two and a half years it gave the firm some two hundred and thirty thousand tons of coal.

The last operation came back again to the Racecourse to the west of the workings of nearly twenty years earlier. It was officially called Harewood West and it was nearly half a mile long passing under Park Hall tramway track to Leek road and stretching south to the old Cheadle Park colliery area. This was worked by Shands and although apparently chasing the Alecs, where it became deeper, this stretch also was quite rewarding, as it produced nearly two hundred and twenty thousand tons. This particular area had probably missed the 1926 outcroppers.

The screening, now that Douglas had left, was from 1960-68, in the hands of a private contractor. After this last operation there had to be some dismantling. Passers by had become used to this activity on the corner at Perkins Lane for twenty years, but it disappeared and turned from black to green with animals feeding as though they had never been disturbed. The fourteen sites were restored after working and in most cases appears to have been of great benefit, especially when hay harvesting is necessary on the land.

## EPILOGUE

The object of this particular piece of historical writing is not merely to retail a list of coal workings through the past few centuries. Much more important, it is to demonstrate how the growth of this industry influenced the growth of the town of Cheadle and the surrounding villages. We know that at the time of the compilation of the Domesday Book in 1087 this place counted but nine families whilst other settlements around, such as Checkley had sixteen families, including Tean. We see that in settling in the area more families had opted for the more productive agricultural stretch of the Tean valley than had chosen the shelter offered by that sandstone hill we now call the Park.

However, there was soon to be an alteration, for a century and a half later a most important event led to a complete change between Cheadle and its neighbouring villages. It was the grant of a weekly market and four annual fairs to the manor of Cheadle and Mr. G. Short's researches enabled these to be dated from 1250. From this date, whatever the district's people needed to buy or to sell it could best be done at Cheadle on Market Day. Later the site for such buying and selling could be marked away from the swelling houses around the Church, some one hundred and fifty yards away where there was open space. Some years later Cheadle copied other market towns and erected a Market Cross around which transactions could be conducted.

There were now two centres of importance to all our lives, the Church and the Market, with the result that, until three centuries ago, that most important lane between became one half Church Street and the other Market Street. Newcomers filled any space on either side the track with their little cottages, perhaps leaving a few paths to get to the common land just behind on either side. This growth continued to spread eastward in an almost straight line of buildings and westward until we felt that was enough, so we called it Town End.

Of the fact that the town was growing there was no doubt so that the Stubbs of Kingsley decided that they should do something about the education of children. These Stubbs, led by the Church Minister at Kingsley, decided that the school attached to the Church there, since 1546, was not of the standard required by 1685. They therefore set up a Grammar School by endowment, behind that Church and Market

*Outcropping at Dandillions on Tean Road*
*From left to right: Tom Timmis, Booth, Fred Booth, Emery, Tom Rogers, Arthur Wilshaw*

Place, approached by a track which climbed up the hill. The endowment insisted that the School should have six poor children from both parishes. This was a definite sign that Cheadle was growing, and furthermore, we have around this time two forms of measuring gauge to give as good a method of number assessment as was possible around the middle of that century.

When Charles II returned to the throne the royal purses had been abolished so that it was necessary to collect money in the form of tax for government use. Hence the Hearth Tax of 1665 by which every Constablewick (group of parishes) checked every dwelling's number of hearths and a tax was levied on most buildings with the exception of those so meanly built and furnished as to be exempt from the tax.

Having completed the schedule for each parish we found not only which house had the larger number of hearths (fireplaces) but which families were of the more important standing, living in the houses we mentioned as being interested in coal mining in that period. In the Cheadle list one hundred and twenty-two people were to pay whilst eightyfour were said to be 'not chargeable', making a total of two hundred and six family heads. The average family at this period had many children but most died young. The average parish's deaths register following this time makes pitiful reading. When historians talk of famine we get the full picture from these registers. It is usually taken that the average family was between four and five persons, so that would give Cheadle a population of 923. By the same reckoning Dilhorne would have 615, Ipstones with Foxt, 490 and Kingsley with Whiston, 340.

The Religious Census of 1676 was designed to check on the rise of certain forms of Non-Conformism which were prohibited at this time. Parsons and their Churchwardens were to make an assessment for the Bishops which would demonstrate how effective was the Parson in keeping his Parish on the straight and narrow path of the Protestant Church. In one or two local parishes the Bishop would find figures to concern him for at Alton fourteen, Ipstones, twelve and Checkley, thirty-nine, were Papists (Catholics) whilst even more alarming was the Ipstones figure of seventy-three NonConformists. These were the very strong group of Quakers centred around Whitehough with a reputation all over the Midlands. It is doubtful whether these were all natives. The totals in the case of Cheadle – one thousand and five – have some relation with the hearth tax count, but there are discrepancies in the case of Dilhorne, only 365. Kingsley had 340 with Ipstones at 488 – very close to the hearth assessment.

Among the Cheadle people caught in the hearth tax we find as expected, those in mining; either ironstone, some seventy years earlier, or in coal at that time:

> "*Edward, Leigh of Woodhead Hall, the founder of the coal family with four hearths.*
> *Geo. Thornbury of Thornbury. Ironstone carting C.1600 – three hearths.*
> *Thos. Mills, Mill House, both ironstone and coal – five hearths.*
> *Ralph Mountford of Cheadle Eaves, later coal – three hearths.*
> *Richard Fowell of Huntley in Coal with Mills – five hearths.*
> *Widow Dorothy Bamford of Park Hall, later coal family – only three hearths.*
> *Richard Whitehurst of Whitehurst, Ironstone, later coal – three hearths.*"

The figures and dates are of more importance since the dates belong to the period of our early mining documents which show an increase in the business of coal getting. We had seen the coal used in lime burning as early as the 1290 document which mentioned a lime kiln on Hounds Chedle. The agricultural community, we were told by Dr. Plot, had increased this practice especially in the Moorlands which he designated as between Three Shires' Head in the north to Draycott or Uttoxeter in the south. A mixture of ess and lime was increasingly used. The ess was made by burning turf and small timber in great heaps for three weeks until large quantities had been accumulated, often for spreading on meadow or arable land. He goes on to describe lime burning in the 1600s and from this description one can understand why there should be an increasing demand for Cheadle coal.

It was not until the iron manufacturers found that coal could be used in the secondary processes at Consall and Oakamoor, that it was in comparatively small quantities purchased from Kingsley and Dilhorne. However, Thos. Patten & Co., the Brass and Copper manufacturers had considered Cheadle's coal when it arrived in 1734 for that later required enough of this fuel to persuade them to operate their own colliery, Deepmoor. It was, in the Deepmoor that John Barnes acted as the sole 'Butty'. He must have made a success of this especially as he also kept the 'Jug and Glass' public house at Town End opposite the 'Swan'. Barnes could pay his men at the little window still facing down to the Church. He paid partly in brass tokens which could be used in this 'beer house', and were eventually made illegal. One or two have been found in the vicinity within the last forty years. Barnes kept the 'Jug and Glass' for about sixty years from 1817.

This was quickly followed by the tin making at Oakamoor and with the extension of the town, with its Lower Street and later Charles Street and Chapel Street meant further local demand.

When the textile industry forsook its domestic character and assembled its looms in factories the owners decided, by the early 1800s, to exchange their water wheels for steam engines as the collieries and all other local industries, even those by the Churnet, had done. Through that same period the spread of the textile industry – one unit from Macclesfield to Cecilly Brook, another from Tean to Tape Street – provided additional female labour to balance the employment position. The Enclosure Acts for the district meant more brickmaking and the building of new farm houses. No wonder Barrow found more than four hundred and fifty shafts plus enumerable old workings in his Survey of 1900, but was unable to date them or report on population effects.

The population figures show that, during the nineteenth Century, the town had doubled in size and although it had not kept pace with the larger industrial areas such as the Potteries or the Black Country, it had maintained a good standard for that small market town of the seventeenth century.

Although its major nineteenth century industries have disappeared with the exception of the Froghall works of Thomas Bolton & Sons, smaller units around Brookhouses have sprung into activity, though the energy source is no longer Cheadle coal. The town's growth, however, is assured situated as it is between its work centres mainly to the west and its opportunities for leisure among the hills and dales of the Peak Park to the east and north.

When we study that rapid upturn in the country's population graph between 1790 and 1810 we must come to the conclusion that, despite the Napoleonic Wars, this country was growing industrially in towns and the growing coal industry was playing its part. During the second half of the nineteenth century it was the major industry in the Cheadle area.Some men worked anything up to sixty years in four or five different collieries and many in the very large Potteries pits. These men had a wealth of experience, knew their work-places, Deputies, Firemen, Managers, Owners and by retirement their jobs became their hobbies.To write a full history I could have spent another ten years listening to these men, their remarkable stories with a liberal sprinkling of humour, viewing their fossils and collections of old photographs. I could have continued making a general re-assessment of the characters of the 'men with the black faces' as we called them in 1920.

*Opencast mining, Kingsley Moor, 1945*

# REFERENCES

Staffordshire Records Office -Sutherland Papers; MF 17 Shrewsbury Rentals; Bill papers, Brett papers; MF 12 - 15, Leveson Rentals 1599-1605; QSO 11 1708/9; MF 58

Chronicles of Croxden Abbey -Sister Mary Lawrence

County Victoria History. Vol 2 p109

Dr Auden - papers unpublished

Blagg documents and papers - unpublished

(D695/1/9/87)  (D2391M/1064)

George Barrow - Geological Survey Cheadle Coalfield, 1903

R S Smith, Willoughby's Iron Works, Renaissance and Modern Studies, Nottingham University, vol XI.

Hereford Records Office *The Foley Papers*

*Ancient Corporation of Cheadle*. T Pape, 1930.

*Robsahm Diary*. Unpublished.

Ecton and Foxtwood Accounts, Devonshire Collection, Chatsworth

Wm Pitt, History of Staffordshire, 1817

*George Chandler*

# INDEX

# LANDM▲RK
# COLLECTOR'S LIBRARY

LANDM▲RK
*Publishing Ltd* ● ● ●

Ashbourne Hall, Cokayne Ave, Ashbourne, Derbyshire, DE6 1EJ England
Tel 01335 347349  Fax 01335 347303
e-mail landmark@clara.net  web site: www.landmarkpublishing.co.uk

## Mining Histories

- Collieries of South Wales: Vol 1   *ISBN: 1 84306 015 9, £22.50*
- Collieries of South Wales: Vol 2   *ISBN: 1 84306 017 5, £19.95*
- Collieries of Somerset & Bristol   *ISBN: 1 84306 029 9, £14.95*
- Copper & Lead Mines around the Manifold Valley, North Staffordshire   *ISBN: 1 901522 77 6, £19.95*
- Images of Cornish Tin   *ISBN: 1 84306 020 5, £29.95*
- Lathkill Dale, Derbyshire, its Mines and Miners   *ISBN: 1 901522 80 6, £8.00*
- Rocks & Scenery the Peak District   *ISBN: 1 84306 026 4, paperback, £7.95*

## Industrial Histories

- Alldays and Onions   *ISBN: 1 84306 047 7, £24.95*
- The Life & Inventions of Richard Roberts, 1789 -1864   *ISBN: 1 84306 027 2, £29.95*
- The Textile Mill Engine   *ISBN: 1 901522 43 1, paperback, £22.50*
- Watt, James, His Life in Scotland, 1736-74   *ISBN 1 84306 045 0, £29.95*
- Wolseley, The Real, Adderley Park Works, 1901-1926   *ISBN 1 84306 052 3, £19.95*

## Roads & Transportantion

- Packmen, Carriers & Packhorse Roads   *ISBN: 1 84306 016 7, £19.95*
- Roads & Trackways of Wales   *ISBN: 1 84306 019 1, £22.50*
- Welsh Cattle Drovers   *ISBN: 1 84306 021 3, £22.50*
- Peakland Roads & Trackways   *ISBN: 1 901522 91 1, £19.95*

## Regional/Local Histories

- Derbyshire Country Houses: Vol 1   *ISBN: 1 84306 007 8, £19.95*
- Derbyshire Country Houses: Vol 2   *ISBN: 1 84306 041 8, £19.95*
- Lost Houses of Derbyshire   *ISBN: 1 84306 064 7, £19.95, October 02*
- Well Dressing   *ISBN: 1 84306 042 6, Full colour, £19.95*
- Crosses of the Peak District   *ISBN 1 84306 044 2, £14.95*
- Shrovetide Football and the Ashbourne Game   *ISBN: 1 84306 063 9, £19.95*
- Historic Hallamshire   *ISBN: 1 84306 049 3, £19.95*
- Colwyn Bay, Its History across the Years   *ISBN: 1 84306 014 0, £24.95*
- Llandudno: Queen of Welsh Resorts   *ISBN 1 84306 048 5, £15.95*
- Llanrwst: the History of a Market Town   *ISBN 1 84306 070 1, £14.95*
- Lost Houses in and around Wrexham   *ISBN 1 84306 057 4, £16.95*
- Shipwrecks of North Wales   *ISBN: 1 84306 005 1, £19.95*